Crypto for Thinkers

Crypto for Thinkers

Understanding the Philosophy of Decentralization

Sameer Khalid

Mindful Pages

Published in 2026

ISBN: 9789374599051(PB)
ISBN: 9789374591598 (eBook)

Published by

Mindful Pages
Imprint of Alpha Editions LLC
312 W. 2nd St #1834
Casper, WY 82601, USA

This book was developed using advanced writing tools to support the drafting and ideation process. All content has been thoughtfully curated, refined, and reviewed to ensure quality and relevance.

Content

Introduction
Rules Without Rulers

There is a peculiar unease that defines our age. We trust our phones more than our governments, our algorithms more than our neighbours, and yet, when the signal fails, we still expect an institution somewhere to fix it. We have never had so much information about how the world works, yet so little faith in those who run it. This contradiction—dependence without trust—is the central paradox of modern civilisation. We suspect manipulation behind every curtain, bias in every platform, capture in every law. Yet we continue to log in, to transact, to comply. The problem is not that we have ceased to believe in institutions, but that we no longer know what could take their place.

The story of crypto begins, then, not with money but with mistrust. It was born from a quiet rebellion against intermediaries—those who hold ledgers, licences, and levers of power. The cypherpunks of the early internet were not gamblers chasing profit, but philosophers disguised as programmers. They imagined a world in which cryptography, not charisma, secured cooperation; in which mathematics could stand where law and loyalty faltered. To them, code was not merely a tool but a kind of moral architecture—a way to build systems that respected autonomy without requiring virtue. Their dream was not utopian anarchy, but a society where verification could replace blind faith.

Yet, as with all human inventions, the dream soon met the market. Bitcoin, Ethereum, and their innumerable descendants carried within them both promise and peril: the possibility of liberation and the risk of new forms of bondage. For every idealist preaching freedom from fiat, there was a speculator counting coins; for every architect of open governance, a carnival of grifters selling digital gold. Crypto became both mirror and magnifier of our moral confusion—an x-ray of the social contract itself. What do we owe each other when the rules are written in code? Who bears responsibility when a line of script decides a fortune?

This book, *Crypto for Thinkers*, begins where hype leaves off. It does not celebrate decentralisation as a slogan, nor condemn it as a fad. Instead, it treats it as a profound philosophical experiment—an attempt to reimagine how strangers coordinate without kings, banks, or bureaucrats. Its concern is not price charts but first principles. What does it mean to trust without trustees? Can autonomy coexist with solidarity? When does freedom become abdication? These are not merely technical questions; they are moral ones, shaping the architectures of power that will define the next century.

The Moral Machinery of Trust

Every civilisation rests upon an invisible machinery of trust. Coins, contracts, courts—all are attempts to translate uncertainty into confidence. For centuries, institutions have performed this alchemy on our behalf. They promise that signatures bind, that balances exist, that justice is enforceable. We accept their mediation because direct verification is costly, and because coordination among millions demands delegation. But the very efficiency that makes institutions powerful also makes them opaque. Their hierarchies blur accountability; their incentives drift from the public good to private interest. The crisis of trust we inhabit is therefore not a failure of technology but of legitimacy.

Decentralisation, at least in principle, offers a remedy: a return of verification to the individual, an architecture where rules are enforced by code rather than decree. Yet this solution carries its own cost. To distribute power is to distribute labour—cognitive, moral, and temporal. The burden of self-sovereignty is heavy; the absence of hierarchy breeds both liberty and loneliness. Crypto's greatest promise—to remove the need for trust—may also be its greatest illusion. For while cryptography can secure data, it cannot secure decency. It can prove that a transaction occurred, but not that it was fair. It can guarantee consensus, but not conscience.

Hence, this book treats decentralisation not as a purely technological phenomenon but as a social philosophy—a re-engineering of the very grammar of cooperation. To understand it demands more than learning the syntax of blockchains; it requires asking why humans delegate, why we obey, and what we fear when control is lost.

The Long Shadow of Institutions

History, too, reminds us that revolutions against intermediaries rarely end as intended. The printing press decentralised knowledge, yet gave rise to censorship bureaus. The Reformation broke the Church's monopoly on salvation, yet spawned new hierarchies of creed. The internet promised a peer-to-peer agora, yet consolidated power in platforms more centralised than any empire before them. Each wave of decentralisation has exposed the same paradox: that coordination at scale requires some structure of trust, even if redefined.

Crypto, in this lineage, represents the latest iteration of humanity's enduring struggle to reconcile freedom with order. Its architects claim to have built systems immune to capture; yet every blockchain reveals, in time, its own priesthood—miners, validators, core developers, foundations. The dream of *rules without rulers* is noble, but power is never absent, only disguised. What matters, therefore, is not whether systems are decentralised in form, but whether they are legitimate in function.

This is where governance, not glamour, becomes the true test. The resilient protocol is not the one with the most nodes or the flashiest roadmap, but the one that endures dispute without disintegrating. Decentralisation without deliberation is mere entropy. The challenge is to design architectures of choice that do not collapse into chaos—to find, as it were, a geometry of freedom.

The New Commons

To think clearly about decentralisation is to revisit an ancient question: how do individuals, each pursuing their own good, sustain a shared world? The commons—be it pasture, data, or code—is always at risk of neglect or capture. Crypto introduces new tools to manage this tension: tokens that encode incentives, ledgers that record contributions, contracts that execute automatically. Yet no algorithm can substitute for civic virtue. Without norms of care, even the most elegant protocol corrodes.

Consider, for instance, open-source maintenance: the silent, unpaid labour that keeps the digital commons alive. Or the governance votes that draw a few dozen participants from thousands of token holders. The myth of full autonomy collapses against the reality of coordination costs. Freedom is expensive, and someone must foot the bill. This book insists that dignity—not efficiency—must anchor our design choices. Systems that forget the human eventually fail the human.

Beyond Hype, Beyond Cynicism

To study crypto seriously is to resist two temptations: evangelism and dismissal. The evangelist confuses novelty with progress; the cynic mistakes imperfection for irrelevance. Both evade responsibility. The proper stance is stewardship: to recognise that technology is neither salvation nor scourge, but a moral amplifier. It scales incentives and intentions alike. The task, therefore, is not to ask whether decentralisation is good or bad, but under what conditions it sustains legitimate order.

In this spirit, each chapter of this book approaches a dimension of the decentralised experiment. We begin with the blind spot of trust, tracing how institutions both fail and remain indispensable. We then explore autonomy at scale, where personal sovereignty collides with collective purpose. From there, we examine the uneasy truce between code and law, the ethics of token design, the fragile commons of open source, the limits of privacy, and the re-centralising tendencies that haunt every distributed system. Later chapters confront global frictions: what decentralisation means for citizens under authoritarian regimes, for workers reclaiming ownership, for educators cultivating digital civics. Finally, we turn to dignity—the moral compass by which decentralisation must steer, lest it devolve into chaos.

Each section builds a single discipline of thought: that governance, not speculation, determines the moral worth of a system. A blockchain's integrity lies not in its cryptography alone, but in how it treats dissent, failure, and the unglamorous work of maintenance.

A Framework for Thinking, Not Trading

This is not a manual for making money. It is a guide for thinking critically about systems that claim to transcend trust. Its goal is to equip readers with conceptual tools: how to discern governance theatre from governance work; how to evaluate a project's legitimacy by its remedy mechanisms, not its rhetoric; how to distinguish decentralisation as design from decentralisation as dogma. To do so, we draw not only from economics and computer science, but from political theory, ethics, and psychology. For crypto is not an alien phenomenon—it is a continuation of our oldest human struggle: to create order without oppression.

The reader need not be a developer or trader to engage here. What matters is curiosity about how humans build and break systems of trust. In the end, decentralisation is less a technical frontier than a civic one. Its fate depends not on hash rates but on habits: how we deliberate, delegate, and doubt.

The Questions Ahead

Can a society function without central arbiters of truth? Can communities self-govern without collapsing into tribes? Can code embody compassion, or must morality remain a human monopoly? These are not abstract puzzles—they will define the institutions our children inherit.

If the twentieth century was the age of institutions, the twenty-first may be the age of infrastructures: invisible, automated, borderless systems that determine how power flows. The question is whether these infrastructures will serve as commons or cages.

Crypto for Thinkers invites you to confront that question without dogma or despair. To think, not trade; to discern, not merely believe. The tools of decentralisation are powerful, but their destiny depends on the philosophies we embed within them. Rules without rulers are not enough. The task before us is to build legitimacy without illusion.

That, in essence, is the wager of this book—and, perhaps, of our century.

Chapter 1
The Blind Spot of Trust

It begins, as so many modern dilemmas do, with a notification that no one sees coming. A global bank's servers freeze without warning; transactions stall, payrolls hang in limbo, and millions of customers discover that the invisible machinery of trust has stopped mid-turn. Within hours, social media fills with outrage and conspiracy, governments issue half-reassurances, and engineers scramble to patch the flaw. The failure lasts a day; the doubt lingers for years. It is in these moments—when trust flickers—that we realise how deeply our lives depend on systems we neither see nor understand. We curse their opacity yet cling to their reliability, despising our dependence while admitting we have no alternative. This is the blind spot of trust: our faith in what we cannot verify, and our helplessness when it falters.

The digital century has magnified this contradiction. Every click, transfer, and agreement passes through an intermediary—a platform, a bank, a regulator—whose credibility we accept as fact. Institutions have become our prosthetic memory and conscience. They arbitrate disputes, record ownership, absorb risk. In doing so, they make modern life bearable. Yet the same concentration that enables efficiency also breeds vulnerability. Power coagulates; accountability diffuses. Scandals of data misuse, financial manipulation, and bureaucratic capture erode belief not just in particular actors but in the institutional form itself. We whisper that the game is rigged, yet continue to play. The paradox is complete: we need institutions precisely because we no longer trust them.

It is from this crisis of confidence that the decentralised imagination emerges. The early architects of crypto looked upon the erosion of trust and proposed an audacious alternative: what if we could build systems that did not require belief at all? Their wager was simple yet radical—replace the fragile authority of humans with the incorruptible certainty of mathematics. Verification, not faith. Rules, not rulers. The slogan carried a moral charge: in a world where institutions lie, perhaps code could tell the truth.

But trust does not vanish when intermediaries do. It merely migrates—from people to protocols, from courts to consensus mechanisms, from law to cryptography. The assumption that trust can be *eliminated* is both the power and the illusion of the crypto movement. In practice, new dependencies arise: on developers, on auditors, on the very algorithms designed to liberate us. The irony is exquisite—systems built to escape institutional capture recreate their own micro-institutions. The question, then, is not how to abolish trust, but how to understand it.

This chapter begins by examining the foundations of that understanding. We start with why institutions fail and still matter: how their purpose—to cut the costs of coordination—makes them both indispensable and dangerous. By analysing their essential functions—rule-setting, dispute resolution, and tail-risk absorption—we can see clearly what any decentralised alternative must replace, not merely reject. If institutions are flawed, it is not because they exist, but because they forget why they were built. Their corruption is not a reason for nihilism but an argument for redesign.

From there, we turn to the cypherpunk diagnosis—a history that predates the coins and exchanges of today. The cypherpunks were not speculators; they were dissidents of a subtler kind. Writing in the 1990s, when the internet still felt like open frontier, they foresaw how surveillance and centralisation would merge into a quiet form of control. Their answer was cryptography as resistance, privacy as political necessity. To encrypt was not to hide, but to assert autonomy; to code was to legislate for oneself. They reframed technology as a non-violent instrument of freedom, a way to carve space for individual dignity in an increasingly monitored world. Yet their vision, too, had limits. Privacy without accountability risks anarchy; autonomy without community degenerates into isolation. Their moral courage reminds us that every tool of liberation is also a test of responsibility.

The chapter then confronts the seductive binary between *trustless* and *trustworthy*. Crypto rhetoric often celebrates the "trustless" system—as though removing human discretion could abolish human error. But even the most elegant code cannot capture the ambiguities of intent, mercy, or fairness. A contract may execute flawlessly and still produce injustice. True resilience lies not in abolishing trust but in layering it: cryptographic verification where precision suffices, human judgement where interpretation is inevitable. The art of governance, decentralised or otherwise, lies in knowing which risks belong to code and which remain human.

Finally, we ask the deceptively simple question: *what problem is crypto for?* Not every inefficiency, not every bureaucratic irritation, is a moral failure that demands decentralisation. A society that routes all frustrations through code risks mistaking design for virtue. The diagnostic lens proposed here distinguishes when decentralisation is justified—when censorship, counterparty risk, or capture risk is so severe that alternatives fail—and when it is self-indulgent theatre. By the end of this chapter, readers will be able to evaluate any crypto claim not by its jargon but by its governance: what human problem it solves, and at what moral cost.

At its heart, "The Blind Spot of Trust" is an invitation to look beneath the slogans of both the old and new orders. Institutions did not arise from malice; they emerged as instruments of cooperation in a world too complex for direct reciprocity. Their decay is tragic precisely because their necessity remains. The decentralised experiment, for all its innovation, inherits this paradox rather than escaping it. Every ledger, whether maintained by clerks or nodes, rests on the same fragile hope: that strangers can coordinate without betrayal.

The coming pages will trace how this hope has evolved—from bureaucratic oaths to cryptographic proofs, from seals on parchment to hashes on chain. Along the way, we will confront the moral arithmetic of trust: how much we must surrender to coordinate, how much we can reclaim without chaos. The lesson, if there is one, is neither nostalgia for institutions nor blind faith in protocols. It is the recognition that trust, however mediated, remains the currency of civilisation.

To see its blind spot clearly is not to despair, but to gain sight.

Why Institutions Fail and Still Matter

On 15 September 2008, in New York City, Lehman Brothers filed for bankruptcy with debts exceeding $600 billion. Within hours, global markets convulsed, and the unthinkable happened: a 158-year-old institution, once a pillar of American capitalism, vanished. What failed was not merely a bank but a dense web of trust that stretched from pensioners in Glasgow to traders in Singapore. For weeks, cash machines trembled, credit froze, and the abstract faith that money would hold value suddenly felt fragile. Yet, within months, the world turned again to the very institutions it had blamed—the central banks, the regulators, the states—to stabilise the wreckage. We cursed their recklessness even as we begged them to save us. That double movement—resentment and reliance—is the signature of our institutional age.

Institutions exist to make strangers predictable. They convert uncertainty into procedure. By standardising contracts, enforcing rights, and absorbing risk, they allow vast numbers of people to cooperate without intimacy. A supermarket shelf, a university degree, a marriage certificate—all are artefacts of institutional coordination. They translate personal intention into collective order. In doing so, they reduce what economists call the "cost of trust": the time, information, and emotional labour otherwise needed to verify every interaction. Without these mechanisms, society would shrink to the scale of personal acquaintance.

Yet every efficiency has a shadow. The very delegation that enables institutions to function also distances them from those they serve. Over time, layers of procedure obscure accountability; incentives drift from purpose to preservation. Max Weber saw this a century ago when he described bureaucracy as the "iron cage" of modernity: rational in design, but cold in spirit. Institutions forget that they are means, not ends. Their leaders defend process as though it were principle. Citizens, sensing this inversion, withdraw trust and substitute compliance. The machinery still turns, but it grinds rather than hums.

Consider the Catholic Church at the height of the Reformation. Its bureaucracy had grown so elaborate that grace seemed purchasable through indulgences, transforming faith into accounting. When Martin Luther nailed his theses in Wittenberg in 1517, he was protesting not belief itself but its capture by institutional self-interest. Five centuries later, the 2008 crisis revealed a similar pattern in finance: complex derivatives masking moral hazard, oversight buried beneath opacity. In both cases, legitimacy failed before legality did. People obeyed the rules long after they ceased to believe in their justice.

This erosion of belief is cumulative. Institutions accumulate what might be called *credibility debt*. Each scandal, delay, or act of hypocrisy compounds the sense that the system serves insiders first. States promise impartial justice yet legislate for donors; universities proclaim truth yet reward citation counts; platforms pledge neutrality yet monetise outrage. When this debt matures, revolts follow—political, digital, or both. But even rebellion depends on institutional scaffolding. Protesters march under permits; journalists report through media outlets; cryptocurrencies trade on regulated exchanges. The aspiration to abolish institutions often collapses into dependence upon them.

To understand why they persist, one must name their indispensable functions. First, **rule-setting**. Institutions articulate boundaries that make coordination intelligible. A traffic light in London means the same as one in Lagos not by nature but by convention. These conventions only endure when backed by authority. The rule may be automated, as in a blockchain protocol, or discretionary, as in judicial precedent, but the function is identical: to prevent collisions.

Second, **dispute resolution**. No system, however precise, can anticipate every contingency. When ambiguity arises, someone—or something—must interpret the rules. Courts, regulators, and professional bodies perform this service imperfectly but necessarily. Decentralised systems attempt to replace judges with algorithms, yet edge cases persist: stolen keys, malicious forks, contested identities. Without legitimate arbitration, every disagreement risks escalation.

Third, **tail-risk absorption**. Institutions exist to bear shocks too large for individuals: floods, pandemics, bankruptcies. In 2020, as COVID-19 paralysed commerce, governments became insurers of last resort. Central banks created liquidity; health systems triaged crisis. The coordination may have been uneven, but no peer-to-peer alternative could have replaced it at scale. This capacity to socialise catastrophe is the essence of institutional value.

None of this is to sanctify institutions. Their failures are real and often self-inflicted. The World Health Organization, criticised for its slow response to Ebola in 2014, revealed how bureaucratic caution can cost lives. Yet the counter-example—the informal volunteer networks that arose in Sierra Leone—demonstrated both the power and the limits of decentralised action. Grass-roots coordination delivered speed and trust, but without stable funding or authority it could not sustain containment. The reconciliation is sobering: legitimacy without capacity is as dangerous as capacity without legitimacy.

Opacity, capture, and inertia are not anomalies; they are by-products of scale. As organisations expand, information filters upward while incentives concentrate downward. The logic of survival supplants the logic of service. Economist Mancur Olson (1982) called this the "institutional sclerosis" that afflicts mature societies: collective action hardens into vested interest. The remedy is neither blind deregulation nor naïve decentralisation, but disciplined renewal. Institutions must periodically re-justify themselves, pruning excess and redistributing authority before stagnation turns to collapse.

Decentralised technologies promise precisely such a reset. By embedding rules in code and transparency in ledgers, they seek to eliminate the human discretion that breeds abuse. Yet the ambition often overreaches. Smart contracts can enforce obligations, but they cannot forgive debt or interpret intent. Distributed ledgers can reveal transactions, but not motives. The ethical labour of judgement remains. A protocol may prevent one kind of fraud while enabling another. Every line of code conceals a political choice: who may act, who may amend, who bears loss when the system fails.

A quiet motif runs through both traditional and decentralised orders—the need for *legibility*. To govern is to make reality readable enough to coordinate. When legibility disappears, chaos follows; when it becomes total, tyranny threatens. Institutions err in both directions: too little transparency breeds suspicion, too much rigidity suffocates innovation. Crypto projects face the same tension. Over-specify rules, and communities lose flexibility; under-specify them, and trust decays. The art lies in calibrating legibility to human scale.

The failure of institutions, then, is rarely a failure of purpose. It is a failure of proportion. They grow faster than their feedback loops, accumulating complexity faster than they learn from it. When Lehman collapsed in 2008, it was not ignorance but overconfidence that killed it—risk models treating volatility as manageable because history appeared stable. When decentralised finance platforms implode, as with the TerraUSD crash in May 2022, the pattern repeats: mathematical assurance masking social fragility. In both cases, opacity was not a bug but a strategy.

Still, to discard institutions altogether would be to discard the memory of civilisation. Each carries lessons encoded in its procedures, scars of past failures that become safeguards. The English common law, for instance, evolved through centuries of precedent precisely because discretion could be abused; case law became a distributed ledger of human judgement long before blockchains. Its strength lay not in infallibility but in iteration. To build decentralised systems without studying such inheritance is to reinvent fragility.

If decentralisation is to mature beyond ideology, it must confront the functions it seeks to supplant. Who writes the rules? Who arbitrates ambiguity? Who absorbs the shock when the improbable occurs? These questions are not relics of centralisation but conditions of collective life. Whether answered by parliament, protocol, or predictive algorithm, the need endures. The danger lies in pretending that mathematics can dissolve moral responsibility.

Institutions fail because humans do. They matter because humans do. The challenge for this century is not to erase them but to make them transparent, accountable, and proportionate—to build systems that remember why they exist. As decentralised networks evolve, their test will be the same that felled Lehman and shamed Rome: can power serve without vanishing into privilege?

The next frontier is not technological but ethical. When the next crisis comes—as it will—will we again look upward to central banks and governments, or sideways to protocols and peers? Or will we have built something humbler and wiser, an institution light enough to bend yet strong enough to bear trust once more?

The Cypherpunk Diagnosis

In June 1991, in Boulder, Colorado, Phil Zimmermann released Pretty Good Privacy—PGP—into the wild. The code spread through bulletin boards and university servers with the velocity of rumour. Within two years the United States Customs Service and the Department of Justice opened a criminal investigation into whether publishing strong encryption violated munitions-export rules. By 1996 the case was dropped; the software remained. No street protests forced that outcome. No party won an election to make it so. A physics graduate, a modem, and mathematics altered the balance of power between citizens and the state. The lesson was stark. Code can act.

Cypherpunks named this act before most had noticed it. In March 1993, Eric Hughes circulated "A Cypherpunk's Manifesto" from San Francisco, arguing that privacy was "necessary for an open society in the electronic age." The claim was not sentimental. It was forensic. Show the vulnerability first: the routine logging of calls and purchases, the casual aggregation of location, the hunger of bureaucracies for metadata. Name the remedy: cryptography, end-to-end, wielded by individuals without permission. Explain the mechanism: by encrypting at the ends rather than in the middle, you deny intermediaries the power to inspect. Implication: you reduce the attack surface not by pleading for restraint but by making the data illegible. This was politics by other means—the quiet politics of a sealed envelope.

Privacy, for them, was not a lifestyle choice but a constitutional safeguard. They watched export controls treat algorithms as weapons; they watched administrators insist that "good people" had nothing to hide. They replied with mathematics. The posture deserves precision. Cryptography did not promise safety; it promised asymmetry. A low-cost act—generating a keypair—could raise the price of unwarranted access to prohibitive levels. A journalist could email a source without betting their freedom on the good faith of a network operator. A dissident could publish under a pseudonym without asking a platform for a waiver. Strong encryption turned silence into a decision rather than a surrender. It was non-violent power when law lagged.

The state responded with a different image: the locked briefcase that policemen must open to find a bomb. In 1993 the Clinton administration pushed the Clipper Chip, a hardware proposal designed in cooperation with the National Security Agency, to embed "escrowed encryption" with government-access keys. The pitch was security with a back door. The reaction from technologists and civil libertarians was swift. The *Electronic Frontier Foundation* and academics at AT&T Bell Labs and MIT demonstrated the technical fragility of key escrow and its political risks. Show: any universal key becomes a single point of catastrophic failure. Name: the *Clipper* proposal, with its *Skipjack* algorithm and the *Law Enforcement Access Field.* Explain: a secret shared that widely cannot remain secret; the mathematics of key management do not bend to policy. Implication: a back door for the "good guys" is a front door for everyone else. By 1996 the project was effectively abandoned. The envelope stayed sealed.

Two years later, a federal appeals court accepted a core cypherpunk contention: code can be speech. In *Bernstein v. United States* (San Francisco, 1999), the Ninth Circuit held that Daniel Bernstein, a mathematician, could publish his encryption algorithm and source code under the First

Amendment. The ruling did not end export controls, but it shifted the presumption. It treated an algorithm not as a grenade but as a pamphlet. Show: a programmer wishes to teach and share. Name: the legal doctrine of prior restraint. Explain: if the state may block the publication of code, it can control a debate long before any harm occurs. Implication: public cryptography becomes a civil right, and the classroom becomes a free press. That jurisprudence later underwrote a global boom in open-source libraries and the routine presence of TLS locks in browsers. The little padlock in the address bar is a monument to a court case most users will never read.

The cypherpunk diagnosis, however, was not purely legal. It was anthropological. It observed that institutions tend to accumulate data faster than they build safeguards, and that individuals trade privacy not in grand bargains but in tiny increments: a postcode for a coupon, a face scan for a faster gate, a contact list for a new app. The diagnosis insisted that consent, if it is to mean anything, must be enforceable by design. End-to-end encryption does not depend on the benevolence of a company policy; it is a cryptographic fact. The quiet motif returns: you seal the envelope yourself, not the postmaster.

When Edward Snowden disclosed secret surveillance programmes in June 2013 from Hong Kong, the cypherpunk intuition—law lags, power accumulates—gained documentary proof. The debates that followed were messy and necessary. Legislative reviews in the United States and Europe led to reforms and a cascade of transparency reports. Yet the change that mattered most was behavioural. Journalists adopted the Signal Protocol; major messaging apps, including WhatsApp, implemented end-to-end encryption at scale in April 2016 (WhatsApp, 2016). The show-to-implication chain is instructive. Show: documents prove bulk collection. Name: the practical response—default E2E. Explain: by encrypting by default, you protect the indifferent as well as the diligent; security ceases to be a hobby. Implication: norms shift. Privacy becomes the baseline rather than the exception.

To present cryptography as pure emancipation would be dishonest. Criminals also use locks. In May 2017 the WannaCry ransomware attack, leveraging a stolen exploit, encrypted computers across more than 150 countries; the United Kingdom's National Health Service suffered cancelled appointments and delayed operations. This is not a footnote. It is a limit case. The sealed envelope can hide a threat as well as a love letter. Here, the cypherpunk claim meets a civic rebuttal: a society must detect and deter harm, not merely defend rights. Reconciliation requires precision. Strong encryption for data in transit need not imply irresponsible software design or negligent patching. Security failures at the NHS were traced to unpatched systems, not to cryptography's existence. The motif adjusts: you can choose to lock the envelope; you must also choose to keep the doorframe sound.

The movement was at its best when it paired principle with pragmatism. John Gilmore's aphorism—"The Net interprets censorship as damage and routes around it"—was less prophecy than programme. The Tor Project, launched in the early 2000s with support from the U.S. Naval Research Laboratory and later civil society groups, manifested the idea that routing itself could confound surveillance. Show: traffic analysis threatens anonymity even when contents are encrypted. Name: onion routing with volunteer relays. Explain: by layering encryption and relays, you obscure who talks to whom, not just what is said. Implication: dissidents in Tehran or journalists in Moscow can publish without flagging their location. But Tor also facilitated marketplaces like Silk Road (shut down in San Francisco, October 2013), where narcotics were traded using Bitcoin and pseudonymous accounts. The double edge cut deep. Policymakers drew a quick line: tool equals harm. The better reading is slower: capacity changes behaviour on all sides—censors adapt, criminals adapt, citizens adapt—so governance must adapt without eroding the capacity of the innocent to act.

The cypherpunk ethic prized autonomy and consent, but it did not deny community. Consider the practice of key-signing parties common among PGP users in the 1990s and 2000s, often held in places like Berlin or London. Show: people meet to verify each other's identities face to face and sign public keys. Name: the web of trust. Explain: no single authority certifies identity; it accrues through interpersonal endorsement. Implication: decentralised identity can scale socially without collapsing into chaos, provided enough participants commit to verification rituals. The ritual matters because it incarnates a value—trust as personal judgement—into a procedure. It turns an abstraction into a weekend decision to bring a passport, meet strangers, and sign.

When law lags, cryptography fills the gap; when law reacts, it often seeks to reassert centralised guarantees. The Apple–FBI dispute in February 2016 following the San Bernardino attack offers a vivid example. The FBI asked a court in Riverside, California to compel Apple to create a custom iOS to bypass security on a seized iPhone. Apple refused, arguing that creating a universal bypass would endanger millions. Show: a single case with human stakes. Name: the All Writs Act and its interpretation. Explain: if a firm can be compelled to weaken its own security, the precedent reaches far beyond one tragedy. Implication: constitutional rights become contingent on the willingness of private actors to resist. The case ended when the FBI accessed the phone via a third party, but the fault line remains. That line is the book's thesis in miniature: legitimacy requires both technology and law, and neither can permanently substitute for the other.

Critics of the cypherpunk view point to a democratic cost. If enforcement agencies cannot access communications even with warrants, the argument goes, the rule of law weakens. This counter-case is serious. It asks whether the sealed envelope should sometimes be opened under supervision. Here, naming matters. The difference between targeted, judicially supervised access and bulk, secret collection is not a nuance; it is the line between a scalpel and a trawl net. Explain: cryptography does not prevent targeted investigation when endpoints are compromised under due process; it prevents dragnet inspection that chills speech. Implication: a liberal society can defend strong encryption while insisting on institutional competence in traditional forms of investigation. The craft lies not in back doors but in warrants that focus on people rather than protocols.

The cypherpunk ethic also misfires when it assumes that transparency alone corrects power. Open-source code is inspectable; most citizens cannot inspect it. Audits exist; few read them. The asymmetry shifts from secrecy to expertise. Show: the 2014 Heartbleed bug in OpenSSL—an open library—exposed vast swathes of the internet despite public code. Name: limits of volunteer maintenance. Explain: openness without sustained funding leaves critical infrastructure under-defended. Implication: privacy requires not only mathematics but institutions that finance the unglamorous labour of upkeep. A sealed envelope posted through a broken sorting office will still go missing.

This history yields a coherent moral origin story without hagiography. The movement taught three durable lessons. First, that privacy is a public good disguised as a personal choice; the benefit of my encrypted message includes your freedom not to be profiled as my associate. Second, that rights defended by architecture degrade more slowly than those defended by policy; standards outlast speeches. Third, that every technical fix migrates the frontier of discretion rather than erasing it; when contents become unreadable, metadata becomes the battleground. Each is visible in behaviour. Journalists change tools; companies publish transparency reports; agencies shift to data-mining traffic patterns. The motif returns: the envelope stays sealed, so the inquisitor studies the postage marks.

The practical implication for decentralised systems is immediate. If code is to instantiate rights, it must be paired with procedures for remedy when code fails. The cypherpunk instinct—to replace discretion with design—meets the reality that harms persist at the edges: lost keys, coerced transactions, compromised devices. It is not a betrayal of the ethic to acknowledge limits; it is fidelity to the deeper aim of preserving human dignity. Zimmermann's PGP did not promise invincibility. It promised a fairer fight. That remains the right standard.

What, then, does "non-violent power" mean in 2025? It is the choice to protect by default, to minimise what is collected, and to design systems in which the cost of mass surveillance exceeds any plausible public interest benefit. It is also the humility to accept that some harms will evade detection because we refuse to normalise suspicion. A society that demands perfect safety will get perfect records. A society that tolerates some uncertainty will keep its interiority intact. Choose.

The sealed envelope sits between us as we end this section: tangible, ordinary, and defiant. The next move belongs to us—law-makers, builders, citizens. We must decide who places the stamp, who holds the key, and under what conditions the paper may be opened. If the law lags again, will we reach for the envelope or the master key?

Trustless vs Trustworthy

On 17 June 2016, at approximately 08:59 UTC, an attacker began siphoning funds from *The DAO*—a decentralised investment fund built on Ethereum and then worth over $150 million. The code was meant to be immutable, its rules public and self-enforcing. Within hours, one-third of the assets were gone. The flaw was not in the blockchain's cryptography but in the logic of a smart contract that allowed recursive withdrawals. No passwords were stolen, no servers breached. The system behaved exactly as written, yet disastrously. What followed—a contested hard fork to restore the funds—exposed a truth that code alone had tried to banish: rules without judgement are brittle. The question returned, sharper than before: can a system be *trustless* if it still depends on people to decide what to do when things go wrong?

The dream of a trustless world has always carried an air of liberation. Bitcoin's white paper promised "a system for electronic transactions without relying on trust." It sounded like emancipation from politics itself: no banks, no arbiters, only mathematics. But every cryptographic guarantee rests on human arrangements—developers maintaining code, validators agreeing on updates, users safeguarding keys. Trust is displaced, not deleted. The motif that runs through this story is *the bridge*: cryptography secures one side, human norms the other. The bridge's strength lies in both pillars, not in denying their existence.

To see this more clearly, start with what cryptography actually does. It constrains discretion. When a transaction is signed with a private key, its authenticity is mathematically provable. When a network reaches consensus through proof of work or stake, no single actor can falsify the record without immense cost. These are extraordinary achievements: they allow strangers to cooperate without intermediaries. Yet cryptography cannot decide *why* a transaction was made, or whether it was fair, or how to respond when it harms someone. The boundary between what can be guaranteed by computation and what requires human interpretation is not a flaw; it is the architecture of trust itself.

The DAO's fork made that boundary visible. Ethereum's developers and community voted to reverse the hack by altering the blockchain's history—an act some saw as moral repair, others as betrayal. Both sides appealed to legitimacy. The "code is law" faction insisted that immutability was sacred; the "justice over purity" faction argued that law itself has always contained exceptions. The fork was a referendum on whether trust should reside in procedure or principle. Its outcome—the coexistence of Ethereum and Ethereum Classic—demonstrated that governance cannot be automated away. It can only be encoded where values are already shared.

A second case, the *Parity wallet freeze* of November 2017 in London, reinforces the lesson. A user inadvertently triggered a flaw in a multi-signature wallet library, permanently locking over 500,000 Ether—then worth roughly $150 million—inside the contract. There was no theft, only paralysis. No amount of cryptographic certainty could restore access. The affected projects petitioned the Ethereum developers for intervention; they refused, wary of repeating The DAO precedent. Inaction was itself a political decision. The chain's integrity survived, but the victims bore irreversible loss. The code had executed perfectly; it had also killed trust.

What these episodes show is not the failure of cryptography but the danger of mistaking *trustless* for *trustworthy*. A trustless system is one where certain operations can be verified independently; a trustworthy system is one where participants believe that, when something goes wrong, the outcome will be legitimate and proportionate. The former is mechanical, the latter moral. Confusing them breeds zealotry: the belief that social problems can be solved by software updates. The proper aim is not to eliminate trust but to distribute it wisely.

That distribution can be described as a layered model. The first layer is **mathematical**: cryptographic proofs that secure integrity and authenticity. These are the "physics" of digital cooperation—predictable, impartial, and mercilessly literal. The second layer is **institutional**: governance processes, dispute mechanisms, and social norms that interpret intent and allocate accountability. The third layer is **legal**: the capacity to enforce rights and remedies in the world of consequences. Each layer addresses a different risk. Mathematics prevents forgery; governance manages disagreement; law deters coercion. To treat any layer as sufficient on its own is to invite failure.

Consider the contrast with the global financial system after the 2008 crisis. Its failures were human—opaque incentives, regulatory capture—but its recovery relied on precisely those human institutions. Central banks restored liquidity because they could interpret context and absorb loss. The crypto world's instinct is to pre-empt such discretion by embedding rules in code, yet the Parity and DAO incidents reveal why discretion, properly bounded, is essential. It is the safety valve that prevents systems from shattering under pressure.

The motif of the bridge reappears. On one side stands algorithmic certainty; on the other, ethical interpretation. Remove either, and the span collapses. The bridge must also bear traffic in both directions: human norms inform code design, while code enforces boundaries that keep power honest. The most resilient systems are those where each side can audit the other.

A credible counter-example might appear in Bitcoin itself, which has functioned without formal governance for over a decade. No hard fork has reversed a transaction; consensus remains purely technical. Yet even here, trust is social. Developers maintain the reference client; miners choose which version to run; users rely on exchanges to convert fiat. When controversies arise—over block size in 2017 or ordinals in 2023—they are resolved not by code but by community preference. The absence of formal institutions masks a dense web of informal ones: mailing lists, conferences, reputations. The code enforces the ledger; people enforce meaning.

Another domain reveals the same pattern at a different scale. Estonia's *X-Road* infrastructure, launched in 2001, uses cryptographic signatures to enable secure data exchange across government agencies. It is often hailed as "blockchain before blockchain." Yet its trust model depends equally on legal oversight and transparency. Every query of a citizen's record is logged and visible to that citizen. The mathematics ensures integrity; the law ensures accountability. The implication is instructive: trustworthiness emerges from the choreography between computation and institution, not from the dominance of one over the other.

The opposite experiment—pure algorithmic order—has not fared as well. In 2020, the decentralised finance protocol *bZx* suffered repeated flash-loan exploits that drained millions of dollars. The smart contracts worked exactly as coded, but they encoded incomplete assumptions about market behaviour. The attackers merely used the rules creatively. No appeal, no arbitration, no repair. The designers promised trustless finance; they delivered systems that rewarded opportunism faster than they could patch it. Each exploit became a reminder that adversarial creativity is also human nature.

To reconcile these extremes, one must re-examine what trust is for. Trust is not the opposite of verification; it is what allows verification to stop somewhere. In everyday life, we accept receipts, signatures, and brands because endless checking would paralyse us. Digital systems face the same trade-off. Perfect verification is infinitely expensive; perfect decentralisation infinitely slow. The point is not to abolish trust but to calibrate it: how much discretion to grant, to whom, under what conditions, and with what remedies. The moral question is proportionality.

This proportionality can be measured by the cost of error. When the downside of failure is trivial—a small payment, a software bug—automation is fine. When the downside is catastrophic—identity theft, life savings, freedom—it demands layered safeguards. A mature decentralised architecture will not be trustless but *trust-minimised*: using cryptography to reduce unnecessary reliance, while preserving human judgement for cases where fairness or mercy must override logic. The engineering term for this is *defence in depth*; the philosophical term is humility.

Humility is often missing from crypto rhetoric. The slogan "don't trust, verify" encapsulates an ethos of scepticism but conceals a dependency on unseen verifiers: auditors, researchers, developers. Each carries its own biases. Mathematical proofs attest only to properties within defined assumptions; social systems inhabit ambiguity by default. The bridge needs maintenance. That maintenance—patching, upgrading, debating—is governance work. Pretending otherwise leaves power to those who control the code repository.

There is also a civic dimension. Law, though slower and softer than code, possesses one virtue algorithms lack: legitimacy through contestation. Citizens can appeal a verdict; they cannot appeal a hash. Courts publish reasoning; blockchains publish results. The distinction matters. When outputs diverge from justice, humans can change rules without pretending that doing so erases trust. The Ethereum community's fork, messy as it was, represented precisely that capacity for self-correction.

The risk, however, is overcorrection—reintroducing arbitrary power under the guise of flexibility. If discretion expands unchecked, decentralisation collapses back into hierarchy. The challenge is to design feedback loops that constrain authority while allowing evolution. Some projects now experiment with *constitutional layers*: explicit meta-rules for how protocols may change. Others, such as *MakerDAO* and *Optimism*, are exploring hybrid governance that blends algorithmic clarity with elected or reputation-weighted councils. These are imperfect but serious attempts to engineer legitimacy rather than assume it.

The layered model also clarifies moral responsibility. When a contract misfires, who bears the loss? If all participants knowingly opted into an immutable system, perhaps no one; if not, the designers and promoters share liability. The deeper question is whether consent can be meaningful without understanding. Most users will never read a smart contract; their trust lies in brand and interface. That reality reintroduces an old figure: the fiduciary. Even in decentralised form, someone designs defaults, writes documentation, and shapes incentives. Their moral duty persists, however diffuse.

The bridge, seen from above, resembles a circuit. Cryptography provides the voltage; norms and laws provide resistance. Without resistance, current burns through; without voltage, nothing moves. Trust, like electricity, requires both flow and limit. The goal is not a perfect insulator but a controlled conductor—enough confidence to cooperate, enough scepticism to check.

The unresolved tension remains: can we formalise discretion without killing its spirit? A machine can prove that signatures match; it cannot weigh mercy against precedent. Yet a society that outsources fairness entirely to code risks moral atrophy. The better path may be iterative—let algorithms handle what they can prove, let humans deliberate on what they cannot, and build visible channels between the two.

The DAO, the Parity freeze, the Estonian data logs—all point to the same frontier. A trustworthy system is not the absence of trust but its architecture. The next design question is simple and severe: which risks belong in code, and which still belong to us?

What Problem Is Crypto For?

In October 2010, Visa and Mastercard cut off payments to WikiLeaks after the release of U.S. diplomatic cables. Within weeks, the organisation published a Bitcoin address and began receiving donations outside the card networks' reach. No court had convicted WikiLeaks. No law had changed. A private chokepoint decided that money should not flow, and it stopped—until a permissionless rail reopened it. The scene was global and precise: payment processors in the United States, an organisation operating from servers mirrored across Europe, and a new, uncensorable conduit born from code. Start with the threat. The lesson is not that crypto redeems every cause. It is that censorship can be exercised by intermediaries long before judges speak, and that alternative rails alter the calculus of who gets to decide.

The central mistake in technical evangelism is to treat decentralisation as a universal solvent. It is not. It is a specific antidote to specific toxins. Three, chiefly: censorship, counterparty failure, and capture. Where these risks dominate, crypto earns its keep. Where they do not, the costs—volatility, complexity, irreversibility, governance overhead—often outweigh benefits. The purpose of this section is a disciplined filter. Think of it as a compass rather than a map. The compass asks which force is strongest, and points you accordingly.

Begin with censorship. Show it, name it, track its mechanism. In February 2022, as Russian forces advanced, Ukraine's Ministry of Digital Transformation posted official crypto addresses from Kyiv and raised tens of millions of dollars within days. Banks hesitated; card processors balked at sanctions exposure; wire transfers lagged. Blockchains settled quickly because there was no bank officer to convince, no correspondent network to placate. The signal was urgent, the donors global, the funds traceable on-chain. Implication: when political bottlenecks, banking holidays, or cross-border friction would choke legitimate aid, crypto is fit for purpose. That fitness is visible in behaviour: a minister posts addresses; a transparent ledger records inflow; NGOs convert to local currency where law allows. Speed is not virtue by itself; here, speed was the difference between kits delivered and kits delayed.

Censorship can also come without war. In October 2020, during protests in Lagos against police brutality, the Feminist Coalition reported that domestic payment links were intermittently blocked; organisers pivoted to Bitcoin to continue receiving support. The decision was not ideology; it was logistics. Funds needed to arrive despite platform risk. When ordinary payments become contingent on official favour, a neutral settlement layer changes the balance of power. The implication is crisp: crypto is not a protest sign; it is a wire that cannot be quietly cut. The compass points north when legitimate speech or association meets private throttles.

The next bearing is counterparty risk. Here, the question is brutally simple: can the intermediary lose, lock, or misallocate your assets? When Canadian authorities in Ottawa in February 2022 ordered banks to freeze certain accounts linked to protests, the episode illustrated a different facet of counterparty risk: the capacity of custodians to alter your financial status with a keystroke. One may applaud or condemn the policy; the risk remains. Self-custody replaces social permission with cryptographic possession. That swap is measurable in behaviour. A user holds a hardware wallet; a seed phrase, not a help desk, determines access. The implication is not that self-custody is superior in all cases—many will prefer recourse over autonomy—but that where custodial discretion threatens livelihoods or lawful dissent, crypto provides a credible escape hatch.

Yet counterparty risk also includes the mundane. Exchanges fail. Bridges get hacked. In November 2022, FTX collapsed in Nassau, wiping billions in customer balances. The failure was not the fault of blockchains; it was classic misuse of client funds. Still, the event revealed a blind spot. Many who sought "crypto" held IOUs at a company rather than keys on a wallet. The compass, properly read, would have flagged the mismatch. If your primary risk is your counterparty, the remedy is not a different counterparty dressed in jargon; it is to remove the counterparty where feasible and prudent. That choice has a visible metric: proportion of assets held in cold storage under your control.

Third, capture. This is the slow, structural risk that rules evolve to favour incumbents at the public's expense. Capture hides in procurement rules, app store policies, rent-extracting tolls. Estonia's *X-Road* achieved interoperability in 2001 because its architects resisted capture; data exchange relied on open standards and auditable logs rather than a single vendor's black box. In commercial platforms, capture looks like a 30% app-store fee, or a social network downgrading external links. Decentralised protocols can counteract such tendencies by making exit cheap and switchability credible. If your firm can migrate data and logic without begging a platform's indulgence, bargaining power resets. The implication is operational: watch for the cost in developer hours to exit a platform; if it approaches prohibitive levels, capture risk is high and a protocol approach becomes attractive.

With these bearings set, the decision tree can be walked in plain language. First question: *Are you facing credible censorship risk?* If yes—because of volatile politics, sanctions, or private chokepoints—then a permissionless settlement layer is not luxury; it is resilience. If no, proceed. Second question: *Is counterparty risk intolerable given the stakes?* If you cannot tolerate account freezes, arbitrary de-platforming, or custodial failure, prefer self-custody and minimise reliance on bridges and wrapped assets. If you can tolerate it because regulated recourse is valuable, proceed. Third question: *Is capture likely to distort rules or fees over time?* If yes, invest in open protocols, portable identity, and public standards at the core. If no, a well-run central service may be cheaper and safer. The compass holds: identify the dominant wind before you set sail.

Examples clarify where the tree sends you. Remittances from migrants in London to families in Lagos or Dhaka sound like a natural crypto use-case. Sometimes they are. If the corridor suffers from punitive fees or capital controls, stablecoins on liquid networks can lower costs and settle fast. But the details decide. If recipients lack reliable off-ramps, or if local enforcement treats crypto conversions as suspect, cash-out risk can surpass fee savings. The relevant metric is not on-chain speed; it is effective time-to-cash in the recipient's hand, including local compliance steps. Where that metric is competitive and legal frameworks are clear, the decision tree says yes. Where not, it says wait.

Consider El Salvador's declaration of Bitcoin as legal tender in September 2021 in San Salvador. As a hypothesis, it addressed financial exclusion and remittance costs. As practice, adoption remained limited for everyday transactions, with many citizens converting to dollars immediately due to volatility and merchant acceptance frictions. The case is not a refutation of crypto; it is a specification test. The dominant risk for a street vendor is price volatility, not censorship. The compass points away from volatile assets for daily pricing. Stable settlement matters. Merchant tools matter. Education matters. Without them, the technology solves a different problem than the one citizens actually face.

Now look at corporate treasuries seeking auditability and tamper-evident records. The capture risk here is low; the counterparty is often your own finance department; censorship risk is minimal. A permissioned ledger might suffice. Many pilots that promised "blockchain for supply chains" stalled because they misread the compass. The real bottleneck was data integrity at the point of entry and incentives for truthful reporting, not consensus among servers. Honduras's land registry pilot with Factom, announced in 2015, struggled amid institutional turnover and unclear legal anchoring. The issue was not hash functions; it was governance of titles and courts. The compass would have pointed to civil service reform and notarisation standards before distributed ledgers.

A strong counter-example tempers enthusiasm. Stablecoins often claim to reduce frictions while preserving purchasing power. Some do, with reserves attested and redemption functioning. Others reveal embedded capture. In August 2022, after the U.S. Treasury sanctioned Tornado Cash, the issuer of USDC blacklisted associated addresses, freezing balances at the smart-contract level. The move may have been lawful and prudent; it also reminded users that certain "decentralised" dollars carry a central switch. The decision tree does not condemn this; it integrates it. If censorship risk is your primary driver, a centrally issued stablecoin may be a poor fit. If your driver is settlement speed within regulatory perimeter, it may be perfect. Context rules.

The decision tree also illuminates public goods. Funding open-source software suffers less from censorship than from free-riding and maintenance fatigue. Tokens can create incentives, but they introduce volatility and governance work. Grants and quadratic funding mechanisms, as seen in Gitcoin rounds since 2019, have directed resources to developers with public matching. The fit emerges when capture risk is low but counterparty trust is diffuse: donors need a credible, transparent allocator; recipients need a predictable process. Where local law permits, crypto-native funding tools can publish every disbursement on-chain, with clear criteria and audit trails. The metric here is grant throughput and completion rate rather than token price.

Motifs steer memory. Keep the compass in hand and ask the same three questions when faced with shiny pitches. A city wants to "put identities on the blockchain." Which risk dominates? If censorship of civic access is the fear, self-sovereign identity with selective disclosure may help. If counterparty risk is low because the city already issues IDs with due process and appeal, the project risks confusing means for ends. If capture is the concern—ids becoming pay-to-play—the remedy is legal protection against exclusion, not Merkle trees. The implication is that some problems are constitutional, not computational.

Behavioural costs must be counted. Gas fees, key management, and recovery all impose friction that moves from centre to edge. Where the dominant risk is modest, that friction becomes hidden labour with little payoff. A university consortium that shares research data across known members achieves integrity and availability through contracts and audits. A public blockchain adds cost without reducing meaningful risk. The metric you track is uptime under stress and incident response time, not "number of nodes." Those numbers impress investors; they rarely protect scholars.

Where the compass points firmly to crypto, design choices still matter. If censorship is the driver, prefer architectures without central choke points: non-custodial wallets, open-source clients, bridges with verifiable proofs. If counterparty risk is the driver, prioritise social recovery and multi-signature setups so that a lost device does not become a lost life. If capture risk is the driver, invest in portability: exportable data, composable contracts, and standards that let you walk away. The visible behaviours are mundane: a CTO runs an exit drill; a journalist stores a shard with a lawyer; a co-op publishes an API so members can switch providers in a day. Competence beats rhetoric.

Counter-arguments deserve respect. Some say that better regulation, not blockchains, solves most frictions. Often true. Strong consumer protection reduces counterparty risk. Administrative law curbs arbitrary censorship. Antitrust action softens capture. Where institutions function well and can be renewed, the tree will often steer you back to them. That is a success, not a retreat. The compass is agnostic; its job is to point, not to flatter.

There is also a democratic concern. Systems that bypass institutions can bypass accountability. Private money with public reach creates policy externalities: tax, crime, systemic stability. The decision tree therefore includes a constitutional mirror. If the remedy for censorship undermines due process, it may cure the disease by killing the patient. The operational test is whether the same transparency that exposes power also disciplines the tool: public audits, clear governance, documented upgrade paths, and the humility to pause when the cure risks a worse harm.

Return to where we began. When card networks severed WikiLeaks, crypto offered a path not subject to corporate gatekeeping. When donations needed to reach Kyiv rapidly, crypto cut the queue. When exchanges re-hypothecated client funds, self-custody provided a backstop. These are not slogans; they are choices visible in keystrokes, custody setups, and timestamps on a public ledger. The compass works because it respects trade-offs.

You now have its bearings. Is censorship plausible and proximate? Is your counterparty intolerably powerful or fragile? Is capture likely to bend rules against you as you scale? Answer those, and most crypto questions become simpler. Not easy—simpler. The unresolved tension is the hardest part: when two risks pull in opposite directions—say, censorship argues for maximal decentralisation while counterparty risk argues for help from a regulated custodian—where do you set the needle? That is the next decision. It is also the honest work.

Chapter 2
Autonomy at Scale

In August 2021, as Kabul fell, an Afghan software engineer tried to withdraw his earnings from an online freelance platform. His account was verified, his balance intact, yet every withdrawal route—bank, PayPal, remittance—was frozen under compliance review. He watched a message flash: *"Service unavailable in your region."* That week, Bitcoin became more than a headline. For a brief, unsentimental moment, autonomy was no longer a slogan; it was an escape hatch. The act of holding one's own keys meant the difference between possession and permission. Yet even as this story spread through crypto circles, a quieter question followed: could a society made of such exits ever cohere?

Autonomy, at small scale, feels like liberation. At large scale, it behaves like entropy. The history of political thought warns us of this paradox. Jean-Jacques Rousseau wrote that freedom is obedience to a law one gives oneself—but who, in a network of millions, is *oneself*? In decentralised systems, every wallet, every node, every validator claims a slice of sovereignty. This dispersal is both thrilling and dangerous. It promises to dissolve domination but risks dissolving coordination too. The chapter that follows asks how autonomy can survive the passage from principle to population—how freedom can multiply without fragmenting into noise.

The core tension is not new. It echoes Albert Hirschman's trinity of *exit*, *voice*, and *loyalty*. Exit means leaving a system that fails you; voice means staying and fighting to reform it. Traditional institutions balance these forces imperfectly: citizens may emigrate or vote, investors may divest or agitate. Decentralised systems, however, hard-code exit. Forks, self-custody, and open-source licences turn the act of departure into a design feature. This power disciplines authority—knowing users can walk keeps governors honest—but it also drains collective stamina. If dissent always means leaving, who stays to mend what breaks? The challenge, therefore, is not to celebrate exit but to cultivate *plural sovereignty*: the capacity to move without erasing community.

The chapter begins by revisiting this idea of sovereignty in the age of open protocols. Unlike nation-states, these digital polities have no borders to guard, only rules to coordinate. A protocol cannot imprison you, but it can exclude you through design choices. A fork is a declaration of independence written in code. Yet every new chain, every new DAO, inherits the same dilemma as postcolonial republics: how to build legitimacy when authority is optional. Through vignettes—from open-source splits that led to flourishing diversity to those that produced exhausted duplication—we will explore how autonomy disciplines power yet also dilutes it.

From sovereignty, we descend to the tool that most citizens of this new order carry in their pockets: the wallet. It is not merely a convenience; it is a constitution rendered in interface. A private key is a clause of ownership; a transaction signature, a ratified act. Each design choice—multi-signature approval, recovery method, fee policy—translates political theory into everyday practice. When a wallet demands your biometric or sends a silent update, it legislates. When it offers social recovery through trusted contacts, it redefines citizenship as networked guardianship. To treat user experience as superficial is to misunderstand power. In decentralised life, *UX is governance*. The smoother the interface, the more invisible its constitutional logic becomes. This section will give readers a framework for dignified design: defaults that protect, permissions that educate, reversibility that respects intent.

The next movement turns to identity, the perennial problem of modern liberty. To act autonomously, one must be recognised without being reduced. Centralised systems verify by storing; decentralised ones verify by proving. The difference is not semantic but ethical. Decentralised identifiers (DIDs) and verifiable credentials promise *plural proofs*—allowing an individual to disclose only what a context demands. A driver may prove age without revealing name; a refugee may verify education without exposing nationality. This reverses the surveillance logic of "collect everything, trust later." But plural proofs also create complexity. Who issues attestations? How are they revoked? When does selective disclosure shade into selective truth? This section will weigh these tensions, showing how self-sovereign identity can uphold dignity only when bounded by revocation and reciprocity.

Autonomy's price is coordination. To act alone is easy; to act together without a master is costly. Every decentralised project, from blockchains to cooperatives, must pay this tax in time, expertise, and patience. Gas fees are the literal manifestation of that cost: computation as friction. Yet the deeper cost is cognitive. Each user becomes an administrator of their own security, an auditor of their own community. Freedom, unmanaged, turns into hidden labour. The final section of this chapter will surface these costs and the design patterns that soften them: sensible defaults, bounded delegation, rotating responsibilities. The aim is not to retreat to paternalism but to cultivate systems where responsibility scales without exhaustion.

The motif that runs through these explorations is the *balancing act*: autonomy as equilibrium, not escape. Like a tightrope walker, the decentralised citizen must lean alternately towards independence and interdependence, self-custody and shared infrastructure. Too much weight on either side, and the structure collapses—into tyranny or chaos. This tension is not a flaw of decentralisation but its test. The art of autonomy lies not in abolishing dependence but in choosing it wisely.

The relevance of this inquiry extends beyond blockchains or finance. The same dynamics shape universities, cooperatives, and online communities. Everywhere we see attempts to rewire trust: users fleeing opaque platforms, workers forming collectives, creators experimenting with direct patronage. Each movement carries the same aspiration—to act without intermediaries—and each discovers, in time, that coordination does not vanish with authority; it merely relocates. The lessons drawn here will therefore speak to a broader audience: anyone designing systems where freedom must meet scale.

Readers who arrive at this chapter already understand decentralisation's moral ambition: to return agency to individuals. What they will find here is its practical anatomy—the frictions, interfaces, and psychological limits that decide whether agency becomes sustainable. They will see that self-sovereignty is not a solitary state but a civic practice; that wallets, far from mere tools, are social contracts; that privacy-preserving identity is not secrecy but selective transparency; and that coordination, wisely designed, is the scaffolding that keeps autonomy upright.

The closing image, perhaps, is of a city without gates. Each citizen owns their key, each house stands independent, yet the streets remain lit because residents agree—implicitly, voluntarily—to pay for the lamps. That is autonomy at scale: not isolation, not anarchy, but a community of self-governing actors who understand that freedom, to endure, must be organised. The pages ahead will explore how to build that city—securely, ethically, and without losing the human warmth that makes liberty worth keeping.

Sovereignty, Exit, and Voice

On 11 March 2021, at 18:33 UTC, a single Ethereum transaction closed the auction for *Everydays: The First 5000 Days* by the digital artist Beeple. The winning bid—42,329 Ether, then worth $69.3 million—was placed through the platform MakersPlace, but the ownership record lived on-chain. No gallery, no clearing house, no customs form. The buyer, Singapore-based programmer Vignesh Sundaresan, known by his pseudonym MetaKovan, took custody of the asset without institutional mediation. A work of art changed hands across continents through code, not contract. The sale was hailed as a revolution in creativity and derided as speculative excess. Yet behind the noise, something subtler was visible: a citizen exercising *exit* from traditional cultural gatekeepers, and doing so in public.

Exit is autonomy's sharpest instrument. It disciplines power not by protest but by departure. When users can walk, monopolies must listen. When they cannot, loyalty turns into servitude. The political economist Albert Hirschman's 1970 treatise *Exit, Voice, and Loyalty* remains the canonical map of this terrain. It proposed that individuals have two main responses to institutional decay: exit—leaving for alternatives—or voice—staying to reform from within. In centralised systems, exit is often costly; hence voice becomes the democratic safety valve. But decentralised architectures invert this ratio. Forks, open standards, and self-custody make exit frictionless, perhaps too frictionless. When exit becomes effortless, voice loses its stamina. This is the paradox that shadows decentralisation: the same autonomy that protects freedom can erode cohesion.

Consider the history of open-source software. In 2014, a dispute within the Bitcoin developer community over block size limits led to the creation of Bitcoin Cash in 2017. The split was meant to scale transaction capacity but became a test of legitimacy. Both sides invoked the same ideals—decentralisation, efficiency, purity—yet could not reconcile governance disputes. The result: two functioning but divergent ecosystems, each claiming continuity with the original. This act of exit demonstrated discipline: Bitcoin Core developers became more cautious about consensus-breaking changes. But it also illustrated fragmentation: resources, community, and credibility were divided. Exit had enforced prudence yet consumed momentum.

Contrast that with another form of exit that strengthened the commons. When Mozilla spun out of Netscape in 1998, it released its browser code under an open-source licence, inviting public contribution. Rather than fleeing a failed company, developers exited into a new structure that amplified their collective voice. Firefox's success in the mid-2000s restored competition and standards compliance to the web. The crucial difference was institutional design: Mozilla combined freedom to fork with governance mechanisms—foundations, councils, meritocratic reviews—that channelled dissent into renewal rather than schism. Autonomy flourished because exit was possible but not casual.

This distinction—between disciplining exit and dissolving exit—matters far beyond software. In 2016, ride-share drivers in Jakarta organised through informal WhatsApp groups to protest unilateral pay cuts by major platforms. With no labour union to mediate, many switched en masse to smaller competitors, forcing rate revisions. Exit substituted for voice. Yet within months, coordination fatigue set in: the market atomised, fares fell, and workers were left with greater exposure and less bargaining power. The gesture of autonomy was real but fleeting. Power, like water, returned through new channels. The lesson applies equally to crypto networks. Forks may punish arrogance but cannot replace solidarity.

Self-custody offers another dimension of exit—individual, not collective. To hold one's own keys is to withdraw from custodial dependency. But sovereignty here is double-edged. The individual gains control yet inherits full liability for error. In April 2022, Chainalysis estimated that over 3.7 million Bitcoin—roughly 20% of total supply—were lost to forgotten keys or inaccessible wallets. Freedom without support structures can turn into paralysis. Sovereignty must therefore be conceived as *institutional plurality*, not isolation. The question is not "who governs?" but "how many forms of governance can coexist without collapse?"

Plurality is already visible in the proliferation of DAOs—decentralised autonomous organisations—each experimenting with hybrid modes of exit and voice. *MakerDAO*, founded in 2017, allows token holders to vote on risk parameters of its stablecoin system. In theory, participants can fork or sell their tokens if disillusioned. Yet its most consequential reforms—adjusting collateral types, creating core units—required sustained debate rather than flight. Maker's endurance suggests that autonomy becomes resilient not when exit is easiest, but when exit exists alongside credible mechanisms of voice. By contrast, *Yearn Finance*'s early "rage-quit" culture, which glorified spontaneous forks, produced speed but also volatility. Over time, it evolved toward structured proposals and delegated representation. The dialectic repeats: freedom without forum breeds noise; forum without freedom breeds capture.

A counter-example illuminates the boundaries of this logic. When Facebook rebranded as Meta in October 2021, it invoked the language of open metaverses while constructing one of the most closed. Its platforms promise user agency but rely on proprietary identity, content, and currency systems. Exit is illusory; data remains captive. Yet Meta's imitation of decentralised rhetoric is revealing. Even dominant institutions must borrow the language of autonomy to preserve legitimacy. The pressure of possible exit—symbolic or technical—disciplines them. In that sense, decentralisation's power extends beyond its adoption. It shifts norms for what control looks like.

The motif that threads these examples is *the door*: every system, however grand, must keep a door ajar for exit to remain credible. But a society of perpetual doorways risks losing walls altogether. Coordination demands thresholds—moments when members commit to shared constraints. Political theory recognises this as constitutionalism: the voluntary limitation of power, including one's own. In decentralised networks, this takes the form of social contracts embedded in code—governance tokens, multisignature treasuries, quorum thresholds. These devices create a middle ground where exit remains possible but costly enough to encourage deliberation first. The door stays open, but it requires intent to walk through.

The empirical test for healthy autonomy, then, lies in balance metrics. How many participants remain active after major governance disputes? What proportion of forks lead to thriving projects rather than abandoned repositories? These are not market indicators but civic ones. A network that never fractures may be complacent; one that constantly splinters is unsustainable. Between these extremes lies what economist Elinor Ostrom called "polycentric governance"—multiple centres of authority coordinating without hierarchy. Crypto networks, properly understood, are laboratories for this principle. Each wallet, DAO, and protocol becomes a micro-sovereign node, testing how much voice and exit a system can bear before coherence gives way.

Still, autonomy at scale cannot rely on voluntary virtue alone. History shows that plural sovereignty requires connective tissue—shared standards, dispute channels, reputational feedback. The early internet's open protocols, from TCP/IP to email's SMTP, succeeded because they defined minimum compatibility while allowing local innovation. Participants could exit a vendor but not the commons. This distinction between protocol and platform is essential. Protocols encode reciprocity; platforms monetise enclosure. Crypto's maturation depends on keeping its protocols genuinely open, its communities aware that autonomy is preserved not by walls but by bridges.

One might argue that exit has gone too far. Decentralised finance, with its endless proliferation of tokens and forks, resembles a marketplace of schisms. Each new chain promises to fix the flaws of the old, while liquidity fragments and security dilutes. Coordination costs rise; attention fractures.

Yet, viewed charitably, this turbulence is adolescence. Political federations, too, began as messy confederacies before stabilising through norms and interoperability. The same may hold for digital polities. Maturity will arrive when exit retains its disciplinary power but ceases to be the default protest.

The door motif returns in closing. Autonomy is not the act of walking out; it is the knowledge that one can. Exit gives leverage; voice gives belonging. The equilibrium of the two defines sovereignty in the decentralised age. When communities design systems that honour both—secure in self-custody yet porous to dialogue—they approach a form of governance that neither dissolves into solitude nor hardens into bureaucracy.

The unresolved question remains deliberately open: how much cohesion can freedom bear before it curdles into control, and how much fragmentation can freedom survive before it turns meaningless? The next sections will test that boundary—not by choosing sides, but by tracing where the door should stand.

Wallets as Constitutional Interfaces

In May 2023, Paris-based hardware wallet company Ledger announced *Ledger Recover*, an opt-in service to shard and escrow a user's seed phrase with third parties. The aim, they said, was mercy for ordinary fallibility. Within days, a backlash rolled across forums and social media. The outrage was very swift. Critics saw an erosion of self-custody's bright line: if firmware could export key material, even under consent, then the device's "offline" sanctity was negotiable. Ledger paused, clarified, and later committed to open-sourcing more of its code. A small firmware flag had become a constitutional crisis. The episode made plain a truth this chapter leans on: wallets are not neutral tools. They are where sovereignty meets policy.

A wallet is a constitution in your hand. Keys delineate rights. Policies constrain powers. Signatures authorise acts. Every prompt, every default, encodes a theory of the citizen. Show this at the interface and you will show the governance beneath. Name it for what it is—*a charter*—and design choices take on the gravity they deserve. Explain it by tracing consequences: a default blind-signing toggle is not UX sugar; it creates a class of citizens who can be tricked into ceding assets. Implication: the craft of wallet design is moral craftsmanship, because the interface allocates risk.

Multisignature wallets make the constitutional metaphor undeniable. In a *2-of-3* scheme, no single actor can move funds; authority requires coalition. That is separation of powers rendered in code. A city treasury using a *3-of-5* Safe (formerly Gnosis Safe) with signers in London, Nairobi, and Lisbon is not just distributing operations; it is disarming opportunism. The behaviour is visible: a proposal submitted, a quorum reached, a movement of funds logged on-chain. The metric is practical: mean time to approve urgent transactions versus median delay for routine ones. Design these thresholds poorly and you create either paralysis or arbitrary rule. Design them wisely and you obtain a living constitution that scales prudence without stifling work. The threshold matters.

Social recovery extends the charter. Argent popularised this model from 2019: a user appoints *guardians*—devices, friends, or institutions—who can collectively authorise recovery after a loss. The idea converts community into insurance. Show: a phone disappears on the Northern line; the owner triggers recovery; two of three guardians attest after a cool-down delay; access returns without seed phrases scribbled on paper. Name: social recovery as *delegated sovereignty*. Explain: rather than centralising trust in a custodian, you distribute it across relationships and time. Implication: dignity endures through mishap, but only if the guardianship graph is legible and revocable. The threshold again governs outcomes: who counts as a guardian, how many, with what delays. Too strict, and users are locked out; too lax, and attackers collude.

Yet wallets can fail constitutionally. In November 2017 in London, a flaw in Parity's multisig library left hundreds of thousands of Ether irreversibly frozen when a user took ownership of the library and killed it. The code obeyed itself; the assets became stone. Limitation, named and sobering: the clause for emergency repair was missing. Explain: a wallet is not a contract isolated in maths; it is a polity with upgrade paths and emergency brakes. Implication: constitutional design must include a narrowly scoped *amendment* process—time-locked upgrades, explicit circuit-breakers, and visible vetoes—without creating a dormant autocracy. The threshold between safety and capture is narrow.

From these episodes a quiet motif runs: *the threshold.* It appears as a multisig number, a recovery delay, a spending limit, a timelock. Each threshold is a judgement about human fallibility and adversarial patience. Too low, and theft thrives. Too high, and coordination dies. The constitutional wallet sets thresholds that educate. It explains, in human words, what is being signed, by whom, under which limits. It slows you down where you ought to slow; it gets out of the way where autonomy pays. This is why "UX is governance". The colour of a button is cosmetic; the second-factor policy behind it is law.

Consider a concrete counterweight: speed. Traders demand rapid execution. Seconds matter. A constitutional wallet that interposes friction indiscriminately will simply be abandoned for riskier tools. This is a real limit. Reconcile it by segmenting rights. Show: a treasury sets a daily spending allowance for small transfers that clear instantly under a single signer, with a hard cap; larger transfers trigger multisig, a 24-hour timelock, and out-of-band alerts. Name: *tiered authority.* Explain: most behaviour is quick within safe bounds; exceptional behaviour is slow by design. Implication: the median user experience remains crisp, while tail-risk receives dignity—not drama. The threshold is tuned rather than preached.

Public goods demonstrate wallets as civic organisers. In February and March 2022, several Ukraine-linked fundraisers routed substantial donations through multisig treasuries to reduce single-point compromise amid wartime uncertainty. The wallets embedded not just custody but process: verifiable proposals, transparent disbursements, roll-up reports for donors. Show: a grant request appears, signers confirm, funds move, beneficiaries publish receipts. Name: *legibility by default*. Explain: the constitutional wallet can make stewardship observable without doxxing. Implication: legitimacy compounds through routines that the interface normalises. The device becomes a civic instrument, not merely a vault.

Identity threads into this too. A wallet that surfaces verifiable credentials—proof of age, proof of membership, proof of solvency—without revealing raw data is not just convenient; it enforces the principle of *minimal disclosure*. Show: a renter proves salary range to a landlord via a zero-knowledge credential, signed by an employer, without exposing account numbers. Name: *selective disclosure*. Explain: the wallet acts as a clerk of the court, presenting admissible evidence under rules that you control. Implication: fewer honeypots of personal data, less collateral damage in breaches, more dignity in the routine humiliations of paperwork. But here again lies a threshold: how easy is revocation? A lost device should not enshrine outdated truths. The wallet must teach expiry, re-issuance, and the politics of who may retract claims.

Now, to the checklist for dignified defaults, expressed not as bullet points but as behaviours a reader could observe. A dignified wallet *describes*, in plain language, the contract you are about to authorise—names, amounts, permissions—before you sign. It *simulates* outcomes and warns when allowances exceed norms. It *stages* authority through sensible tiers: small payments fast, large ones slow, with timelocked windows that allow a human to wake, think, and veto. It *notifies* across channels you control, not ones an attacker can easily hijack, and it makes silence an alarm: if a critical alert cannot reach you, certain actions pause. It *teaches* recovery by rehearsal—an exit drill run quarterly, a guardian ping confirmed, a backup key rotated on calendar. It *declares* upgrade powers prominently and *binds* them—say, a supermajority and a delay—so that even the maintainers' good intentions require time and consent. It *exposes* provenance with clarity: which library this signing screen depends on, which build, which audit, with links that a sceptical professional can verify. It *refuses* dark patterns. No hurry, no hiding. Finally, it *makes leaving easy*: export keys, revoke permissions, uninstall in peace. This is what dignity looks like in software. Not sparkle. Structure.

Sceptics will ask: is this too much to expect from a wallet used on a bus in rush hour? Will people tolerate friction, read disclosures, appoint guardians? Behavioural reality: many will not. The answer is not moralising; it is design that *defaults wisely*. Think of contactless payments with spending caps; think of banking apps that delay new payee transfers for a day to frustrate fraud. Users accept well-targeted friction when it protects them from adversaries and from their tired selves. The lesson for wallets is to commit to a small set of defaults that pay for themselves: clear-text transaction simulation by default; delayed first transfer to a new contract; address books with human names; automatic warnings on infinite token approvals. Short, specific, enforced. The threshold, again, separates theatre from care.

There are hazards on the other side. Over-constitutionalisation can become paternalism. If every action requires a gauntlet of prompts, users will jailbreak or migrate. Worse, over-centralised recovery services may recreate banking by another name. The remedy is modularity. Allow those who need more protection to opt into it, visibly and reversibly, without coercing experts into friction they do not want. Permit multiple guardianship models to coexist—human guardians, hardware guardians, institutional guardians—so citizens can assemble the authority pattern that matches their risk and culture. Autonomy is not a monolith; it is institutional plurality inside one device.

Transparency must also include the platform itself. If a wallet bundles an internal exchange, a bridge, or staking, it holds policy levers that resemble ministerial portfolios. Which validators are whitelisted? Which networks are supported? Which fees are hidden in a slippage slider? These are not mere product decisions; they are budget lines and trade agreements. A constitutional interface declares them plainly, and offers portability. The respected test is simple: could a competent user replicate their setup elsewhere within an afternoon—contacts, whitelists, credentials, keys—without begging? If not, the interface is a platform in constitutional clothing.

Jurisdiction matters. A wallet with corporate presence in a given country inherits that legal system's demands. Declare them. If sanctions trigger address blacklists or if a court can compel software changes, the citizen deserves to know. This does not make the wallet untrustworthy; it makes it honest. Some will choose another tool. Others will accept the constraint. All are better citizens for seeing the threshold where law and code meet. Better a known boundary than a false absolution.

Finally, the human factor. A wallet is a mirror of its maker's ethics. Teams that publish threat models, describe their telemetry, and invite independent audits demonstrate a habit of mind that users can rely on. Those that treat users as metrics rather than citizens reveal themselves in their prompts and defaults—hurry, nudge, capture. A government of software is still a government. It deserves scrutiny, rotation, and dissent. A constitutional wallet should celebrate this: a public changelog, an archive of past errors, an attitude that treats criticism as a civic asset.

We return to the motif. The threshold is everywhere. Between convenience and consent. Between recovery and capture. Between speed and prudence. The work of the wallet is to place that line where humans can live with it, and to mark it so clearly that moving it requires ceremony. The forward question is pointed: when the next convenience arrives—a biometric that signs for you, an AI that "reads" contracts, a custody-as-a-service that promises fewer headaches—what threshold will you accept, and which constitutional clause will you refuse to trade away?

Identity Without a Master

On 1 July 2021 in Brussels, the European Union's Digital COVID Certificate entered into force across twenty-seven member states. Travellers presented a QR code at airports from Lisbon to Berlin; border officers scanned the code offline and saw a cryptographic signature verifying vaccination or test status. There was no central server queried at the gate, no dossier assembled in the shadows. A public key, published by each member state, allowed instant validation. The system was blunt in purpose yet subtle in method: prove *this* claim, disclose nothing more. In a season of polarised debate, the certificate revealed something quieter—identity could be reconstructed as a set of verifiable claims rather than a permanent file. The card defined the person.

Identity has long been managed by accumulation. Ministries, banks, and platforms collect, store, and correlate, asserting that more data means more confidence. The result is brittle power: a breach leaks everything; an error follows you for years. Decentralised identifiers (DIDs) and verifiable credentials invert the logic. They make identity a choreography rather than a hoard—a dance of proofs supplied for a purpose, withdrawn when the purpose ends. The motif here is the *aperture*: open only as much as the light requires. Too wide, and glare blinds; too narrow, and nothing can be seen. Getting the aperture right is the work of design, not dogma.

Start with the mechanics you can touch. A DID is a persistent identifier controlled by the subject, resolvable to a DID Document that lists public keys and service endpoints. The *W3C DID Core* became a Recommendation in July 2022, giving this pattern a canonical shape. A verifiable credential (VC), standardised by the *W3C Verifiable Credentials Data Model* in November 2019, is a digitally signed statement—"over 18", "licensed architect", "resident at this postcode"—issued by some authority and presented by the holder. Show: you open a wallet, select "proof of age", and share a cryptographic presentation with a nightclub. Name: selective disclosure via zero-knowledge proofs or predicate proofs. Explain: the verifier checks the issuer's signature and the freshness of the proof without learning your full date of birth or home address. Implication: you enact the aperture—purpose-limited, minimally invasive, resistant to correlation.

Centralised KYC, by contrast, conflates verification with storage. A bank in London takes scans of your passport, a utility bill, and a selfie, then retains them for years to satisfy audits. This is understandable—regulations bite—but it creates honeypots. When compromised, they spill not a claim but a life. A VC-based workflow reframes the dependency. Show: the same bank requests a credential from the UK Passport Office attesting "document valid"; a proof from your employer that salary exceeds a threshold; a credential from a credit bureau attesting you're not on a sanctions list. Name: privacy-preserving onboarding. Explain: the bank sees yes/no predicates and cryptographic signatures; it stores just enough to meet regulatory tests. Implication: compliance survives; surveillance shrinks. The make-or-break detail is revocation: the bank must be able to check, without phoning home for every login, that a credential has not been withdrawn. Status lists or revocation registries handle this quietly—small, cacheable data structures that flag invalid credentials without revealing who checked what and when. The aperture moves, but the room stays dark.

Consider a second verifiable example. Estonia's digital identity, built on national PKI and the *X-Road* data exchange layer since 2001, allows citizens to sign legally binding documents with smartcards and mobile IDs. It is not "self-sovereign" in the ideological sense—the state is the root issuer—but it embodies two decisive principles: user-controlled signatures and transparency of access. Every query against your population registry or health record is logged; you can inspect who looked and why. Show: a citizen files taxes in minutes because salary and deductions are pre-filled; they approve with a PIN and see a ledger of data flows. Name: accountable issuance. Explain: strong cryptography anchors authenticity; institutional rules govern scope. Implication: centralised issuance need not mean centralised surveillance; the aperture is narrow because law and interface insist. Estonia is no utopia, but it demonstrates how *legibility without exposure* can be built into identity infrastructure.

A credible counter-example tests the promises. Worldcoin, a project announced in 2021 and launched more broadly in 2023, proposed that biometric uniqueness—iris codes captured at physical "Orbs"—could provide Sybil resistance for global digital identity. Proponents touted privacy-preserving hashes; critics raised concerns about coercion, consent, and the governance of biometric templates. Show: people in Nairobi or Buenos Aires queue for scans in exchange for tokens; regulators in Kenya pause operations (August 2023) pending data protection reviews. Name: the biometric bind. Explain: even if the iris code cannot reconstruct an image, the act of collection centralises intimate risk; revocation can stop future use but cannot retrieve the past capture. Implication: a proof of "personhood" may be safer when built on plural, revocable attestations—proof-of-uniqueness via web-of-trust, device attestations, behavioural signals—than on immutable bodily signatures. The aperture cannot be closed once the eye has been mapped.

What, then, counts as *identity without a master*? Not an absence of authorities, but a change in relationship. Instead of one registry dictating who you are everywhere, many issuers attest different facets of you somewhere. Your university asserts your degree; your local council asserts your address; a professional body asserts your licence; a charity asserts your membership. You carry these as credentials. You present only those relevant to a request. You rotate keys when compromised. You revoke claims when they expire. The behaviour is mundane: you open a wallet, choose proofs, consent to share, and watch the audit log fill. The metric is practical: average number of attributes revealed per transaction; median revocation latency; false rejection rate at gates. Identity becomes operationally plural and measurably cautious.

The ethics are correspondingly modest and exacting. Minimal disclosure is not a slogan but a discipline. Show: a landlord asks for three months of payslips; you present a signed statement from your employer that income exceeds a threshold and is current as of last week. Name: least-privilege verification. Explain: the less raw data you expose, the less damage a breach can do; the fewer fields a verifier collects, the less they must secure. Implication: privacy stops being secrecy and becomes hygiene. A good verifier asks for a proof they can actually defend in court and manage in storage; a good wallet makes the safer path the default.

Revocation is the second pillar. Centralised identity often treats revocation as administrative—flip a switch in a database—but the social harm persists; the traces remain copied in caches and warehouses. VC ecosystems are healthier when revocation is *cryptographically explicit* and *locally checkable*. Show: a professional's licence is suspended in

Manchester; their credential's status list is updated by the issuing council; hospitals that check the credential see the red flag even while offline or behind restrictive firewalls, because the revocation list is a signed, periodically fetched artefact. Name: revocation legibility. Explain: if revocation requires phoning a remote database at the moment of care, failures of connectivity become failures of duty. Implication: dignity is protected not only by who can issue, but by how quickly harm can be halted without breaching privacy for every routine check. The aperture narrows on demand.

Of course, credentials can be weaponised. A state could require a "good behaviour" credential to access services, chilling dissent. A platform could tie reputation to wallet-bound attestations, making mistakes hard to escape. Here, the constraint must be constitutional rather than technical. Limit linkability through pairwise DIDs—unique identifiers per relationship. Forbid coercive coupling of credentials in law and procurement: a library should not demand proof of political donations; a delivery app should not demand complete social graphs. And embed the right to *credential amnesty*: the legal power to retire certain attestations after adjudication. The remedies are dull but crucial—appeal processes, sunset clauses, and independent auditors who test for overreach. The aperture must be adjustable by citizens, not simply by issuers.

One might object that selective disclosure complicates compliance. Regulators need audit trails; banks require continuous monitoring; health systems need reliable identities to prevent fraud. Fair concerns. The reconciliation is architectural. Separate *real-time verification* from *post-event audit*. Permit point-of-care checks to use minimal proofs, then allow accredited auditors, under lawful process, to reconstruct context from issuers if misconduct is suspected. Show: a suspicious pattern triggers an audit request; the auditor asks specific issuers for confirmations tied to pseudonymous transaction IDs; each issuer reveals only its piece under warrant. Name: delayed transparency. Explain: this preserves the aperture at the moment of service while maintaining societal capacity to investigate. Implication: privacy and accountability become complements rather than antagonists.

We should be clear about the limits. DIDs and VCs do not themselves solve Sybil attacks in open networks; they solve *overexposure* in closed ones. They do not, by themselves, end data broking; they give individuals and verifiers a tool to refuse it. They cannot guarantee honesty; they can constrain the damage of deceit. And they introduce new failure modes: key loss, guardian collusion in social recovery, issuer insolvency. Designing around these means borrowing from the preceding subchapter's constitutional toolbox: thresholds, timelocks, transparent upgrade paths. When identity is a portfolio of proofs, the custody of that portfolio needs the same care as assets. The behaviour, again, is visible: a quarterly "credential drill", revocation rehearsed, trusted contacts confirmed, replacement keys issued.

The EU's certificate, Estonia's signatures, and Worldcoin's controversy show the spectrum. At one end, credential systems that minimise disclosure and permit revocation without surveillance. At the other, biometric ambition that risks irrevocable exposure. Between them, a host of experiments: India's Aadhaar, launched in 2009 under the Unique Identification Authority of India, provides a single national number for welfare distribution and KYC; its courts and civil society have wrestled over scope, consent, and private-sector use. Aadhaar's scale is astonishing; its architecture centralises power. The lesson is not to reject national IDs outright but to insist on selective disclosure at the edge, independent audits of authentication logs, and legally enforceable purpose limits. Identity is not a database; it is a contract with a populace.

For enterprises, the calculus is pragmatic. Measure *time-to-onboard* with VCs; measure *breach exposure* by counting the sensitive fields you no longer store. Compare *false-positive rates* at gates before and after predicate proofs replace full-data checks. If the numbers improve, the system respects people and reduces cost. If they do not, you have built privacy theatre. The aperture has been painted on the wall.

For citizens, the shift is behavioural. You begin to collect attestations from a mosaic of issuers—university, employer, union, charity, credit union—and you present them piecemeal as needed. You rotate keys annually. You subscribe to revocation notifications from issuers that matter. You treat your wallet as a clerk who works for you, not a portal that works for someone else. The change is small in gesture and large in consequence. Agency becomes routine.

The idea of identity without a master is not an invitation to solipsism. It is an argument for *plural masters with bounded reach*. A city, a guild, a hospital, a platform—all may speak about you, but none may speak for you everywhere. When their claims conflict, there must be process. When their claims expire, they must withdraw. The aperture lives in that discipline. It opens so that society can function; it closes so that a life can be private.

The unresolved test is the hardest: when harm prevention demands stronger linkage—say, to stop subsidy fraud or coordinated harassment—how far should the aperture widen, and who decides? A magistrate? A multiparty council? An algorithm with appeal? We will need procedures, not slogans. The architecture can support either virtue or vice. The hinge is will.

The Cost of Coordination

In December 2017 in Vancouver, Axiom Zen's game CryptoKitties clogged the Ethereum network within days of launch. Transactions queued. Fees spiked. Traders, gamers, and small developers discovered the same bill on the same day: autonomy demands capacity, and capacity is scarce when everyone tries to act at once. No court failed. No bank froze accounts. The network did exactly as designed, yet coordination costs surfaced in the only currency all systems recognise—delay. Here was a plain lesson. Freedom has a receipt.

The receipt takes many forms. Gas at the point of use. Time sunk into wallet hygiene. Hours spent reading proposals. A founder clicks through three multisig prompts, a volunteer reviews governance threads, a designer replays failed transactions to understand nonce gaps. Each act is a grain of sand that does not ruin the machine but slows it. Call it the coordination tax. It is paid by the edges rather than the centre, and therefore vanishes from dashboards until it threatens to stall momentum. This is the paradox of decentralised success: when autonomy scales, the bill arrives late and large. It arrives everywhere at once. This matters.

Show first, then name. In December 2017, CryptoKitties consumed blockspace that other applications needed. Ethereum's miners processed the highest-fee transactions first; everyone else waited. Name the phenomenon: *congestion externality*. Explain: permissionless access means one popular app can raise the marginal cost for all others, because throughput is a commons. Implication: autonomy without capacity planning converts choice into queues. The mechanics were unromantic—mempools swollen, confirmation times stretched—but the social lesson was sharp. When everyone is their own bank, everyone is also their own queue manager.

A second scene, three and a half years later, points to a remedy with limits. On 5 August 2021, Ethereum activated the London upgrade—EIP-1559—introducing a base fee that adjusts block by block and burns rather than pays it to miners. The change did not magically cheapen blockspace; it made fees more predictable and tamped down bidding wars. Show: users saw fewer "stuck" transactions and clearer fee suggestions in wallets. Name: *fee legibility*. Explain: by establishing a protocol-level default for how prices move, the network reduced cognitive load at the edge. Implication: defaults are governance. They shrink decision fatigue without withdrawing agency, the first pattern in a repertoire for managing autonomy's tax.

Decision fatigue is harder to perceive than fees, yet it corrodes more. A simple token transfer now asks a human to pick a network, a gas priority, a nonce strategy, and a signing device. Choices multiply. Errors multiply with them. In this respect, autonomy externalises *learning*. Every user becomes a novice auditor. The wrong signature on an "infinite approval" screen can drain a wallet. The wrong bridge can bleed funds. To name this is to change it. When we call these burdens *hidden labour*, we remind designers that they are movable, not inevitable. The implication is operational: push common, safe paths into defaults; let expertise express itself in opt-ins, not traps.

Delegation, when bounded, is a second pattern that pays for itself. Consider Bitcoin's Taproot activation on 14 November 2021. Taproot introduced new script capabilities and privacy improvements after a year of discussion and testnet trials. The activation method—Speedy Trial—asked miners to signal readiness within a short window; if enough hash power signalled, the change locked in with a delay. Show: node operators chose clients that implemented the rules, miners signalled, and activation occurred with minimal drama. Name: *bounded delegation*. Explain: authority to set a default path (activation upon threshold) existed but was constrained by time, signalling, and a clear exit (node sovereignty). Implication: you can reduce decision overhead for most participants while preserving the right of dissenters to hold the line. The receipt shrank without confiscating choice.

Now a caution. In September 2021 in San Francisco, an upgrade to Compound's protocol—Proposal 062—introduced a bug that miscalculated rewards, erroneously distributing millions of dollars' worth of COMP. No theft occurred; no adversary breached servers. Coordination itself failed. Show: a proposal went live, users harvested mistaken rewards, and governance scrambled to pass patches under a time delay. Name: *governance execution risk*. Explain: even with audits, upgrade paths convert social approval into code paths; staging and kill-switches are constitutional clauses, not niceties. Implication: bounded delegation must include bounded blast-radius. Stage changes. Use canary deployments. Tie large powers to timelocks long enough for humans to wake, read, and veto. Autonomy that never slows for risk is bravado.

The motif of this section is the *receipt*. We return to it because it keeps us honest. Where do you see it? In a DAO where every grant requires a forum post, a temperature check, a snapshot, and an on-chain vote—weeks of attention to send a small stipend. In a wallet that forces you to type a 24-word seed on a cramped touchscreen when a single YubiKey plus social recovery would have managed risk better. In a public-goods round where donors must bridge, wrap, and sign three transactions for £20 of support. Each is a choice. Each is chargeable to no one and paid by everyone.

There are countervailing successes. Gitcoin's quadratic funding rounds, running since 2019, show how design can compress coordination cost while amplifying plural preferences. Show: small contributions from many donors unlock matching from a central pool, with anti-sybil checks and transparent payouts. Name: *scaled pluralism*. Explain: by rewarding breadth over depth, the mechanism converts scattered voice into decisive allocation without forcing everyone into one committee room. Implication: we can buy back some of the time autonomy stole, provided we measure what matters—donor participation rates, matching effectiveness, and completion rates for funded work—rather than fetishising token prices or dashboard gloss.

Defaults do heavy moral lifting elsewhere too. A multisig treasury can set a daily allowance for low-risk payments that clear under one signer, escalating to two or three signatures and a timelock only when thresholds are crossed. Show: routine expenses flow; exceptional ones slow. Name: *tiered authority*. Explain: the shape of friction fits the shape of risk; humans spend attention where it earns interest. Implication: the tax is progressive. Those who impose outsized risk also bear more of the coordination cost. A fair bill finds the right payer.

Bounded delegation extends beyond protocol upgrades and treasuries. It stabilises social recovery. Argent's guardianship model, for example, allows a user to appoint devices, people, or institutions as guardians who can collectively approve recovery after a cool-down delay. Show: a theft attempt triggers alerts; guardians refuse; funds stay put. Name: *distributed custody*. Explain: you move trust from a single custodian to a threshold among parties you chose, with delays that favour defenders. Implication: the learning burden declines—the user rehearses recovery quarterly; the edge does less frantic work because the centre (your social graph) absorbs the shock. The receipt shrinks again.

Not all defaults help. Some harden into theatre. A project that requires five separate votes to grant a £1,000 research stipend is not stewarding funds; it is laundering responsibility. Conversely, an interface that hides infinite token approvals behind a cheerful button is not respecting autonomy; it is taxing the future for speed now. The diagnostic is behavioural. Measure median time-to-decision for routine matters, and the abandonment rate for partially completed proposals. Track how often timelocks trigger community review rather than rubber-stamp. Attention is scarce. Design must spend it like cash.

Fragmentation compounds costs in subtle ways. Each new rollup, wallet, and bridge adds choice, yet also adds new failure modes. A researcher, wishing to fund a grant, confronts five possible networks, three wrapped assets, and a dozen bridges. The cognitive meter spins before the first pound moves. Here, composability and portability are not slogans but relief valves. A healthy ecosystem commits to portable credentials, standard transaction simulation, and shared address books. Show: a user switches wallets on a new device and sees the same human-readable contacts and contract warnings. Name: *interoperable caution*. Explain: when safety cues travel with the person, not the app, learning amortises. Implication: the receipt is paid once, not at every till.

There is a rejoinder worth respecting: some coordination costs are the price of self-respect. You *should* pause before moving treasury funds. You *should* learn the basics of key hygiene. A democracy asks citizens to read and vote; a decentralised network asks them to deliberate and sign. The counter-example is the centralised exchange that makes everything smooth—until it fails catastrophically. FTX's collapse in November 2022 reminded millions that outsourcing all coordination to a fast-talking centre ends with a larger bill. The reconciliation is not to romanticise friction but to be choosy. Keep the pauses that prevent irreversible harms; remove the hurdles that merely protect designers from writing better software.

We can name three habits that convert philosophy into practice without listing them like a brochure. First, rehearse. Run quarterly "exit drills" for treasuries and personal wallets: rotate a guardian, restore from backup, revoke stale approvals. The visible behaviour trains muscle memory and reveals broken paths before crisis. Second, stagger. Stage changes with canaries and thresholds, so that failures fail small. Third, narrate. Write proposals and wallet prompts in clear language that states the power being exercised, the limit being crossed, and the time left to object. The implication across all three is the same. Coordination costs fall when systems teach while they run.

The state of fees remains the bluntest instrument. When blockspace grows scarce, prices rise. Some will insist that more throughput solves all. It does not. Higher capacity lowers the unit cost but raises expectations and invites heavier use. Demand expands to meet supply. The humane answer is a portfolio: scalable execution for the everyday, and settlement layers that favour finality and auditability for the consequential. Give people trains for commuting and courts for disputes. Price each accordingly. The choice is architectural, not ideological.

The final place to look for the receipt is within ourselves. Voluntary coalitions decay, not from malice, but from neglect. We ghost meetings. We skim long posts. We rubber-stamp because we are tired. Designing for that human fact is not cynicism; it is care. Rotating stewards, explicit time-bounds on roles, and sunset clauses keep responsibility light and fresh. A system that assumes everyone will behave like a monk will exhaust saints and empower opportunists. A system that assumes most of us will be busy most of the time will protect us from ourselves.

Return to Vancouver for a moment. The kittens taught a generation that a network is not a cloud but a street with finite lanes. Since then, we have widened roads, improved tolling, and built bypasses. Yet the deeper work is cultural and procedural. It asks whether we can teach millions to be sovereign without making them clerks, and whether we can distribute power without warehousing attention in committee rooms. That is the unresolved test. The forward question is practical and hard: which decisions will you pre-commit to automate, which will you delegate with brakes, and where, precisely, will you keep the pause that saves you when everything moves too fast?

Chapter 3
Code, Law, and Legitimacy

On 17 June 2016, a vulnerability in *The DAO*—a decentralised investment fund running on Ethereum—was exploited. Over three million ether, roughly a third of its holdings, began draining into a child contract. Panic spread across message boards and chat rooms. No one disputed what the code was doing. Yet what it *meant* was another matter entirely. Some argued that "code is law": the attacker had simply followed the contract's logic. Others called it theft by algorithmic loophole. The blockchain was immutable, but the community was not. In the end, Ethereum forked—one chain reversing the attack, another refusing to. Both claimed legitimacy; both survived. The episode was not a glitch in digital utopia. It was a constitutional moment.

That phrase—*constitutional moment*—captures the tension at the heart of this chapter. Code promises certainty where law wavers, but it cannot yet contain the full complexity of human life. A smart contract can transfer tokens flawlessly, yet cannot weigh intent, duress, or fairness. Law, by contrast, is slow, interpretive, and often messy—but it absorbs the shocks of ambiguity. When software steps into the role of sovereign, we must ask: what does it mean to govern without recourse to mercy or discretion? And when humans amend or override code, under what authority do they act? The line between enforcement and exception becomes the site of legitimacy itself.

The twentieth century built institutions on paper and trust: courts, registries, banks. The twenty-first is rebuilding them in code, seeking incorruptible execution. But incorruptibility and justice are not synonyms. A network may be secure yet unjust, efficient yet illegitimate. *The DAO* fork showed that integrity of code and integrity of community are distinct currencies, and that systems survive only when both are honoured. This is where the conversation must mature—from whether law or code "wins" to how they coexist in disciplined tension.

The first section of this chapter explores *when code is law—and when it isn't*. The slogan, popularised by Lawrence Lessig in the late 1990s, was descriptive before it became dogmatic. Software constrains behaviour more reliably than statutes do. You cannot jaywalk across a smart contract. Yet its precision is brittle. Oracles fail. Time zones shift. Hackers exploit edge cases that judges would recognise as absurdities. The mature answer is hybrid: pre-agreed legal interfaces that define how disputes, reversals, and emergencies are handled without surrendering automation's strength. The reader will see that code's perfection is not an end but a boundary condition, within which legal and ethical reasoning must still breathe.

Next comes *property, custody, and remedies*. The law of possession evolved for objects that could be fenced, handed, or seized. Bearer assets on a blockchain complicate this—possession becomes control of keys, and control may be automated or fractional. What happens when those keys are lost, or misused, or held jointly? Without a clear concept of remedy, even well-built systems can incubate moral hazard. This section argues for a remedy-first mindset: design protocols with their worst day in mind. Who can make whole, and how, when something goes wrong? The sober lesson is that freedom without restitution breeds fragility, while restitution without freedom breeds dependency. The art lies in balance.

The third section, *forks as constitutional crises*, examines how decentralised systems rewrite themselves under duress. Forks are secessions with shared ancestry; they preserve the chain of blocks but split the chain of legitimacy. Power in such moments does not flow solely from hash rate or software control. It flows from narrative coherence—from whose version of events persuades the greatest plurality of users. Bitcoin, Ethereum, and countless smaller projects have lived through these moments, each time revealing that governance is a performative act: authority is asserted, contested, and stabilised through coordination, not decree. Readers will learn to interpret forks not as technical schisms but as civic dramas, where sovereignty, consent, and precedent are redefined in real time.

Finally, *regulators as system actors* closes the circle. For years, the crypto field cast regulation as an external threat, a cold hand from a decaying order. But as networks mature, the line between system and regulator blurs. Tax authorities, central banks, and financial watchdogs are not monoliths of repression; they are participants in the coordination field. Their demands—clarity of custody, anti-fraud provisions, consumer protection—can harden systems rather than neuter them. Policy, approached intelligently, becomes a constraint that defines legitimacy, not an apocalypse that ends innovation. The chapter will trace how regulatory clarity, far from extinguishing decentralisation, can make it sturdier by aligning it with public accountability.

Threading through all these themes is a quiet motif: *the handshake*. Code executes trustlessly, yet humans still meet in metaphorical handshakes—agreements about dispute processes, revocation, or recovery. Each handshake carries a moral texture. Too few, and systems fracture under rigidity. Too many, and they revert to bureaucracy. The challenge of hybrid governance is to script the handshake, to decide when and how to allow discretion without unravelling predictability.

The stakes are civilisational. As more of public life migrates into code—money, contracts, speech, voting—the infrastructure of justice must follow. If every transaction is irreversible, we must decide what mercy looks like in irreversible systems. If every decision is programmable, we must decide who writes the exceptions and who watches them. Code is not replacing law; it is becoming law's latest theatre. The actors are not judges and clerks but developers, auditors, node operators, and users whose clicks enact statutes. They must be taught to reason as legislators, not just as engineers.

This chapter will not tell readers to trust law over code or vice versa. It will show that legitimacy arises where each checks the other: law reminding code of humanity, code reminding law of its promises. Between them lies a frontier where design meets ethics—a zone of uncertainty that deserves governance as refined as the systems it regulates. That is where the next generation of civic architecture will be built.

The question that hovers at the chapter's edge is simple but radical: when the next crisis comes—another exploit, another fork, another regulatory showdown—who decides what justice looks like in a world that executes itself?

When Code Is Law—and When It Isn't

At 10:34 a.m. on 17 June 2016, an automated contract began draining ether from *The DAO*, a decentralised investment vehicle built on the Ethereum blockchain. Within hours, roughly 3.6 million ether—valued at more than £40 million at the time—had been transferred into a subsidiary contract. There was no server breach, no forged signature, no criminal intrusion as conventionally defined. The system was functioning precisely as coded. Yet to the thousands of investors watching helplessly as funds moved beyond recall, this was not functioning—it was failure. The attacker had exploited a recursive call vulnerability: a logical flaw in the contract's design, not in its syntax. The community's dilemma became existential. Should they treat the transaction as legitimate because the code permitted it, or reverse it to preserve fairness? The ensuing "DAO fork" split Ethereum into two chains, two communities, two definitions of justice.

That episode crystallised the paradox of digital governance. Code is supposed to enforce without discretion, but discretion is often what prevents ruin. The phrase *code is law*, coined by legal scholar Lawrence Lessig in 1999, captured the idea that software architectures regulate behaviour as effectively as legal ones do. A website can make plagiarism impossible, a wallet can make theft unprofitable, a smart contract can make promises self-executing. Yet these mechanisms operate without empathy, context, or appeal. When things go wrong—as they always do—the community discovers that the final court of appeal is not code but coordination.

Smart contracts deliver a narrow kind of perfection. They execute exactly what is written, not what is meant. Their strength lies in predictability, their weakness in interpretation. Show: in August 2020, an automated market maker called Yam Finance collapsed within 48 hours of launch after a one-line arithmetic error caused token inflation to spiral. Name: *deterministic fragility*. Explain: the contract could not distinguish between valid and absurd outcomes—it simply executed. Implication: systems built for certainty must also prepare for absurdity, because in code, absurdity is still valid input.

Legal systems evolved precisely to handle the grey zones that machines cannot. A judge can weigh intent, mitigate harm, or apply precedent. A smart contract cannot. The law accepts that fairness sometimes requires contradiction: contracts can be voided for mistake, duress, or misrepresentation. Code cannot void itself on moral grounds. To function in a messy world, automated systems must therefore meet the law halfway. They need explicit procedures for dispute, rollback, and repair, not ad hoc interventions when calamity strikes. The DAO crisis was costly not only for its victims but for the credibility of decentralisation itself—it showed what happens when "unstoppable" code meets a community that still expects justice.

The motif throughout this discussion is the *boundary*. Every digital system defines boundaries: between what it will execute automatically and what it will defer to human judgment. Pretending those boundaries do not exist is itself a design flaw. The most resilient systems write the boundary into their constitution. The *MakerDAO* project, for instance, learned from 2016's chaos. When a severe market crash in March 2020 left its lending contracts undercollateralised, MakerDAO's "Emergency Shutdown" procedure allowed token holders to freeze the system and settle positions through a controlled unwind. Show: human actors used pre-agreed governance powers to halt a crisis without arbitrary interference. Name: *procedural discretion*. Explain: discretion is not the enemy of automation—it is the circuit breaker that keeps autonomy from burning down the house. Implication: we can automate execution, but we must never automate forgiveness.

Contrast that with the 2022 *Solana* network outage, which halted block production for seventeen hours due to a flood of validator messages exceeding capacity. There was no exploit, only congestion. The developers coordinated on Discord to restart the network—an act of centralised control inconsistent with the ethos of unstoppable systems. Yet the alternative was paralysis. This case exposes a hard truth: when systems lack pre-agreed emergency procedures, power defaults to whoever can act fastest. Unwritten authority fills the vacuum. The law has a word for this—*equity*: the discretionary power to prevent manifest injustice when rigid rules fail. Code, if it is to govern fairly, must acknowledge the same necessity and predefine its forms of equity.

So far, the examples speak of crisis. But even in routine use, law and code coexist uneasily. Consider how stablecoin issuers design redemption clauses. Circle's *USDC*, for instance, promises one-dollar redemptions under a framework governed by U.S. regulations, banking audits, and contractual terms. Its convertibility depends as much on legal enforceability as on smart contract logic. Compare that with *DAI*, a decentralised stablecoin issued by MakerDAO, whose peg is maintained algorithmically through collateral and incentives rather than contractual obligation. One depends on courts, the other on markets. Yet both rely on trust—legal in one case, technical in the other—and both are vulnerable if their respective systems lose credibility. The implication is that no architecture escapes the need for legitimacy; it merely shifts where that legitimacy is tested.

The counter-example is worth inspecting. In 2020, *Harvest Finance*, a DeFi yield aggregator, suffered a $34 million flash-loan exploit. The code executed flawlessly; the attacker exploited pricing oracles to drain value. The developers publicly pleaded for the return of funds, posting an address and a "bounty" for the hacker's conscience. None came. Without legal recourse, the victims were left to social pressure and moral suasion. Show: technical autonomy without legal interface collapses into impotence. Name: *jurisdictional vacuum*. Explain: when neither contract law nor criminal law can reach the actor, the system's rules end at its boundary. Implication: if you cannot articulate what justice looks like outside the blockchain, you have no justice inside it.

To bridge that gap, hybrid governance models are emerging. *Aragon Court* (launched 2020) and *Kleros* (founded 2018) use decentralised juries to arbitrate disputes arising from smart contracts. Each relies on cryptographic randomness to select jurors, token-based incentives to ensure diligence, and transparent verdicts anchored on-chain. These systems are not replacements for national courts but complements—fast, narrow, and self-contained. Their legitimacy, however, still rests on human participation: people must volunteer, deliberate, and enforce judgments socially. The boundary reappears. Show: a dispute over escrowed funds in Kleros resolves through crowd-sourced verdicts; enforcement depends on network recognition. Name: *layered legitimacy*. Explain: each layer of adjudication—code, jury, court—handles what it is best suited for. Implication: governance matures not by abolishing layers but by aligning them.

Legal interfaces outperform afterthoughts because they anticipate failure before it happens. The 2019 *LexDAO* initiative exemplifies this. A group of lawyers and developers collaborated to draft smart contract templates that embed references to off-chain arbitration bodies and applicable law. Each contract includes clauses defining jurisdiction and remedy, enforceable both on-chain and off. The innovation is not technical but conceptual: treating law not as an adversary of code but as an API. When parties dispute a transaction, the smart contract knows where to look for human judgment. The implication extends beyond DeFi: any autonomous system—from supply-chain provenance to algorithmic insurance—needs a pathway for moral repair.

Critics sometimes argue that adding legal backstops reintroduces the very intermediaries blockchain sought to remove. But the goal of decentralisation was never to abolish all discretion; it was to make discretion accountable. A pre-agreed human procedure differs from arbitrary intervention. When encoded transparently and invoked under defined conditions, human governance enhances rather than undermines autonomy. The difference lies in timing. Afterthought governance breeds suspicion; constitutional governance builds resilience. The line between tyranny and stewardship, digital or otherwise, is whether authority is consented to in advance.

We can measure this maturity. Look at a protocol's "crisis drill". Does it have an explicit recovery mechanism, quorum thresholds, and time delays? Does it publish minutes of emergency interventions? These are not bureaucratic ornaments; they are the civic hygiene of decentralised systems. Ethereum's post-DAO governance now includes *EIP-Process Guidelines*, outlining how proposals move from idea to implementation with community sign-off. Bitcoin's conservatism—its refusal to change easily—serves the same function in a different register. Both have learned the same lesson: rule by code alone is rule without memory.

The motif of the boundary returns one last time. Every functioning society, analogue or digital, depends on the maintenance of boundaries—between rule and exception, automation and appeal, execution and interpretation. The future of smart contracts will hinge not on greater precision alone but on the humility to admit where precision ends. Hybrid governance is not compromise; it is realism. It recognises that code can execute law but not embody it. The moment law and code acknowledge their shared frontier, legitimacy stops being an accident and becomes a design principle.

The unresolved tension, then, is not whether code should replace law but how societies will decide *who interprets the code when it breaks*. Should every protocol embed its own court? Should national law assert primacy through regulation? Or will legitimacy migrate to networks whose governance earns trust through transparency rather than jurisdiction? The answers will determine whether the next generation of digital institutions remain merely efficient—or become just.

Property, Custody, and Remedies

On 24 February 2014 in Tokyo, Mt. Gox halted withdrawals and filed for bankruptcy days later. At least 650,000 bitcoins were missing. Years of litigation followed, and only in 2018 did the Tokyo District Court shift the case from bankruptcy to civil rehabilitation, opening a path for partial creditor recovery. No vault door had been blown off. No paper certificates were forged. Control of private keys—pure possession—had slipped, and with it the meaning of ownership in a system that treats control as title. The question landed like a gavel: if value is a bearer asset secured by a string of secrets, what does restitution look like when the secret is gone? Plan for the worst day.

A different drama unfolded in Halifax in January 2019. QuadrigaCX's founder, Gerald Cotten, died in India. According to court filings in Nova Scotia, he alone held the private keys to the exchange's cold wallets. The funds proved irretrievable. Clients who thought they held "accounts" discovered they were unsecured creditors in an insolvent estate. The law could not conjure keys from a will; it could only distribute losses. These paired scenes—Tokyo and Halifax—frame the stakes. Bearer assets compress property and custody into a single act: keep the key, keep the value. Lose the key, lose the remedy.

Show the mechanism before naming the doctrine. A bearer instrument confers rights by possession, not by identity. In the physical world, a banknote serves as bearer paper: whoever holds it spends it. On a blockchain, the private key is the bearer instrument. There is no ledger entry tagged "belongs to Alice" beyond the cryptographic fact that Alice's signature can spend. Name the consequence: *possession-as-title*. Explain: where legal systems once separated ownership from custody—think of a share certificate held by a transfer agent—blockchains collapse the categories. Implication: if we want restitution when things go wrong, we must add back structure—technical, contractual, or legal—that reintroduces pathways to repair.

Start with law catching up to property. In *AA v Persons Unknown* (England and Wales, November 2019), the High Court recognised cryptoassets as property capable of being the subject of proprietary injunctions. In *Ruscoe v Cryptopia* (New Zealand, April 2020), the High Court held that a failed exchange held crypto in trust for account holders, separating client assets from the company's estate. Show: courts issue freezing orders; liquidators distribute per-asset trusts. Name: *legal characterisation*. Explain: where the law sees property, it can order remedies—trace, freeze, recover. Implication: if a platform segregates client assets in trust, customers avoid standing in the queue of general creditors during insolvency. If it does not, they do not. The distinction is not philosophical; it is a chequebook on the worst day.

We can classify custody models by the remedies they enable. Self-custody puts the human at the helm. It maximises sovereignty and minimises counterparty risk. But its remedies are internal: backups, social recovery, and multisignature arrangements that survive device loss or duress. Behaviour signals competence: a quarterly recovery drill, a guardian reconfirmation, a time-locked "panic button" that pauses large transfers. The metric is dull and decisive: recovery success rate in staged tests. If that number is unknowable, the risk is unpriced.

Pooled custody at a centralised exchange flips the bargain. Users outsource key management and gain ease: password resets, customer support, liquidity. Remedies become external—insurance pools, legal claims, and regulated capital buffers. But they are conditional. When the exchange fails badly enough, as FTX did in Nassau in November 2022, the remedy is court-supervised redistribution, not instant restitution. The visible decision is where to hold balances before the sky darkens. The metric is withdrawal latency under stress—minutes not days—and the proportion of assets demonstrably held in segregated cold storage. If an institution cannot answer those questions in writing, it has already answered them.

Between these poles lie hybrid arrangements: institutional-grade custodians with segregated on-chain wallets, client-specific whitelists, and multi-party computation (MPC) that distributes signing across hardware in separate jurisdictions. Remedies improve: a lost device does not erase title; a compromised signer cannot spend alone; a court order can instruct a custodian without handing them your key. Show: a UK charity holds reserves with a custodian using 2-of-3 signing, with one key held by the firm, one by a specialist escrow agent in Zürich, and one by a board-controlled hardware module. Name: *distributed custody with legal fail-safes*. Explain: the arrangement blends cryptographic thresholds with contractual duties; it creates a "who to call" on the worst day that does not reintroduce a single point of capture. Implication: properly staffed and audited, such models give institutions a remedy envelope closer to traditional finance while preserving exit if confidence fails.

A credible counter-example tempers the enthusiasm. In August 2016, Bitfinex in Hong Kong suffered a breach of its multi-signature wallet system and lost roughly 120,000 bitcoins. The architecture employed a third-party signer (BitGo), suggesting that threshold signatures would prevent single-party abuse. They did not prevent coordinated or systemic failure. Bitfinex then issued BFX tokens to haircut customers and later redeemed them as the firm recovered—a financial remedy rather than a technical one. Reconciliation matters: multisig and MPC do not abolish risk; they reshape it. Where key compromise becomes harder, insider collusion or software supply-chain attacks step forward. Remedy-first thinking still applies: assume threshold compromise and ask what can be made whole, by whom, and under what binding commitments.

The motif that threads this section is the *worst-day plan*. It is not romantic. It is the unglamorous script that determines whether autonomy is dignified or punitive. A worst-day plan in self-custody names guardians, specifies a cool-down period, and rehearses loss. A worst-day plan at an exchange specifies segregated client accounts, independent trustees, audited proof-of-reserves, and pre-committed insurance triggers. A worst-day plan in a protocol sets timelocks for upgrades, circuit-breakers for liquidity cascades, and "last clear chance" mechanisms that give honest users time to react to exploits. If these elements do not exist *before* the crisis, someone will improvise them *during* the crisis, and improvisation is a tax paid by victims.

Moral hazard deserves candour. If users expect that "the community" or "the foundation" will reverse losses after a hack, they behave less cautiously and projects cut corners on safeguards. Remedy-first is not rescue-first. It is the discipline of specifying which harms are reversible, under which conditions, and which are not. The visible behaviour is a protocol publishing its reversal envelope: what events trigger pauses; who can vote to enact a patch; what quorum and delay apply; where appeals go. The metric is not feel-good participation; it is how often emergency powers were attempted, how often they succeeded, and how often they were rejected after debate. A culture of measured refusals is as important as a culture of care.

Legal remedies bite hardest when technical ones fail. That requires mapping custodial models to legal theories of responsibility. If a retail exchange represents itself as an agent holding assets in trust, then directors and custodians accept fiduciary duties. If it represents itself as a counterparty, it becomes a debtor: your "balance" is a promise, not a segregated asset. The frontline decision for a regulator is to force that disclosure; the frontline decision for a user is to read it. Behaviour measures respect: institutions that publish trust deeds, name trustees, and disclose governing law signal a remedy culture; those that bury terms in marketing pages trade on confusion.

Jurisdiction matters. In England and Wales, proprietary injunctions can restrain unknown defendants and exchanges from dissipating misappropriated cryptoassets once a claimant links addresses to harm. In the United States, courts have increasingly treated crypto as property subject to constructive trusts and tracing. In New Zealand, *Cryptopia*'s estate was distributed per-asset to account holders because the court found a trust. The implication is practical. Keep assets with firms whose legal structures allow proprietary claims, not merely unsecured ones, and choose venues where procedural tools—freezing orders, Norwich Pharmacal orders, disclosure orders—can operate quickly. Speed is remedy.

The self-custody camp confronts a different law: the physics of memory. Keys must be generated, stored, backed up, and rotated. Where human fallibility meets cryptography, design must absorb reality. Social recovery, as pioneered by wallets like Argent from 2019, brings family, devices, or institutions into a guardianship graph with thresholds and delays. The worst-day plan here is not a call to customer support but a drill: reconstitute a wallet using guardians every quarter; replace a compromised guardian; test travel-mode restrictions that block high-value transactions from unfamiliar locations. The metric is completion: did the last drill succeed in under an hour? If not, adjust the graph. Sovereignty without rehearsal is theatre.

Institutions require variants of the same dance at scale. A university treasury that uses a 3-of-5 multisig to authorise payments can commit to a rhythm: small disbursements under a single signer up to a daily cap; larger ones require two or three, plus a 24-hour timelock that triggers clear, multi-channel alerts. The worst-day plan becomes a calendar entry. On the day an attacker compromises an email account, the timelock provides a human window for doubt. On the day a signatory is away, the threshold holds. Decisions become explicit: who counts as a signer; how many; how quickly can they be replaced; which jurisdictions they sit in. Measured in minutes and names, not slogans.

Where property meets protocol, remedies become design primitives. Consider collateralised lending. A liquidation is a remedy for undercollateralisation; the contract specifies oracle sources, discounts, and auction mechanics. The worst-day plan defines the "oracle of last resort": how to proceed when primary price feeds go dark or are manipulated. MakerDAO's Black Thursday in March 2020 exposed this fissure when oracle updates lagged during market stress. Changes that followed—circuit-breakers, auction tweaks, keeper incentives—were not aesthetic; they were a remedy architecture. The metric to watch is simple: loss-given-failure on oracle disruptions measured across test scenarios, and time-to-recovery for the peg.

We should also talk about impossibility. Some losses are philosophically irreparable. A coerced transaction signed at gunpoint is valid on-chain. A phishing attack that tricks a signature produces the same irreversible state as a legitimate payment. Remedies here shift from reversal to *containment*. Defaults can limit blast radius: per-transaction spending caps, velocity limits, session keys with narrow permissions, and alert windows that allow a veto from a pre-registered safe device. The worst-day plan is to design a future you can survive. Accept the unfixable and plan for the avoidable. That is not doom; it is prudence.

A brief return to Mt. Gox clarifies how legal and technical remedies entangle. The shift to civil rehabilitation in 2018 changed who could be made whole and how: creditors would be repaid in a mix of bitcoin and cash under court supervision rather than receiving pennies in bankruptcy. The decision reflected a moral intuition—victims should share in the asset's appreciation rather than be trapped by a 2014 price. Law, here, supplied mercy that code could not. The implicit instruction to designers is plain. Build systems that retain the capacity for equitable correction without normalising bailouts. Encode pauses and appeals; publish reversal envelopes; refuse to promise miracles. Legitimacy grows when worst-day stories end with process rather than panic.

There is a final asymmetry to note. Traditional finance tolerates some fraud and mistakes because reversals exist; crypto reduces many fraud vectors but turns some mistakes into monuments. Remedy-first design is the moral middle: do not promise to catch every fall; commit to catching the catastrophic ones. That means committing budget, not just rhetoric—insurance pools sized to historical losses plus stress multipliers; funding for independent response teams who can triage incidents; and explicit agreements with forensic firms to trace stolen funds quickly. Measure these by response time to freeze orders, average recovery percentages in past incidents, and the transparency of post-mortems. Culture shows in the autopsy.

We end where we began, on the worst day. In Tokyo and Halifax, property bled into custody and custody into remedy. Some harms were unmade; others became casebooks. The future will offer new variants: cross-chain bridges with complex failure modes; custody governed by MPC across continents; courts that grow more fluent in tracing orders and digital trusts. The unresolved question is the one every designer and trustee must answer in advance: when possession is title and finality is default, what combination of keys, contracts, and courts will you rely on when the phone rings at 3 a.m., and who has the authority to make you whole without making everyone else reckless?

Forks as Constitutional Crises

On 1 August 2017, at block 478,559, Bitcoin split. In Hong Kong meeting rooms and Reddit threads, in miners' warehouses from Inner Mongolia to Iceland, an argument about block size became a referendum on authority. The result was Bitcoin Cash—a chain with a larger block limit and a claim to truer continuity with Satoshi's design. Exchanges listed both. Wallets updated. Users chose. Nothing exploded, yet a constitution was rewritten in public view. Forks decide who we are. The ledger kept its history, but its future diverged. That is the paradox of secession with shared ancestry: both children inherit the archive; each insists the archive means something different.

A fork is not a bug but a ballot. It asks which rules govern, who interprets them, and how exceptions are handled. Hash power counts, of course, but so do story, stewardship, and staying power. In constitutional terms, legitimacy flows from a coalition that can coordinate over time: developers who continue to ship, users who continue to sign, businesses that continue to integrate, and validators who continue to secure. Raw computation is muscle; narrative is motive; coordination is movement. When these align, a chain survives a split without losing itself. When they do not, the branch withers into a ticker.

Start with what a fork does that law recognises. It redraws jurisdiction without relocating citizens. Accounts, contracts, and balances exist on both sides at the instant of the split. Property becomes duplicated state; consent becomes choice at the edge. Show the behaviour, then name the doctrine. When Ethereum forked in July 2016 after *The DAO* exploit, two chains emerged: Ethereum (ETH), which implemented a state change to unwind the attacker's gains, and Ethereum Classic (ETC), which refused. Name this for what it is—*a constitutional schism*. Explain: both sides appealed to the same founding text—immutability, openness, resistance to capture—but weighed principles differently. Implication: forks are not technical errors; they are referenda on first principles, with code as the ballot and history as the witness.

Legitimacy in such moments rarely flows from hash alone. It flows from credible narratives that mobilise coordination. Ethereum's majority argued that "code is law" was never absolute; that law, even when codified, contains doctrines of equity; that a one-off surgical remedy prevented a systemic injustice. Ethereum Classic argued that the promise of finality was the social contract; that ad hoc corrections created precedent for future capture; that bearing a loss preserved a higher order of trust. Both sides were coherent; only one drew the larger coalition for longer. The metrics told the story: developer commits, client diversity, application adoption, fee revenue, and node counts. Social capital compounded as technical capital.

Bitcoin's 2017 split illustrates a different route to the same question. The block size debate—years of it—was not only about throughput. It was about who should decide trade-offs between scale and verifiability. Supporters of big blocks emphasised cheaper transactions and mainstream viability; opponents emphasised decentralised verification for anyone running a modest node. Segregated Witness (SegWit) activated on Bitcoin in August 2017, moving witness data outside the traditional block and enabling second-layer capacity like the Lightning Network, while Bitcoin Cash launched larger blocks and a different roadmap. The result was revealing. Bitcoin's cultural constitution—skepticism of governance by convening elites, bias for conservatism, and a strong norm against hard-forking—held. BCH kept miners and momentum for a time, then fractured again in 2018 and 2020 over rule changes and developer funding. Coordination frayed because narrative splintered. The constitutional centre did not hold.

A credible counter-example cautions against deterministic readings. In November 2017, the *SegWit2x* proposal—an agreement among major firms and miners to double Bitcoin's block size months after SegWit—failed to activate despite substantial corporate support. Signatures on a New York hotel letterhead could not summon legitimacy. Why? Because the proposal misread the constitution. It conflated hash power and exchange dominance with consent. Users and many developers refused the change, signalling by running clients that rejected the fork. The visible behaviour mattered: node operators upgraded to implementations without 2x, exchanges prepared contingency tickers, and the proposal's backers withdrew days before the flag date. Implication: even overwhelming hash power cannot write a constitution if citizens refuse to read it.

The motif that threads these cases is *the record*. A fork preserves the record while disputing its meaning. Whose interpretation governs the next page? That question is answered by coalitions that can keep time. Sustained release cycles, predictable governance processes, and institutional memory all contribute to what political scientists would call *state capacity*. In decentralised networks, state capacity is the ability to coordinate upgrades, maintain clients, manage incidents, and defend against adversaries without a monarch. It is measured in maintenance as much as in miracles. Chains that continue to ship boring fixes keep legitimacy even when their slogans do not trend.

Consider a different kind of split: not over code limits but over social capture. In March 2020, after the Steem blockchain's largest token holder changed hands through the acquisition of Steemit Inc., a controversy ignited. Exchanges temporarily mobilised customer deposits to influence validator elections; community members decried it as a hostile takeover. In response, a portion of the community "hard-exited" to form Hive, a fork that excluded the disputed stake. Exchanges later relented; the Steem network continued; Hive gained traction with a clear identity centred on community autonomy. Show the behaviour: validators co-ordinated snapshots, applications migrated, and users chose homes. Name: *exit as remedy*. Explain: when voice fails in delegated governance, the fork becomes a constitutional *vote of no confidence*. Implication: in delegated systems, a credible path to exit disciplines actors who might otherwise treat their mandate as a license.

Not every fork clarifies; some diffuse responsibility into haze. In September 2022, Ethereum's transition from proof of work to proof of stake—the Merge—completed without a contentious split on the main stage. An attempted PoW continuation chain, ETHW, launched days later with modest hash rate and limited ecosystem support. Here, hash did not conjure culture. ETH's narrative—environmental efficiency, finality improvements, and years of public rehearsal—had prepared the ground. Coordinated client teams, extensive testnets, and clear communication gave the move the feel of a constitutional amendment rather than a coup. The counter-chain, lacking an organising story beyond inertia, struggled to attract builders and liquidity. Again, the record remained; meaning consolidated around the coalition that had done the work.

Forks expose a fundamental asymmetry: speed privileges the prepared. When a split approaches, exchanges that pre-announce ticker policy, replay-protection rules, and deposit/withdrawal halts set expectations; those that improvise feed chaos. Wallets that show users what chain they are signing on reduce accidental double spends; those that do not become vectors for confusion. Developers who publish contingency clients and emergency communications earn trust. The behaviour is public, countable, and remembered. These are civic duties, not product niceties. The constitution lives in release notes.

Hash rate still matters, but as part of a bundle. Its meaning is contingent on costs, client diversity, and social acceptance. In Bitcoin's case, miners with abundant hash could not push through 2x because the validating base refused; in Ethereum's case, miners' exit during the Merge mattered less than stakers' entry because clients, applications, and users had prepared for years. These examples complicate any claim that "the longest chain" always carries sovereign grace. Legitimacy is closer to H.L.A. Hart's "rule of recognition" than to an engineering metric: it is the set of criteria a community in fact uses to determine what counts as valid law. In blockchains, those criteria are encoded partly in software and partly in practice—exchange listings, index inclusion, widely used libraries, default client settings, and the moral authority of maintainers who have earned their reputations by tending the commons.

Boundary cases test the doctrine. What if a minority chain nurtures a thriving subculture, superior tooling for a niche, or a governance model that better fits a community? Ethereum Classic survived with a clear story—immutability—and a constituency that preferred that anchor to the larger ecosystem's pragmatism. Its hash rate and market capitalisation never overtook ETH's, but legitimacy at a smaller scale was real. The constitutional reading here is pluralist: federations can coexist when their charters are clear and their borders are respected. The metric is not only price; it is persistence across cycles, developer retention, and resilience under stress (for ETC, including surviving 51% attacks in 2020 by revising confirmation practices and client defences).

To read forks constitutionally is to watch for four habits rather than worship one number. First, do leaders narrate constraints as well as goals? A credible amendment begins by naming what cannot change lightly. Second, do processes stage dissent? Off-chain deliberation, on-chain signalling, and time-locked activations create places where disagreement can be expressed without breakage. Third, do institutions practice restraint? The refusal to use emergency powers is as constitutive as their use; a culture of no-drama releases accumulates authority. Fourth, does the network retain *repair capacity*—the ability to identify, triage, and patch defects across clients and versions under pressure? Each habit manifests in behaviour: meeting minutes published, dissenters cited with respect, testnets rehearsed, RCs signed and verified by multiple teams. Legitimacy accrues like compound interest on these routines.

There are dangers. Forks can be weaponised to expropriate; snapshot exclusions can punish political opponents; premines can be smuggled in during upheaval. The constitutional antidote is bright light: explicit criteria for snapshotting, independent audits of genesis allocations, and clear, dated statements by recognised stewards *before* activation. When promises move from talk channels into signed artefacts, opportunists lose room to manoeuvre. Again, watch the record. It remembers.

The history of political constitutions suggests that amendments must be difficult but not impossible. Too easy, and the charter becomes whim. Too hard, and injustice calcifies. Networks find this balance by embedding meta-rules: thresholds for activation, windows for review, mutexes that prevent conflicting changes, and norms about what constitutes a "rough consensus". Bitcoin's extreme caution is one expression; Ethereum's more activist posture is another. Neither is automatically superior. Each is a temperament with trade-offs. What matters is coherence: that the temperament be stable enough for citizens to plan their lives, yet flexible enough to correct error.

Forks, then, are less about victory than about verdicts on governance. They reveal whether a community can change rules without changing character. They teach that authority in decentralised systems is earned through care for the shared record: who tends it, who interprets it, who resists the temptation to scrawl graffiti when the room is dark. The constitutional reader looks past the ticker to the rituals—client meetings, EIP discussions, BIPs, release cadences—and asks whether this polity deserves continued allegiance.

The unresolved tension remains sharp and useful. When a fork looms, which coalition should claim the mantle of continuity—the group that protects formal properties like immutability, or the group that protects substantive justice by repairing harms? When miners and businesses align but users resist, which consent matters more? And how many amendments can a chain survive before the story that binds it snaps? The next crisis will pose these questions again. The record will be ready. The meaning will be contested. The decision, as ever, will be yours.

Regulators as System Actors

On 20 April 2023 in Strasbourg, the European Parliament voted through the Markets in Crypto-Assets Regulation (MiCA). The roll-call was not a skirmish in a culture war but a piece of plumbing: a framework for issuance, custody, stablecoins, and disclosure across twenty-seven states. Clarity arrived by formal vote. In June 2024, parts of MiCA began applying to asset-referenced and e-money tokens; the broader regime followed later in the year. A lesson surfaced immediately for builders across Paris, Berlin, and Tallinn: policy can be a scaffold, not just a wall. Get the footings right and the structure hardens. Ignore them and the ground gives way at the first tremor.

Regulation is usually framed as a threat to autonomy. Yet systems that never meet law rarely meet reality for long. The most honest way to read a rulebook is as a set of constraints under which resilient architectures can emerge. Show first, then name. When the Monetary Authority of Singapore (MAS) announced its stablecoin framework in August 2023, and began granting recognitions through 2024, it set unambiguous expectations for reserve quality, redemption timelines, and disclosure (MAS, 2023/24). Name the effect: *predictable obligations*. Explain: issuers who commit to verifiable, high-quality reserves and to timely redemption design their contracts and operations around worst-day behaviour—queues, run dynamics, communication cadence. Implication: clarity disciplines both code and treasury long before a crisis arrives. The scaffold holds because it is visible.

Clarity also puts borders around legitimate exit. Law can fortify systems without forbidding departure. The United Kingdom's Financial Conduct Authority (FCA) brought financial promotions rules for cryptoassets into force on 8 October 2023, insisting that firms make fair, clear, and not misleading offers and give risk warnings with "cooling-off" for retail. Skeptics read only friction. Yet the deeper move was to draw a perimeter inside which voluntary exchange could proceed with fewer ambushes. Behaviour changed. Interfaces slowed first-time purchases; firms cut the most egregious inducements; compliance teams began to measure not clicks but complaint rates and time-to-redress. The scaffolding nudged design towards duty of care while leaving the door open for those who insisted on walking out.

A counter-example cautions against overreach. In 2021 China banned crypto mining; in 2017 and 2021 it clamped down on trading. Hash power emigrated to Kazakhstan, then to the United States and elsewhere. Liquidity routed through offshore venues. Bans preserved perimeter optics but exported activity to jurisdictions more prepared—or less scrupulous. The lesson is not that rules are futile. It is that blanket prohibitions channel rather than erase flow. Where the scaffold is demolition, the structure simply reassembles elsewhere, often flimsier. Good law aims to shape load paths, not to pretend gravity will change.

The central claim of this section is simple: treat regulators as actors inside the system, not referees shouting from the stands. That means forecasting their most likely moves and designing *with* them. The likely vectors are not mysterious. Consumer protection drives transparency; market integrity drives surveillance of manipulation; financial stability drives reserve quality and segregation; tax compliance drives reporting; sanctions and AML drive screening and the "travel rule". Each vector maps to a design response that can both harden a protocol and preserve credible exit. The motif throughout is the *scaffold*: constraints that enable height without collapse.

Start with custodial safeguarding. MiCA and several national regimes converge on segregation of client assets, governance of key material, and proof that liabilities match reserves. Show: a custodian that publishes cryptographically verifiable proof-of-reserves *and* a third-party assurance over liabilities, on a cadence that matches market velocity, gives users a live picture of solvency and a paper trail for courts. Name: *two-sided attestation*. Explain: Merkle proofs without liabilities are theatre; audit letters without on-chain verifiability are opacity. Implication: custody that takes regulation seriously is not

"CeFi by another name"; it is a layered design where code, process, and law check each other. The exit remains because assets are actually segregated, redemption times are published, and withdrawal circuits are tested and timed.

Stablecoins expose the same logic. MAS's framework requires S$- and G-10-linked tokens to be fully backed by low-risk assets with daily valuation and prompt redemption. MiCA's Title III and IV do likewise for "significant" tokens. Builders can treat those rules as a drag, or as a spec. Show: an issuer structures its reserve as short-dated government paper held with bankruptcy-remote custodians; it automates daily NAV publication and commits to T+1 redemption with a guaranteed floor. Name: *redemption discipline*. Explain: code enforces transfer, but the promise that a token is worth a currency unit in bad weather is a legal and operational affair. Implication: the token's ledger becomes credible money not because it lives on a chain but because it can be cashed out—fast, fairly, and under scrutiny—without quietly trapping holders. Exit is preserved by design.

Policy also shapes interfaces to permissionless rails. The U.S. Treasury's designation of Tornado Cash smart contracts in August 2022 reminded everyone that sanctions obligations attach to persons and services, not to math itself. Circle's USDC responded by blacklisting sanctioned addresses at the contract level within days. Show: a centralised issuer exercised a policy lever; non-custodial users felt the freeze. Name: *chokepoint realism*. Explain: the state does not need to "ban DeFi" when it can shape the assets that touch it. Implication: build with asset pluralism and graceful degradation—design systems that continue to function when a centralised stablecoin freezes assets, by routing through censorship-resistant collateral, time-locked escrows, or community-governed redemption queues. Exit survives because there are alternate load paths when a policy lever is pulled.

A second vector is market abuse. Even without bespoke crypto law, many jurisdictions have anti-manipulation and fair-dealing standards that de facto cover token markets. Show: after the U.S. CFTC's 2020 action against BitMEX for BSA/AML failures and supervisory gaps, offshore derivatives venues changed margining disclosures, KYC, and surveillance. Name: *integrity pressure*. Explain: when surveillance becomes baseline, credible venues instrument their books: they publish API-level latency, match-engine fairness audits, and outlier-trade incident reports. Implication: these are not performative reports. They are design primitives that keep markets hard to game and easy to trust, while preserving the right to take assets out the moment faith falters. The exit door is clear; the room is safer while you are in it.

Tax is a third vector that too many designers treat as an afterthought, until it is not. The OECD's Crypto-Asset Reporting Framework (CARF), approved in 2023, gives tax authorities a schema for cross-border reporting similar to the Common Reporting Standard for bank accounts. The design response is not hand-wringing; it is *selective traceability*. Show: a wallet ships exportable, human-readable transaction histories and cost-basis tools; exchanges issue standardised statements keyed to CARF fields; protocols adopt optional memo fields for provenance without doxxing. Name: *auditable minimalism*. Explain: serve the legitimate need for audit without building surveillance honeypots; remove raw identifiers, keep hashes and proofs. Implication: users can comply without surrendering every detail; regulators receive decision-useful data; exit remains because the system does not depend on permanent dossiers to function.

There is a temptation to declare DeFi out of reach. It is pseudonymous; interfaces are forks and front-ends; the contracts are immutable. Yet policy can still act as a system parameter rather than a prohibition. The appropriate target is *gateways*. Jurisdictions can and increasingly do regulate how professional front-ends, custodians, and fiat ramps interact with permissionless contracts: disclosures about risks; filters for obviously sanctioned addresses; increased scrutiny for governance tokens that behave like securities. Builders can treat this as sabotage or embrace it as a way to raise the floor. The practical design pattern is layered access: full-power tools for sophisticated users who attest competence; safeguarded paths for retail with simulations, spending caps, and default revocations. Exit is preserved across layers; harm migrates down.

A credible limitation must be faced. Heavy regimes sometimes freeze innovation. New York's 2015 BitLicense pushed several start-ups to leave the state; years later, only larger firms could afford compliance. Yet the state also created a stable charter for trust-company custodians that helped institutionalise client-asset segregation. Reconcile this by seeing policy as a spectrum. Poorly designed rules compress the ecosystem into oligopoly; well-designed ones make safety cheap enough for smaller actors to adopt. The test is behavioural: do entry costs fall over time as templates, audits, and standard controls are commoditised? If not, the scaffold has become a cage.

Foresight comes from modelling the *feedback loop*. Regulations land; actors adapt; second-order effects appear. When promotions rules in the UK curbed wild inducements, scams did not vanish; they migrated to messaging apps and foreign sites. The thoughtful response is not to double bans, but to flood the commons with safer defaults: wallet prompts that flag infinite approvals; interfaces that simulate transactions in plain language; exchanges that delay first withdrawals to new addresses by a day unless a user overrides with additional checks. These behaviours are measurable: reduced fraud claims per thousand users; lower complaint rates; faster dispute resolution. The regulator's vector meets the designer's counter-vector and the public sees the benefit.

To keep regulation as constraint rather than doom, three habits must become routine—habits that this book has already argued for under other names. First, *pre-commitment.* Publish reversal envelopes, emergency procedures, and upgrade paths before trouble. Supervisors prefer transparent knobs to secret levers. Second, *portability.* Make leaving easy: export keys, revoke allowances in one tap, and move attestations between wallets. Regulators who fear capture fear it less when credible exit exists. Third, *proportionality by default.* Set spending caps, timelocks, and risk tiers so the smallest actions fly and the largest slow. That earns regulatory patience because it demonstrates prudence in code. Each habit shows in behaviour, not rhetoric.

Jurisdictional arbitrage remains a fact. Builders will cite Zug, Dubai, London, or Hong Kong as venues offering a better blend of clarity and ambition at any given moment. Arbitrage need not be nihilism. It can be discovery. Different regimes test different scaffolds; the market observes which ones produce fewer collapses, fewer scams, and more useful products. Over time, good patterns travel: reserve rules, disclosure templates, incident-reporting standards, even vocabulary. The risk, as ever, is that the "race to the bottom" outpaces the race to the useful middle. The antidote is data: public post-mortems, incident registries, and metrics that emphasise resilience—withdrawal latency under stress, redemption reliability, custody segregation rates—rather than vanity.

One last example closes the circuit. In September 2024, the European Securities and Markets Authority (ESMA) issued technical standards under MiCA for market abuse in crypto-asset markets. Rather than criminalise volatility, the standards demanded surveillance and disclosure practices familiar from equity venues. Several exchanges responded by publishing suspicious-activity typologies and by instrumenting wash-trade detectors that quarantined volumes from incentive programmes. It looked bureaucratic. It was civic. The *scaffold* acted as expected: it made manipulation costlier and honesty cheaper, while leaving the right to withdraw or delist intact. Exit remained the final accountability mechanism.

We return to the opening vote in Strasbourg. MiCA's passage did not anoint a winner in an old argument; it set a playing field on which better and worse architectures will reveal themselves. Treat regulators as system actors and the design questions sharpen: which disclosures buy trust at minimal privacy cost? Which redemption commitments make a token money-like without creating a single point of policy capture? Which gateway obligations keep the door open while reducing harm at the threshold? The unresolved tension is the one worth holding: how far can we formalise duty without dulling freedom, and how do we prove, in behaviours and metrics rather than slogans, that exit is preserved even as the scaffold rises?

Chapter 4
Incentives, Commons, and Capture

In May 2020, a smart contract called YFI was deployed with no premine, no venture allocation, and no privileged minting rights. Within days, it became the nucleus of what would later be called "DeFi Summer". Andre Cronje, the developer behind it, declared YFI to have "*no intrinsic value*". Yet within weeks, the token governed billions of dollars of liquidity. Participants called it a *fair launch*; cynics called it a mirage. Both were right in part. For a brief moment, the ideals of permissionless coordination and collective reward aligned. Then came derivatives, yield vaults, imitators, and accusations of extraction dressed as empowerment. The question lingered: can incentives be moral?

Every system of coordination hides a theory of virtue. Whether through subsidies, inflation schedules, or governance rewards, token design decides who benefits from collective effort and who quietly pays for it. It is a moral architecture disguised as mathematics. Each emission curve is a theory of time preference; each vesting schedule, a view of patience; each vote weight, a claim about merit. This chapter asks how those design choices build or corrode the commons—and how the rhetoric of decentralisation can mask new forms of rent-seeking. The paradox of digital commons is not that they are unowned, but that they are owned too diffusely to be defended.

The first problem is generosity without durability. Open-source infrastructure—protocols, libraries, client software—underpins every blockchain system, yet remains chronically underfunded. The failure is not technical but economic. The incentives that fuel token speculation rarely fund the maintenance of public goods. We have seen the pattern before: the tragedy of the commons becomes the tragedy of maintenance. After the DAO hack of 2016, security audits became urgent; by 2021, their budgets were an afterthought again. Predictability, not drama, sustains civilisation. The challenge is to design treasuries and reward flows that reward upkeep, not hype.

Treasuries themselves are moral actors. They represent collective surplus converted into power. A treasury that funds independent audits, infrastructure grants, and translation work signals stewardship. One that recycles funds into governance bribes and self-referential liquidity schemes signals capture. The same code primitives—multi-signature vaults, time-locked disbursements, budget proposals—can serve either ethos. The difference lies in what political economists call *agenda control*: who proposes, who executes, who vetoes. Governance theatre—polls with preordained outcomes, votes timed for apathy, token-weighted quorums dominated by whales—can mimic democracy while entrenching oligarchy. Real governance work, by contrast, requires visible accountability. It is measured not by the number of votes cast, but by the number of proposals implemented and reviewed.

The motif that threads through this chapter is *care as currency*. Incentives are declarations of care—what a system rewards, it multiplies. Yet care can be faked. Mining rewards once paid for securing networks; now they often subsidise speculation. Inflation, justified as decentralised funding, can become disguised extraction from late entrants. The moral test is simple: who gains when the music stops? A fair launch distributes uncertainty symmetrically; a rent-seeking design guarantees asymmetry from the start. Tokenomics, at its best, is not about yield—it is about stewardship through time.

Power hides most effectively in what looks neutral. The order of transactions in a block—the domain of *miner* or *maximal extractable value* (MEV)—creates silent hierarchies of advantage. Bots front-run trades, reorder transactions, and drain value from ordinary users without touching a rule. The rails appear neutral; the profits say otherwise. Ordering is governance by another name: it decides who speaks first and who is heard last. Ethical engineering must surface those hidden politics, build guardrails—commit-reveal schemes, batch auctions, inclusion lists—and measure success by reduction in extractable value, not by slogans about "efficiency".

Incentives shape not only markets but morals. A system that rewards early exit over long-term contribution breeds opportunism. One that rewards visibility over substance breeds theatre. The incentive designer, knowingly or not, becomes a legislator. That legislator must confront the same questions as any constitutional drafter: what is owed to the future, what is owed to the present, and how much trust should any citizen place in the next generation's restraint. Tokens, treasuries, and governance contracts are constitutions written in syntax instead of statutes. They require amendment mechanisms, term limits, and rituals of renewal no less than political charters.

The deeper question—how to prevent capture while sustaining commons—runs through all four sections that follow. *Token Design as Moral Choice* examines how emissions, distributions, and governance rights encode ethics in arithmetic. *Open Source and the Tragedy of Maintenance* confronts the economics of decay, tracing why collective infrastructure falters once speculation wanes. *Governance Theatre vs Governance Work* exposes the techniques by which coordination rituals mask agenda control. *MEV and the Politics of Ordering* reveals how supposedly neutral rails redistribute value and agency in silence.

Yet the thread uniting them is not cynicism but agency. To design incentives is to decide who will have the freedom to say no. To fund maintenance is to acknowledge that the unglamorous sustains the extraordinary. To govern without capture is to resist comfort, to choose friction when ease would corrode legitimacy. The lesson is older than code and broader than crypto: every commons survives only by aligning self-interest with duty. The question we now face is whether decentralised systems, so proud of disintermediation, can rediscover what civilisation learned painfully long ago—that without a shared ethic of care, even perfect markets eat themselves.

This chapter stands at that crossroads. It asks how digital constitutions distribute not only power but responsibility; how we can encode restraint, patience, and fairness into mechanisms that cannot feel; and whether the next generation of systems can balance reward with repair. The reader will find no comfort in purity, only in clarity. Incentives will always tempt capture; commons will always demand maintenance. The test is whether we can make both productive—whether design can turn greed into gardening, and coordination into care that endures after the harvest.

Token Design as Moral Choice

On 17 July 2020, Andre Cronje deployed a token called YFI on Ethereum. There was no pre-sale, no venture allocation, and no founder's reserve. Participants had to deposit liquidity to earn it, and Cronje explicitly declared the token to have *no intrinsic value*. Yet within days, YFI's market capitalisation crossed one billion dollars. The project—Yearn Finance—was hailed as a "fair launch", the first in a decade of self-dealing token distributions to look genuinely egalitarian. For a brief moment, incentives and ethics aligned. But soon came imitators: "fair" launches that pre-mined secretly, redistributed rewards to insiders through side channels, or locked out the very communities they claimed to empower. What looked like progress towards financial democracy became another round of rent extraction. The moral was simple: in crypto, code may automate trust, but distribution automates power.

Token design is political economy written in syntax. It defines who benefits from coordination and who carries the risk when coordination fails. Every emission schedule, every vesting clause, and every voting weight is an ethical choice disguised as arithmetic. The common claim that tokenomics is "just economics" misses the point. There is no neutral distribution of rights or rewards. Every curve privileges one temporal horizon over another: fast emission favours speculators, slow emission favours builders, perpetual inflation rewards incumbents. Token design, therefore, is moral architecture—one that decides which virtues a system amplifies: patience or predation, care or capture.

The YFI experiment captured a hunger for justice in decentralisation. By contrast, projects like EOS (2018) and Filecoin (2017) raised billions of dollars through token sales long before shipping viable networks. EOS's initial coin offering, raising over $4 billion in a year, created a massive treasury controlled by a few entities. Filecoin's allocation granted substantial shares to venture capital backers under multi-year vesting but without corresponding obligations to maintain infrastructure. Show: the distribution patterns were public. Name: *front-loaded extraction*. Explain: those early investors captured most of the future's optionality before the network produced social value. Implication: when wealth precedes contribution, governance becomes theatre; legitimacy decays from the start.

Fair launches like Bitcoin's in 2009 or Monero's in 2014 attempted the opposite: distribution through open participation, not pre-allocation. Yet even these models embed politics. Bitcoin rewarded those with early access to computation and information. Monero, more inclusive at launch, still rewarded technical literacy. Visibility replaces capital as the gatekeeper. The moral claim of "fairness" must therefore be tested by outcome, not rhetoric: who can realistically participate, and how quickly do asymmetries re-emerge? The question should haunt any designer tempted to believe distribution can be neutral.

The motif that runs through this subchapter is *stewardship versus extraction*. Stewardship designs distribute wealth to those who maintain the commons; extractive ones reward those who exit earliest. The distinction often hides behind technical jargon. Inflation funding for validators, for instance, can be stewardship if it sustains security and public goods; it becomes extraction when validators collude to raise rewards beyond necessary costs. The difference is not inflation itself but its moral calibration: whether issuance reflects contribution or control.

Show the principle through visible behaviour. In 2021, Osmosis, a decentralised exchange on the Cosmos network, allocated a portion of block rewards to a community pool managed by on-chain proposals. It funded audits, educational content, and integrations. By contrast, in 2022, several so-called "governance tokens" on Ethereum diverted treasury funds to influencer partnerships and yield subsidies, generating short-term volume but long-term disillusionment. The same instrument—treasury emission—produced opposite moral outcomes because the criteria for disbursement diverged. Name the distinction: *budgeting for maintenance versus marketing of illusion.* Explain: predictable, rule-based funding sustains the commons; arbitrary discretionary spending invites capture. Implication: fairness in token design requires not only symmetry at genesis but discipline in perpetuity.

Power in token systems comes not from ownership alone but from time. Early buyers and insiders accumulate compound governance—votes multiplied by duration. Delegated voting compounds it further. The result is plutocracy by inertia. In 2023, Uniswap's governance remained dominated by a few addresses controlling over half the voting power through delegation. No law was broken, yet legitimacy eroded. Formal democracy concealed oligarchic control. Moral design, in this context, would have included sunset clauses on delegation, decay functions for inactive votes, or time-weighted redistribution. Such mechanisms do not remove wealth; they reintroduce movement. They make power circulate.

A credible counter-example demonstrates restraint without regression. The Nouns DAO, launched in August 2021, auctions one NFT per day, with proceeds funding the DAO treasury. Each token equals one vote; no dilution, no inflation. Over time, the DAO funded open-source projects, public art, and software experiments. Critics note that the system concentrates ownership among wealthy collectors. They are right. But its design also channels proceeds into a shared pool with transparent spending. Extraction exists, but stewardship coexists. The moral trade-off is visible, not hidden—a critical improvement over opaque allocations. Moral design does not eliminate inequality; it makes it accountable.

To moralise tokenomics is to face uncomfortable arithmetic. Consider emissions. Fixed supplies like Bitcoin's produce deflationary behaviour—users hoard rather than spend, strengthening incumbents. Perpetual inflation like Dogecoin's dilutes long-term holders, rewarding constant miners. Dynamic supply adjustment, as in Terra's algorithmic stablecoin (before its 2022 collapse), aimed to stabilise value but instead centralised risk into feedback loops that few understood. Each mechanism encoded a moral wager: should wealth reward patience, labour, or adaptability? The disasters that followed Terra's collapse were not merely economic failures—they were ethical failures of design imagination.

The second axis of morality lies in *rights*: who can change the rules. Immutable contracts promise fairness but resist repair. Upgradeable ones enable adaptation but invite tyranny. The DAO hack of June 2016 revealed this tension. Ethereum's community chose to hard fork, reversing the theft and restoring balances; Ethereum Classic refused. Both invoked justice—one distributive, one procedural. The fork, as discussed earlier, was constitutional. What it proved for token design is this: rights are never purely technical. They are negotiated between code, community, and conscience.

Good designers accept that every incentive creates shadows. Liquidity mining, for instance, attracts capital quickly but loyalty slowly. Voting rewards produce engagement but can entrench mediocrity. "Vote bribing" platforms such as Convex Finance (2021) illustrate how rational incentives can erode legitimacy: participants rent governance power to the highest bidder, turning decision-making into an auction. It is efficient but not dignified. Stewardship requires periodic friction—grace periods, quorum thresholds, or retrospective funding—to resist the tyranny of instantaneous greed. Moral systems, digital or human, survive through delay.

A deeper question follows: can a token system express care? The answer lies in *recurrence*: the rhythm of distribution and renewal. Bitcoin's halving every four years, a simple decay schedule, taught millions of users that time itself is policy. Ethereum's switch to proof of stake in September 2022 reduced its issuance rate by around 90%, effectively making it deflationary after fees. The change aligned incentives with sustainability: validators earn from security, not inflation. That was a moral pivot, not a marketing one. The network began to reward patience instead of throughput.

Yet moral clarity can fade with scale. When financialisation accelerates, every design choice is reinterpreted through speculation. "Fair launch" becomes meme, not principle. Stewardship retreats before opportunism. The quiet motif of *care*—who tends the commons—is replaced by the louder one of *yield*. To restore balance, designers must embed care in architecture, not expectation. Time-locked treasuries, rotating councils, non-transferable reputation scores, and clawback clauses are not paternalism—they are pre-commitments to civility. They force communities to slow down, to think about those who come after.

A pattern from political history helps frame the dilemma. After the South Sea Bubble of 1720, British lawmakers imposed restrictions on joint-stock companies. The goal was to prevent reckless speculation; the effect was to slow legitimate innovation for decades. Regulation, like emission curves, can overshoot. The moral lesson is the same: restraint must be measured, not absolute. Over-correct and you freeze initiative; under-correct and greed consumes the commons. Token design must internalise that equilibrium. It must make virtue cheap enough to compete with vice.

The next generation of designers faces a frontier beyond yield: *credibility by conduct.* The question will no longer be which tokenomics model generates the most liquidity, but which sustains the most trust. We will judge systems not by total value locked but by total value retained when incentives end. That metric—retention after reward—is the moral barometer of any decentralised economy.

The unresolved tension endures. When we design tokens, we legislate the future: who inherits power, who carries cost, who has the right to repair what breaks. The fair launch, the emission curve, the voting scheme—all are drafts of a constitution. The challenge is not to make them perfect but to make them decent: to encode enough humility that correction remains possible. The moral lens, once applied, makes tokenomics less about price discovery and more about principle discovery. The real question, one that no spreadsheet can answer, is simple and enduring: when the incentives end, what kind of people will remain?

Open Source and the Tragedy of Maintenance

In April 2014, a tiny flaw in the OpenSSL library—known as Heartbleed—exposed millions of websites, including Yahoo,

GitHub, and Canada's tax agency, to potential data theft. The bug's estimated cost exceeded half a billion dollars in mitigation, yet the software it stemmed from was maintained by just one full-time developer earning less than a typical systems administrator. OpenSSL was not neglected because it was obscure; it was neglected because it was free. Its ubiquity became its curse. Everyone depended on it; no one budgeted for its survival. When the Linux Foundation announced the Core Infrastructure Initiative weeks later, pooling corporate donations to stabilise critical open-source software, it looked like a permanent fix. Within years, interest waned. The same structural problem persisted across blockchains: shared infrastructure without shared maintenance.

Public goods decay not through malice but through diffusion. In decentralised systems, the absence of ownership is treated as a virtue. Yet maintenance—patching clients, updating libraries, auditing contracts—is ownership by another name. It demands care over time. The tragedy of the commons reappears, coded this time in Solidity and Rust. Ethereum's clients, Bitcoin's core software, and countless dependencies such as LevelDB and Libsecp256k1 are maintained by small teams who bear disproportionate responsibility for global stability. Maintenance, measured in merged pull requests or patched vulnerabilities, is unglamorous labour; it yields no airdrops, only gratitude. And gratitude does not pay salaries.

Blockchain communities have tried to address this through treasuries, grants, and so-called "MEV-sharing" schemes. Each promises sustainability, yet each tends to fail in predictable ways. Treasuries accumulate funds from inflation or protocol fees, but politics soon corrodes intent. Show: in 2021, MakerDAO held over $60 million in its surplus buffer, but governance paralysis delayed even basic infrastructure grants. Name: *capital without cadence*. Explain: when disbursement depends on sporadic votes, urgency dies in debate. Implication: funding public goods through direct democracy produces accountability without execution.

Grants aim to be more nimble. Gitcoin, launched in 2017, pioneered quadratic funding to match community donations with larger pools. Its model rewarded projects that inspired broad small-scale support. For several rounds, it funded core Ethereum tooling and public education. But as Gitcoin Grants scaled, campaigns skewed towards popular marketing, not maintenance. Developers who wrote tests or fixed edge-case bugs could not compete with meme tokens that mobilised votes. Name this drift: *attention capture*. Explain: funding tied to visibility rewards charisma over reliability. Implication: the invisible work that keeps systems alive must be financed by mechanisms insulated from spectacle.

The third experiment, MEV-sharing, tried to convert the invisible tax of transaction reordering into a revenue stream for users or developers. In 2023, Flashbots' "MEV-Share" protocol proposed redistributing a portion of miner or validator profits back to end-users. It sounded like justice: take from extraction, give to participants. Yet the captured value proved volatile, dependent on arbitrage flows and liquidity spikes. The result was income without predictability. Developers cannot plan salaries on uncertainty. A maintenance budget that fluctuates with mempool congestion is not a budget at all.

Predictability, not novelty, sustains the commons. The Core Infrastructure Initiative worked temporarily because its funding was committed over multiple years. Similarly, Ethereum's Protocol Guild—a collective of core developers—launched in 2022 with retroactive funding from donors and DAOs, designed to vest over time. The idea was modest: reward those maintaining consensus clients, not just building new features. By 2024, the Guild had received commitments exceeding $10 million from major protocols including Uniswap and Lido. Show: stability emerged from continuity. Name: *maintenance as endowment*. Explain: by decoupling support from hype cycles, the Guild made maintenance legible work. Implication: blockchains that wish to last must internalise such funding as core policy, not charity.

Yet every solution reveals its cost. Treasury-based funding risks bureaucracy; grant-based funding drifts towards fashion; MEV-sharing dissolves into noise. The limitation is not financial innovation but human attention. Maintenance competes with novelty in a culture that valorises launch over upkeep. Codebases sprawl while teams fragment. The paradox is visible: decentralisation expands participation but diffuses responsibility. Who upgrades the upgrade?

A quiet motif runs through this problem: *entropy*. Systems, left alone, drift towards disorder. Without planned maintenance, entropy accumulates as technical debt and security risk. The collapse of the Terra network in May 2022 was not solely an economic failure; it was an operational one. Its maintainers ignored the growing mismatch between algorithmic assumptions and on-chain behaviour. Patches could have reduced feedback instability. None were applied. Entropy, unbudgeted, became catastrophe.

Predictability also means cultural rhythm. Ethereum's "Merge" in September 2022, after years of preparation, demonstrated that disciplined iteration can coexist with innovation. The network's switch from proof of work to proof of stake required synchronised upgrades across dozens of teams and clients. Each step had a named maintainer, a clear specification, and a calendar. The effort was bureaucratic, even dull—but precisely that dullness prevented chaos. The quiet success of the Merge contrasted with the drama that often defines decentralised projects. It proved that maintenance can be an act of collective maturity.

A counterpoint lies in Bitcoin's austerity. Its development ethos prizes minimal change; proposals undergo years of debate. Taproot, activated in November 2021, was the first major upgrade in four years. Critics call the process glacial;

supporters call it prudent. Both views hold. Slow governance ensures stability but risks stagnation. Reconcile this by recognising that maintenance comes in two forms: *preservation* and *evolution*. Preservation defends what works; evolution adapts to new conditions. A credible funding system must distinguish between them and support both with distinct rhythms.

The politics of open-source maintenance reveal another asymmetry: who pays and who decides. Large exchanges and custodians rely on client developers yet rarely contribute proportionally. They rationalise this as market efficiency—if the software is open, why pay? But free-riding corrodes legitimacy. In 2019, Chaincode Labs and Blockstream funded Bitcoin Core developers directly, setting a precedent. Later, the Human Rights Foundation began microgrants for independent maintainers. These acts restored balance. The visible metric is not donation size but diversity of sponsors. Concentrated funding creates new dependency. True stewardship spreads patronage thinly enough that no donor can dictate roadmap priorities.

In the broader economy, governments fund public goods through taxation. Blockchains resist central taxation but can mimic its function through automated endowments. Some networks dedicate a fixed share of block rewards—often 1–2%—to a community pool. Yet without predictable disbursement, such pools become political theatre. The design challenge is to transform volatility into stability: convert transaction fees into slow-releasing trusts, time-locked contracts that disburse at a steady rate, audited and renewed by contributors rather than speculators. Predictability is not bureaucracy; it is oxygen.

The counter-example that proves the rule is the short life of DeFi grant programmes during 2021–2022. Funded by exuberant treasuries, they showered money on hackathons and integrations. Within a year, as token prices fell, budgets evaporated. Maintenance work halted. Documentation lagged. Infrastructure degraded quietly. The visible metric was GitHub activity: commits fell, issues multiplied, response times stretched from days to months. Reconcile this failure with the earlier claim: systems thrive when their funding horizon exceeds their hype horizon.

This subchapter's argument can be summarised through a behavioural lens. Healthy systems institutionalise care. They build maintenance into their rituals: release cycles, audits, retrospectives, predictable pay. Unhealthy systems outsource care to volunteers and call it community. In open-source culture, the line between passion and exploitation is thin. A sustainable design treats maintenance as labour, not love.

The tragedy of maintenance, then, is not only economic but moral. When users assume someone else will patch the bug, write the test, or maintain the library, they rehearse the same delusion that doomed Heartbleed: that dependence without contribution is sustainable. Yet the cure is within reach. Predictable funding, transparent stewardship, and modest expectations can turn entropy into order. The quiet motif returns—*entropy managed is civilisation.*

The unresolved tension remains: decentralised systems reject central authority but crave reliability. Can they cultivate a culture that rewards those who keep the lights on, not only those who light new fires? The forward test is this: a network's durability should be measured not by how quickly it launches the next upgrade, but by how predictably it maintains the last.

Governance Theatre vs Governance Work

On 30 September 2021, a Compound governance vote labelled "Proposal 062" passed on-chain and executed in San Francisco's morning. The change looked procedural: adjust reward parameters. Hours later, users began claiming millions of dollars in COMP they were never owed. A single arithmetic mistake in the proposal's code had slipped through discussion, audits, and voting. The vote passed. The code broke. For a week, patches crawled through time locks while the wrong incentives spooled out to anyone quick enough to harvest them. The episode was not merely a bug; it was a biopsy. It showed how a pageant of forum posts, token-weighted votes, and ornate dashboards can hide the real levers of power: who writes proposals, who controls execution keys, and who can hit pause when the calendar turns against you.

The term *governance theatre* names that gap between ritual and authority. The DAO wears a crown of ballots while the sceptre sits elsewhere. To read these systems honestly, ask three questions before you admire a vote: who can put an item on the agenda; who can execute it once passed; who can stop it at the last minute. If those answers point to the same small set of hands, you have ceremony, not self-rule. The motif that will anchor this section is *the agenda*. Agendas make and unmake power: they decide what is thinkable, what is discussable, and what gets buried in a week of other business. Watch the agenda, and you will see governance work.

Show, then name. In Compound's case, an apparently routine parameter change exposed a structural asymmetry: proposers possessed the practical monopoly on code that could be voted upon; most voters assessed prose, not bytecode. Name the pattern: *proposer's prerogative*. Explain: when only a narrow circle can craft executable proposals, the electorate becomes an audience, not a legislature. Implication: the metric that matters is not voter turnout but proposer concentration—how many distinct entities authored the last twenty proposals—paired with execution pathways—how many distinct entities actually pressed the buttons that changed contracts.

Another scene, from March 2020, reveals a different mask. On the Steem blockchain, after a change in ownership of Steemit Inc., major exchanges mobilised customer deposits to vote in a new set of witnesses favourable to the acquirer. The move complied with the letter of stake-weighted rules. It violated the spirit of consent. Community members forked to create Hive within weeks, explicitly excluding the disputed stake. Name the manoeuvre: *agenda capture by stake mobilisation*. Explain: when voting power can be borrowed or rehypothecated, the calendar gets weaponised—snap elections, rapid recalls, surprise votes at thin-liquidity hours. Implication: an honest governance design must control agenda timing (minimum discussion periods, weekend locks, time-of-day distribution) and stake provenance (guardrails against using unconsenting deposits for votes).

Where theatre thrives, signals multiply and substance shrinks. You see temperature checks that never reach code, opinion polls that are never followed by drafts, and "request for comment" threads that end with "defer to core contributors." The work, by contrast, occurs off-stage: in repos, timelocks, and multisig consoles. The reliable diagnostic is behavioural: measure the proportion of passed proposals implemented within their stated windows; measure mean timelock durations relative to the risk of the change; measure how often a veto or guardian pause is exercised and later reviewed in public minutes. Numbers, then names. Execution makes authority visible.

Examples at scale help distinguish ritual from rule. In June 2022, Lido DAO debated whether to self-limit its share of staked ether to preserve validator diversity. The proposal failed. Critics saw the vote as proof of capture by tokenholders with aligned financial interests; supporters framed it as market realism. What matters analytically is not the outcome but the anatomy. Who set the question? Who drafted the options? Who controlled the timetables and the interfaces where votes occurred? Lido's process surfaced the central friction of token governance: the largest stakeholders can simultaneously be the most informed operators and the most conflicted participants. A theatre reading stops at turnout percentages. A work reading interrogates agenda formation and conflict management, then asks whether institutional design—delegate councils, independent risk committees, rotating agenda-setters—could have improved deliberation without smothering it.

Contrast that with Ethereum's Merge in September 2022—a monumental change with no token vote. Client teams proposed, debated, tested, and executed a multi-year transition from proof of work to proof of stake. Users, miners, and exchanges expressed voice by choosing clients, scheduling downtime, and listing the chain they recognised. The core ritual was not a poll but a public process: AllCoreDevs calls, testnets, shadow forks, and release candidates. Name the model: *rough consensus and running code*. Explain: authority emerged from public repetition and demonstrated competence rather than from token counts. Implication: legitimacy can arise from transparent craft where agenda-setting is plural (multiple client teams), execution is distributed (no single switch), and veto is real (any client or user could refuse). For many protocols, this is impractical; for those that can manage it, it is governance work in its most adult form.

To make theatre tangible, keep the motif of the agenda in view. Agenda power has three valves: *propose, sequence, scope*. Propose: who can draft code that reaches a vote? If "proposers" are de facto a single lab, stop pretending you have a parliament. Sequence: who decides when the vote happens? If timing routinely favours low-attention windows, you have a manipulation channel, not a calendar. Scope: who decides what a proposal may include? Logrolling—bundling unrelated changes—forces voters to swallow poison with medicine. Real governance work separates concerns and staggers changes so that dissent can be precise rather than self-destructive.

Two more cases show how to read authority in practice. First, Uniswap governance (2020–2023) demonstrated the power of *agenda brokers*—large delegates who control proposal pipelines. Many community ideas died at the "temperature check" stage because no high-status account adopted them into code. Meanwhile, proposals shepherded by major delegates sailed through, even when controversial. The metric here is *delegate gatekeeping rate*: count community threads with clear support that never reached a formal vote; compare with the pass-through rate of proposals championed by top delegates. If the ratio skews heavily, theatre prevails; a handful write the playlist.

Second, MakerDAO's long march toward its "Endgame" restructuring showed governance work's drudgery and risk. Over 2022–2023, Maker's forums, risk teams, and core units processed dozens of proposals reshaping collateral, budgets, and organisational structure. Some votes were performative; many were operational. The telling numbers were not quorums but *implementation velocity* and *reversal rate*: how long from "green" to live contract, and how often changes were reverted after side effects appeared. A low reversal rate paired with steady throughput indicates real administrative capacity; a high rate flags agenda churn and thin execution muscle.

Heuristics expose capture early if you choose ones tied to behaviour, not branding. Who proposes? Count unique proposers over a rolling window; a healthy polity shows dispersion that persists beyond market cycles. Who executes? Trace multisig signers and client maintainers; if the same three names touch every critical pathway, label that risk—not to shame, but to plan. Who vetoes? Examine guardian roles, emergency brakes, and their invocation history; a veto that exists but never explains itself erodes legitimacy faster than no veto at all. Who controls narrative? Identify who moderates the forum, who curates the newsletter, who hosts the calls; speech organisation is agenda control by another name. These heuristics are not cynical; they are civic. They turn vibes into verifiable signals.

A credible counterpoint warns against fetishising dispersion. Some protocols with widely distributed proposers and long timelocks ship little and break often. Creaking calendars protect against capture but smother responsiveness. The reconciliation is design, not rhetoric. Use *bounded delegation*: allow specialist councils to propose within narrow domains—risk parameters, documentation budgets, client maintenance—subject to broad, slow-moving constitutional limits. Reserve heavy quorum and long delays for powers that alter rights or treasuries. Measure the result. If emergency patches stop requiring theatrics, you have found a better balance; if councils ossify into fiefdoms, rotate them by term and enforce cooling-off rules before members can stand again.

Theatre also flourishes in the shadows of incentives. Vote buying—rebranded as "incentive alignment"—turns deliberation into an auction. Platforms that let protocols pay for votes promise efficiency; they sell legitimacy. The worst outcomes are subtle: policy tilts towards short-term fee extraction because that is what pays delegates today. A governance system that wants to resist this drift must break the link between immediate payout and lasting power. Time-weighted voting decay, long timelocks on treasury distributions, and reputational scoring for delegates (based on implementation follow-through, not speeches) are constitutional tools that convert heat into light. Again, watch the agenda: when money can schedule the day, citizens eventually stop showing up.

Users can learn to diagnose theatre at a glance. Enter a forum and ask: are most threads authored by the same logo? Are proposal templates uniform, with clear sections for scope, risks, and rollback, or are they baroque sales decks? Do maintainers post timelines and changelogs after each vote? Does the multisig publish signer rotations and key-ceremonies? Is there a public cadence—weekly calls with minutes, monthly retrospectives, quarterly roadmaps—and does it persist when prices fall? Theatre slips when the lights dim; work keeps its diary.

The master key, as ever, is exit. When agenda control calcifies, credible exit makes voice meaningful. Steem's fork to Hive was painful but clarifying; it converted a captured agenda into a new one with different stewards. Still, exit is not cheap. Bridges, application migrations, and social graphs are sticky. This is why governance work must include *portability engineering*: standards for data export, APIs for contract state replication, and tooling that lets users and developers move without begging. A captured agenda loses power when deserts have roads.

None of this absolves citizens of attention. Participation is labour. Delegation helps, but it must be earned, not inherited. Follow the diary: read one implementation diff per week; track one multisig each month; learn the names of those who routinely propose without drama and execute without fanfare. They are your civil service. Fund them. Hold them to account without burning them out. A polity that rewards only fireworks ends with arsonists in charge.

The unresolved tension remains live and useful. How much friction should we deliberately add to guard the calendar from capture, knowing that friction also slows repair? When should we entrust agenda-setting to experts, and how do we rotate that trust before it fossilises? When a vote passes but no one with keys commits the change, which legitimacy should prevail—the will of tokenholders or the conscience of maintainers? The next crisis will not be a shortage of opinion; it will be a shortage of well-placed brakes. Before you vote again, ask the only question that turns theatre into work: if the forum went dark tomorrow, who could still set, execute, and halt the agenda—and do you trust them with your name?

MEV and the Politics of Ordering

On 3 September 2020, during a period of heavy decentralised exchange (DEX) activity, a single Ethereum block contained over 400 transactions battling for position. One trader's swap on Uniswap was sandwiched—bought before, sold after—by a bot that earned roughly $13,000 in profit in 12 seconds. The trader's loss was invisible in the interface, but perfectly legible in the block: a reorder of transactions that reshuffled wealth without breaking any rule. This, in miniature, was *miner extractable value*, or MEV—a term coined months earlier by Phil Daian and colleagues to describe how those who decide transaction order can quietly collect rent. When Ethereum shifted from miners to validators in September 2022, the term evolved into *maximal extractable value*. The practice stayed the same. Whoever sets the order, sets the odds.

Ordering is the quiet constitution of every market. Before any price is discovered, someone decides *who goes first*. Traditional finance regulates this through queueing rules and oversight: exchanges like NASDAQ or the London Stock Exchange must timestamp and sequence orders under scrutiny. Blockchains, by contrast, expose this ordering to whoever assembles the block—miners, validators, or specialised intermediaries. Neutral rails, it turns out, are never neutral. The ledger's fairness depends on a thousand micro-decisions about order, and those who profit from it often justify their actions as arbitrage or efficiency. Yet each reordered transaction subtly taxes coordination and corrodes legitimacy.

MEV is not an exotic edge case. It is structural. In May 2021, Flashbots—a research collective formed to mitigate and measure MEV—reported daily extractable value exceeding $5 million on Ethereum during peak volatility. Most of it came from front-running, back-running, and liquidations: bots inserting their transactions around user activity. These bots rely on mempool visibility: the waiting room where pending transactions are broadcast before inclusion. Whoever monitors it with speed and capital can reorder the queue for gain. The behaviour mirrors high-frequency trading in equities—same physics, different governance.

Show the mechanics. A user sends a swap. The transaction enters the mempool with a gas fee attached. A bot detects the likely price impact, replicates the swap with higher gas, and ensures it lands first. The user pays more, receives less, and sees none of it. Name this act plainly: *priority theft*. Explain: blockspace is auctioned, but knowledge of others' intentions gives insiders a second auction for advantage. Implication: the very mechanism that secures consensus—ordering—becomes a site of hidden power.

Yet MEV is not inherently malicious. Arbitrage maintains price parity across markets; liquidators keep lending platforms solvent. The harm lies not in value capture but in opacity and externality. In early DeFi, liquidations often failed to compensate borrowers fairly, and sandwiching inflated transaction costs system-wide. Every user paid for someone else's latency. Mitigations arose: batch auctions, sealed mempools, and *fair ordering services*. The most ambitious, Flashbots' *MEV-Boost* (2022), separated block building from block proposing, introducing competition among builders and transparency around bids. For months, this modularity reduced visible front-running and channelled rewards back to validators. But it also centralised block construction among a few sophisticated actors—Blocknative, Flashbots, bloXroute—creating new choke points.

This tension—between mitigation and monopoly—is the core political drama of MEV. Each attempt to reduce extraction redistributes it. The 2023 introduction of "private mempools" and "order flow auctions" promised user protection but also enabled new forms of pay-for-access. Wallets and aggregators began selling their users' transaction flow to preferred builders, echoing *payment for order flow* in traditional markets. The pattern repeated: moral justification wrapped in efficiency language. The central question re-emerged—who earns by seeing first?

Consider a counterpoint. Cowswap, a DEX launched in 2021 by Gnosis, uses *coincidence of wants* batch auctions. Orders are aggregated off-chain, matched where possible, and only net settlements reach the blockchain. This design minimises MEV by reducing opportunities for reordering. Measurable effect: users saved over $20 million in avoided sandwich attacks by mid-2023. Yet Cowswap relies on trusted *solvers*—entities that batch and match orders. They hold temporary discretion, a soft form of order control. MEV shrinks, but delegation rises. Reconcile this: mitigation always introduces governance; fairness without authority is a mirage.

To perceive MEV ethically, we must recast it not as an engineering flaw but as a distributive choice. Every ordering system allocates visibility, priority, and surprise. Ethical bounds arise where that allocation intersects dignity. A trader expects risk, not ambush; a borrower expects rules, not opportunism. Systems can encode these expectations by design. Batch auctions limit ambush. Commit-reveal schemes hide intentions until locks expire. Randomised sequencing, as proposed in 2023 by Ethereum's *Proposer-Builder Separation* roadmap, adds uncertainty for bots while preserving throughput. These are not silver bullets but civic compromises: they slow the powerful without paralysing the system.

Show where ethics and efficiency meet. In December 2022, Coinbase's *Base* network proposed *fair sequencing services*—specialised actors randomising transaction order post-collection. This introduced a measurable fairness metric: *expected inclusion delay*. By bounding delay variance, Base signalled that fairness can be audited, not just promised. Contrast that with Binance Smart Chain's opaque validator rotation, where ordering often correlates with off-chain deals.

The former turned ordering into accountable infrastructure; the latter, into silent hierarchy. Ethics here is procedural: transparency converts dominance into duty.

A deeper political lens clarifies the stakes. MEV is extraction without representation. Those most affected—users—rarely participate in rule-making. Builders and validators negotiate over revenue splits, not rights. When Flashbots published its *MEV-Share* proposal (May 2023), offering partial rebates to users, critics noted that it still privileged intermediaries who could access the relays. Redistribution replaced fairness. The visible behaviour—complex dashboards, rebate metrics—masked the unchanged asymmetry: who watches the mempool still decides who profits.

To grasp the motif of *ordering as power*, imagine the ledger as a queue outside a rationed shop. The order of service defines the distribution of goods. Blockchain systems claim impartiality—first come, first served by gas price. But gas price itself is a social signal: those with better bots, faster networks, or insider information cut the queue legally. The mempool is not a democracy; it is a bidding war disguised as access. The question becomes not whether MEV exists, but how to civilise it.

Ethical mitigation does not demand purity; it demands containment. The aim is to turn zero-sum edges into bounded margins, transparent enough for users to accept as cost rather than theft. Proposals like *encrypted mempools* (e.g., SUAVE by Flashbots, 2023) attempt this by hiding transaction content until block inclusion, reducing front-running. Yet encryption adds latency, complexity, and trust in relay operators. The counter-example of *dark MEV*—private order flow invisible to public relays—illustrates the danger: too much opacity births oligopoly. The cure for MEV can become its mutation.

The most instructive precedent comes from traditional market structure. After the 2010 "Flash Crash", regulators forced exchanges to publish trade data and implement circuit breakers. These did not eliminate high-frequency trading but bounded its damage. Blockchain analogues—open MEV registries, slashing for manipulative reordering, or protocol-level limits on gas bribes—could play a similar role. The principle is the same: treat ordering as public infrastructure, not private turf. Transparency does not prevent exploitation, but it changes its cost curve. When sunlight raises the price of cheating, darkness becomes expensive.

Measurement grounds ethics. Flashbots' open-source dashboard remains the best tool for tracing MEV's flow. It shows concentration: by mid-2024, three builders produced over 70% of Ethereum blocks. Such numbers should alarm any decentralisation advocate. The metric of decentralisation is not node count but *ordering diversity*. When a handful decide order, consensus is cosmetic. Fairness decays quietly, one block at a time.

Still, eradication is impossible. MEV will persist as long as blockchains host markets. The task is containment and cultural realism. Systems should make extraction predictable, measurable, and taxable to the commons. A portion of builder profits could automatically fund public goods—an *MEV tithe*. Such mechanisms exist in spirit: Flashbots' open research, the Protocol Guild's retroactive grants, or Cowswap's solver rebates. They transform hidden rents into explicit support for maintenance. If profit is unavoidable, at least make it civic.

The unresolved tension, however, is philosophical. Fairness requires friction; efficiency rewards its removal. Randomisation lowers capture but raises latency; transparency deters abuse but exposes intent. Each mitigation redistributes advantage rather than erasing it. The forward test for designers and citizens alike is diagnostic: when you next send a transaction, ask not only *whether it will be confirmed*, but *who will decide its place in line*. That line—quiet, invisible, yet monetised—has become the real parliament of the blockchain. The question is timeless and political: can a system that lets anyone reorder you ever truly call itself neutral?

Chapter 5
Privacy, Security, Responsibility

In December 2022, journalists at *The Guardian* revealed that the identities of Iranian protesters had been sold on the dark web for less than the cost of a cinema ticket. The leak traced back not to a hacked intelligence service but to a poorly secured petition site hosted abroad. A single misconfigured spreadsheet—names, emails, city of residence—had become a weapon. The story barely made headlines in the West, yet it marked a quiet moral turning point. Privacy, long framed as a personal preference, had once again proven itself a civic infrastructure—one that, when neglected, endangered not just individuals but movements.

Privacy is the precondition of dissent. It is what allows a journalist to meet a source, a donor to support an unpopular cause, a citizen to test an idea without fear of reprisal. Yet privacy's cousin, secrecy, has long sheltered fraud, evasion, and corruption. The tension between the two is not technical; it is moral. Encryption, anonymity, and data minimisation are only as virtuous as the purposes they serve. The technologies themselves are neutral, but the architectures we build around them encode values—who must justify exposure, who earns opacity, and under what rules exceptions are made. The twenty-first century's most urgent political question may not be *who governs*, but *who knows*.

This chapter begins from that contradiction. It treats privacy not as an accessory to freedom but as a public utility: invisible when it works, catastrophic when it fails. From decentralised ledgers to encrypted messaging, our systems of coordination now run on visibility gradients. The harder question is how to preserve accountability without constructing a panopticon. Civic privacy is not the absence of visibility; it is its calibration—seeing enough to trust, but not so much as to coerce.

In this light, the privacy debate shifts from metaphysics to design. The tools we choose define our social contract. Consider the dilemma faced by donation platforms during the 2022 Russian invasion of Ukraine: platforms like Patreon and GoFundMe suspended some campaigns citing sanctions compliance, while crypto-based initiatives like UkraineDAO raised millions with full on-chain transparency. Donors faced a moral puzzle—visibility proved authenticity, but also exposed identities. In journalism, similar trade-offs appear daily: the decision to encrypt communications through Signal or ProtonMail may protect a whistleblower but complicate editorial verification. Each tool carries an implicit theory of responsibility—toward subjects, audiences, and the state.

The core argument here is that privacy and responsibility are not opposites but reciprocals. To handle data with discretion is to accept the duty of care that privacy demands. The responsible use of anonymity does not mean opacity from all scrutiny; it means submitting to the right kind of scrutiny. That distinction—the difference between protection and concealment—will frame the first section of this chapter, *Privacy as Civic Infrastructure*. It will explore how societies balance rights to privacy with obligations to prevent harm, and why moral literacy, not just encryption, is the first defence against both authoritarianism and impunity.

The second movement, *Threat Models for Citizens, Not Engineers*, leaves ideology for pragmatism. For most people, the frontier of digital safety is not an intelligence agency but an opportunist with a phishing link or a stolen phone. We will examine why security culture must be lived, not laminated. Real resilience begins with mundane routines: compartmentalising devices, verifying identities, rehearsing recovery. The image of the lone cryptographer gives way to the ordinary citizen who updates passwords before dinner. In the networked century, heroism is replaced by hygiene.

Still, trust demands more than habit. The section *Audits, Assurances, and What Can't Be Proven* examines how we measure reliability when no system can prove virtue. Audits, bug bounties, and proofs of reserve create partial windows into integrity, but they also invite performative compliance. The reader will learn how to read disclosures sceptically yet fairly—how to distinguish between an honest uncertainty and a marketing gloss. The lesson is that transparency without interpretation is noise. Assurance is a relationship, not a report.

Finally, *The Ethics of Irreversibility* confronts a uniquely digital paradox: systems built for censorship resistance also make honest mistakes permanent. Blockchain finality protects political dissidents; it also traps mis-sent funds and enshrines code errors. We will explore experiments in reversible wrappers, time-bound locks, and community-managed restitution—all ways of restoring mercy without reintroducing tyranny. Here, responsibility takes its hardest form: acknowledging that freedom includes the burden of repair.

Across these sections runs a quiet motif—*the trace*. Every act in a digital system leaves one, whether visible or encrypted, deliberate or residual. Traces connect accountability and vulnerability. They are the fingerprints of both truth and abuse. To live ethically with traces means accepting that we are all archivists now—each message, key, and signature part of a collective memory we can neither fully erase nor fully trust.

The stakes are more than technical. As governments expand surveillance in the name of safety and private firms monetise intimacy as data, the boundaries of responsibility blur. Ordinary citizens are caught between two imperatives: protect themselves and participate. A society that chooses transparency without limits invites conformity; one that fetishises secrecy breeds suspicion. The humane path lies in designing systems where choice and consequence stay proportionate—where privacy protects the weak and accountability disciplines the strong.

If earlier chapters asked what decentralisation makes possible, this one asks what it obliges. It invites the reader to think less about the code and more about the covenant—to see security not as armour but as architecture, privacy not as retreat but as right, and responsibility not as compliance but as conscience. The following pages will move from the personal to the structural, from the keypad to the polis, tracing how our digital defences mirror our moral priorities.

The question to carry forward is deceptively simple: when visibility becomes infinite and reversibility impossible, what does it mean to act responsibly? The answer cannot be automated. It must be learned, tested, and lived—block by block, habit by habit, in a civilisation that now runs on code but still depends on trust.

Privacy as Civic Infrastructure

In August 2020, the Belarusian authorities raided the offices of *Tut.by*, the country's largest independent news outlet, and seized servers after reporters published footage of protests in Minsk. The crackdown was swift, the justification bureaucratic: a violation of "data handling laws". Yet the underlying truth was simpler. The government wanted names. It sought the identities of those who had filmed, uploaded, and shared evidence of state violence. What followed was not just the silencing of journalists but the intimidation of anyone who had trusted their digital footprints to the wrong infrastructure. Privacy, in that moment, ceased to be a personal preference and revealed itself as a civic necessity—the invisible scaffolding that upholds free association, dissent, and truth.

The paradox is enduring. The same opacity that protects whistleblowers can shield embezzlers. Privacy defends conscience; secrecy breeds impunity. Democracies must distinguish between the two without collapsing into surveillance. The distinction rests not in technology but in intent and accountability. A society that treats privacy solely as an individual right will tolerate its erosion whenever fear or profit demands it. A society that understands privacy as civic infrastructure—a public good like clean water or reliable transport—recognises that protecting it sustains everyone, including those who never encrypt an email or join a protest.

To see privacy as infrastructure is to trace its civic function: coordination without coercion. Just as a city relies on roads to connect strangers safely, a polity relies on informational boundaries to let citizens exchange ideas, dissent, and organise. When these boundaries dissolve, participation becomes perilous. The effect is measurable: in countries with pervasive surveillance, turnout in opposition demonstrations falls by 30 to 50 per cent (Chen & Xu, 2019). Fear travels faster than data. Privacy failure is not a technical glitch; it is a public health event of the civic sphere.

Show, name, explain, imply. The first and clearest arena where privacy functions as civic infrastructure is charitable giving. In February 2022, *GiveSendGo*, a Christian crowdfunding platform hosting the "Freedom Convoy" protests in Canada, was hacked. Donor identities—including thousands of small contributions from the United States and Europe—were leaked and published online. Some donors lost jobs; others received threats. The moral argument over the protests is irrelevant here. The breach exposed a structural hazard: when civic participation leaves an indelible, searchable trace, conscience becomes costly. Philanthropy—once protected by quiet envelopes and anonymous tithes—now requires cryptographic prudence. Privacy safeguards the pluralism that democracy depends on.

Contrast that with the *Panama Papers* leak (April 2016), where secrecy, not privacy, sustained corruption. The release of 11.5 million documents from the law firm Mossack Fonseca revealed offshore accounts of politicians, executives, and public figures worldwide. The infrastructure of concealment—shell companies, nominee directors, encrypted channels—was built to evade scrutiny. The same technical tools that could have protected journalists or dissidents instead protected rent-seekers. The difference between privacy and secrecy lay in reciprocity: privacy defends individuals from unjust intrusion; secrecy denies the public its rightful knowledge. Both hide, but only one hides fairly.

The motif that threads through this subchapter is *the wall*. A wall can protect or imprison, depending on who controls the gate. Privacy erects walls that shield the weak from the strong; secrecy builds walls that shelter the strong from the weak. The art of democratic design lies in knowing where to place the door.

The ethics of tool use follow naturally. End-to-end encryption, zero-knowledge proofs, and decentralised identity systems do not absolve their users from judgement. They distribute power, not wisdom. When activists in Hong Kong adopted Telegram for coordination in 2019, the encrypted chat protected them from interception but exposed metadata that revealed group sizes and timing. The platform's partial opacity became a tactical liability. A civic frame would have asked: who needs to see what, and when, to preserve both safety and accountability? Rights imply duties. Privacy technologies are civic instruments, not magic shields.

Journalism offers a sharper test. In 2013, Edward Snowden's leaks to *The Guardian* and *The Washington Post* required operational security as complex as the revelations themselves. Encrypted drives, air-gapped laptops, and secure meeting points were not romantic flourishes; they were civic hygiene in the face of systemic intrusion. But Snowden's act also revived an uncomfortable question: when does revealing secrets serve public accountability, and when does it endanger legitimate confidentiality? The journalists faced a duty to redact identities of field agents and limit technical detail that could compromise ongoing operations. Privacy, here, was not a right to conceal but a responsibility to discriminate—to protect individuals without erasing the truth.

A counterpoint comes from the 2021 *Pegasus Project* investigation led by Amnesty International and *Forbidden Stories*, which exposed the global use of spyware developed by Israel's NSO Group. The project relied on collaboration across 17 media outlets in 10 countries, all handling sensitive data on targeted journalists and activists. Their coordination required a disciplined privacy framework: shared protocols for data storage, verification, and publication. No major leak compromised sources. The implication is clear: privacy as infrastructure works when maintained collectively, not hoarded individually. It behaves like a commons—sustainable only through shared norms.

Treating privacy as civic infrastructure shifts the argument from ideology to maintenance. Like roads, it requires upkeep, audits, and adaptation. Legal frameworks such as the European Union's GDPR (2018) enshrine data minimisation and consent as civic standards, but enforcement remains uneven. Meanwhile, mass data brokers in the United States operate with impunity, trading in the granular habits of millions. The civic equivalent would be allowing private contractors to run city traffic lights for profit, optimised not for safety but for surveillance. The infrastructure metaphor reveals what is often obscured: privacy is not an obstacle to governance but its precondition. When citizens know that observation is bounded, they engage more freely and contribute more honestly.

The economic argument complements the civic one. According to a 2021 study by the Norwegian Consumer

Council, over 70 per cent of apps analysed shared behavioural data with advertising networks without informed consent. The profit model of surveillance capitalism treats personal data as extractive resource rather than civic trust. When that model scales, societies inherit two deficits: informational inequality and moral fatigue. The former allows a few firms to know everything about everyone; the latter convinces citizens that resistance is futile. Both corrode democracy by eroding reciprocity.

A credible counter-example, though, deserves attention: public health data during the COVID-19 pandemic. Governments needed granular information to track contagion. Some, like South Korea, used real-time location tracking to enforce quarantines; others, like Germany, relied on decentralised exposure notification apps that preserved anonymity. The former produced rapid containment but provoked unease; the latter preserved privacy but relied on voluntary uptake. The reconciliation lies in proportionality and consent. Civic privacy does not forbid data use; it demands purpose limitation and sunset clauses. Infrastructure earns legitimacy when it retires itself.

The civic lens also clarifies personal ethics. Citizens who encrypt their messages but dox opponents on social media betray the very principle they invoke. Privacy without empathy becomes secrecy by another name. A civic conception requires mutual restraint—the recognition that other people's boundaries are as vital to the commons as one's own. This is not sentimentality but design discipline: social norms must evolve with technical affordances. The right to encryption must coexist with the duty to transparency in public office; the right to anonymity must coexist with mechanisms to redress harm. The infrastructure analogy forces these dualities into view.

There is, however, a deeper cultural battle beneath the legal and technical debates. In many liberal democracies, privacy has been marketed as a luxury: a premium feature, a subscription benefit, a choice. Yet when basic protections—encrypted messaging, secure browsing, data deletion—depend on price or expertise, the civic function collapses. Privacy becomes privilege. Infrastructure is the opposite: it must be universal, boring, and reliable. The transition from luxury to infrastructure is a moral project. It demands that we treat privacy as we treat clean air—something too fundamental to be optional.

The motif of *the wall* returns here as both defence and temptation. Walls keep danger out but can keep scrutiny out too. The challenge for modern governance is to build walls with windows—transparent enough for oversight, opaque enough for safety. Blockchain systems, with their radical transparency, confront this directly. A donation made on-chain can prove authenticity but exposes donor identity. A journalist's payment for leaked documents can be traced to their address. Cryptographic advances like zero-knowledge proofs hint at a future compromise: proving legitimacy without revealing specifics. These are not mere technical tricks; they are moral architectures—walls learning to breathe.

To argue privacy without caricature is to accept discomfort. Absolute transparency breeds conformity; absolute secrecy breeds corruption. The civic challenge lies in cultivating partial sight—enough to coordinate, not enough to control. The question is not whether societies value privacy, but whether they are willing to pay for its upkeep: in budget lines, in habits, and in restraint. Civic infrastructure costs money and discipline. Its failure costs trust.

The unresolved tension remains deliberately open. If privacy is civic infrastructure, who owns its maintenance? Should encrypted communication be treated like public transport—funded, regulated, and accessible to all—or like private property defended by self-help? When governments demand backdoors in the name of security, do they repair the walls or crack their foundations? The test for any democracy, digital or otherwise, is whether it can preserve the spaces where conscience can breathe without allowing those same spaces to suffocate accountability. The blueprint exists; the upkeep is our task.

Threat Models for Citizens, Not Engineers

On 15 July 2020, Twitter's public conscience was hijacked. From San Francisco to Lagos, blue-tick accounts—from Joe Biden and Apple to Bill Gates—suddenly promoted a bitcoin scam. The breach was not an elite zero-day. It was a phone call. Attackers phoned Twitter contractors, posed as IT, and coaxed credentials for internal tools. The email looked utterly, painfully ordinary. Hours later millions saw a lesson usually buried in technical manuals: the most effective attacks are mundane, and they exploit people rather than code.

A year later, in September 2021, Coinbase disclosed that around 6,000 customers had been phished with convincing emails that redirected them to spoofed websites; the attackers then exploited an SMS multi-factor flaw to drain accounts (Coinbase, 2021). This was not Lazarus Group versus a national grid. It was a patient adversary with a list, a script, and a weekend. These cases anchor the premise of this subchapter: for most citizens, the real threats are predictable—phishing, device loss, and the industrial trade in personal data. Security, then, is not a stunt. It is routine. The routine is *the drill.*

Start with phishing because it is how most storms begin. Show the behaviour. You receive a message that your delivery failed; you tap a link; a page that mimics your bank opens; you type credentials; nothing seems to happen. Name the tactic: *credential harvesting*. Explain: attackers exploit urgency and familiarity to push you into the wrong reflex. Implication: the effective countermeasure is not higher IQ but slower hands and a *second channel*—verify requests for money or secrets using a different medium than the one that asked. A fraud email gets a phone call to a known number. A WhatsApp request gets confirmed face to face. Systems improve when citizens practise that choreography. The drill is dull. It is also civilisation.

Phishing thrives because personal data is cheap and abundant. The Equifax breach in 2017 exposed the personal information of roughly 147 million people (Equifax, 2018). Data brokers compile the rest—addresses, phone numbers, relational maps—then sell lists that turn into targeted scripts. Name the adversary: *the data broker economy*. Explain: when your details can be bought for pennies, attackers don't need sophistication; they need volume. Implication: treat exposure as ambient and plan for *resilience over secrecy*: assume adversaries know your name, job, and close contacts; invest instead in friction they cannot bypass easily—hardware keys, time-delayed transfers, and out-of-band confirmations.

Device loss is the second great leveller. A lost phone on the Piccadilly line can be more dangerous than a remote hacker. Show the mundane catastrophe: a journalist leaves a handset in a taxi; the device has email, cloud storage, and a password manager unlocked by a short PIN. Nothing is breached at first. Everything is exposed in potential. Name the discipline: *compartmentalisation*. Explain: separate identities across devices and accounts so that one failure is not *total*. Keep sensitive accounts behind hardware security keys, not SMS. Disable previews on lock screens. Require a second factor that is not on the same device. Implication: security becomes architecture. A wall here, a door there, a gate you must rattle twice. The drill is spatial as much as mental.

Citizens do not need threat maps with exotic acronyms. They need pictures of *what goes wrong*. Consider a small NGO in Nairobi coordinating legal aid. The director uses a personal Gmail, a shared Dropbox, and a group WhatsApp. A volunteer receives a PDF "invoice" carrying malware macros; another volunteer forwards a spreadsheet with participants' names to a personal email; the director's phone dies the night before court. No spies, no zero-days. Just work, haste, and entropy. Name the frame: *operational hygiene*. Explain: move the most sensitive material into a shared vault with roles; restrict edit rights; ensure two people, not one, can access critical accounts; pre-arrange a replacement phone with a spare SIM and a written set-up checklist. Implication: responsibility becomes a schedule. The drill is calendared, not heroic.

Verification is where citizens win cheaply. Show: a family receives a message from a "bank" demanding a transfer to resolve a fraud hold. The son calls the number on the back of the card, not the one in the text. The hold was fiction. Name: *second-channel verification*. Explain: most fraud collapses when forced into a path the attacker doesn't control. Implication: teach this once, strongly; repeat it monthly; rehearse with elderly parents and teenagers. Culture beats configuration. The drill repeats.

Security habits stick when they have a story. In March 2019, Twitter's CEO, Jack Dorsey, suffered a SIM-swap attack; his phone number was taken over and used to post offensive tweets. The swap succeeded because a support agent at a mobile carrier was convinced to port the number. Show the fixable weak link. Name: *SIM-based identity*. Explain: if your second factor relies on a phone number, your security is outsourced to call-centre scripts. Implication: wherever possible, replace SMS codes with app-based OTP or, better, security keys (FIDO/U2F). The habit costs minutes. It saves weeks. The drill is to notice where you still trust the phone company.

Data brokers, meanwhile, enlarge every small breach. In the Cambridge Analytica scandal (2018), data consent theatre allowed the profiling of voters at scale; individual indiscretions became aggregate manipulation. Citizens cannot opt out of entire industries. But they can blunt the edges. Show: a researcher uses email aliases for each major service and a private relay for newsletters, then watches which company leaks which alias. Name: *attributional compartmentalisation*. Explain: by segmenting identifiers, you quietly create a tripwire; when spam arrives, you learn which relationship failed. Implication: evidence creates leverage for complaints, and your world stains less when one stain spreads. The drill is a habit of names.

Some will raise the counter-example: what about nation-state malware, Pegasus-grade intrusions, baseband exploits? The answer is neither denial nor melodrama. These threats exist, but they are rare and targeted. If you are a high-risk journalist, activist, or official, you will need specialist support, managed devices, and strict protocols. For most citizens, such measures are performance. Reconcile the fear with proportion. Name: *risk stratification*. Explain: match control to plausibility. Phishing and device loss are universal; supply-chain firmware implants are not. Implication: spend your attention where it pays—on the drill you will actually keep.

Recovery turns accidents into anecdotes rather than trauma. Show: a researcher drops a phone in Lisbon; within an hour, they restore a new device from a cloud backup; within a day, two hardware keys re-enrol their critical accounts; within a week, they rotate passwords for the handful of services that still used SMS. Name: *recovery choreography*. Explain: rehearsed recovery prevents opportunists from turning mishap into breach. Implication: schedule a quarterly "fire drill": simulate loss, restore from backup, re-authenticate, rotate one stale secret. Time the drill. Track the snags. Make it shorter next time. A calendar, not courage, protects futures.

Small patterns compound. Use *least privilege* at home: create a separate standard user on your laptop; keep admin passwords in a manager; install software only after a cooling-off hour. Keep two browsers: one for work logins, one for the wild. Arrange a "dead man's handle" with a spouse or colleague—a shared envelope, physical or digital, that contains the keys and instructions they would need in a crisis. None of these acts requires a manifesto. They require a page in a drawer and a reminder that repeats. The drill, again.

Measurement creates belief. Abstract promises rarely shift behaviour, but a number can. Track one metric per quarter. For phishing, measure *false-login attempts prevented*—how many times did the second channel catch a fraud? For device loss, measure *time-to-restore* from a simulated wipe. For data exposure, measure *leaked-alias detections*—how many unique email aliases ended up with spam, and from which services? Transparency turns security from superstition into craft. You can decide where to aim the next improvement because the last improvement is written down. The drill produces proofs.

Institutions can make citizens safer by default. Banks that delay first transfers to new payees for 24 hours give humans time to think. Messaging apps that default to end-to-end encryption keep mistakes quiet. Wallets that simulate transactions and flag infinite approvals prevent "click-through" regret. These are not niceties; they are democratic design. Show the behaviour: when a default asks for patience, fraud curves bend. Name: *consent-preserving friction*. Explain: tiny delays at critical thresholds protect outsize value. Implication: ask your vendors one simple question: where are your pauses? If they cannot answer, the product treats your attention as revenue, not as a right.

Journalists, whose livelihoods strain against these risks, often model practical discipline. A small newsroom in Warsaw keeps a *go-bag* laptop with a clean OS for source meetings; two reporters share control of the encrypted drive containing sensitive documents; a shared chart records who accessed what, when. Every six months, they conduct a breach role-play: one reporter plays the attacker; another traces logs; the editor times the recovery. Nothing advanced. Everything deliberate. The drill gives them confidence to promise protection—and the humility to admit its limits.

There are limits. Even careful routines can fail under duress. Coercion defeats consent screens; border agents can compel device unlocking; cloud providers can be subpoenaed. The point of citizen threat modelling is not invincibility. It is damage control. Name: *bounded failure*. Explain: assume that some layer will break; design so that a breach at one layer does not reveal everything. Implication: accept imperfection early, not after catastrophe. Security, like health, is a practice you maintain, not a state you achieve. The drill is life-long.

Culturally, we must retire the myth of the brilliant defender and embrace the rhythm of teams. Families, small businesses, and volunteer groups can and do share security chores. One person handles backup checks; another verifies bank changes by phone; a third rotates shared secrets on a calendar. The group builds a tiny civil service for itself. Heroics entertain; routines endure. The drill becomes communal, which makes it stick.

The motif returns to where it began: the drill. You run it because you will forget under pressure; you run it to turn panic into a list. Attackers rely on tiredness and hurry. Your countermeasure is boring, repeatable, and slower than a click. A second channel. A second key. A second device in a drawer. And a second look at any message that demands speed.

The unresolved tension is practical and moral. How much friction will you add to make tomorrow survivable, knowing that too much friction keeps people outside the system altogether? Where is your line between helpful delay and paralysing process? When the next "ordinary" email arrives—and it will—will your habits fire before your hope does? The answer will never be a tool. It will be the drill you kept when there was no crisis, and the calm you earned by practising when no one watched.

Audits, Assurances, and What Can't Be Proven

On 17 June 2016, *The DAO* exploit began to siphon funds from a smart contract celebrated as the future of decentralised investment. The code had been public for weeks; multiple pairs of expert eyes had combed through it; the rhetoric around "audited" and "open source" floated like incense above the altar. Yet a re-entrancy flaw—subtle, legalistic, devastating—slipped through review. The fork that followed was constitutional theatre; the lesson that followed was practical. An audit is a boundary, not a guarantee. The seal did not save.

Five years later, on 30 September 2021, Compound's governance "Proposal 062" passed and executed. Within hours, users claimed millions in unintended rewards owing to a one-line arithmetic mistake embedded in the change. The protocol had audits on earlier versions; the vote had discussion; the forum had consensus. A small defect still propagated at the speed of automation. Again the pattern held: the badge of "audited" reduced risk; it did not certify virtue or competence tomorrow. What people needed was calibrated confidence, not borrowed certainty.

Audits do useful, humble work. They reduce unknowns within a declared scope. That scope is the first truth to read. Show, then name, then explain. A competent security review states its boundaries: commit hash, time window, threat model, and exclusions. Name this candour: *scoped assurance*. Explain: by declaring what was and wasn't examined, auditors constrain false comfort. Implication: responsible readers treat an audit as a snapshot with margins, not a vaccine. Confidence grows when those margins are explicit and when the team responds visibly to findings—fixes merged, tests added, changelogs written in plain English. Trust is a verb.

The second layer is technique. Static analysis, differential testing, property-based fuzzing, and formal verification each catch different families of error. Formal methods can prove that under specified assumptions certain behaviours cannot occur; they cannot prove that your assumptions describe the messy world. Oracle manipulation, economic attacks, or governance timing games live outside a function's logic. The implication is clear: read methods like you read instruments in a cockpit. Each tells the truth about one variable. No dial shows the horizon.

A third layer lies outside code entirely: *operational assurance*. If a protocol can upgrade, who holds the keys? How long is the timelock? Are emergency pauses staged and documented? A project that publishes signer identities, quorum rules, rotation schedules, and incident drill summaries communicates something no code comment can—the willingness to be accountable. In practice, this social clarity reduces the damage radius of inevitable defects. You see the same humility in post-mortems that name human error as readily as edge cases, and that attach follow-through: dated tasks, owners, and deadlines. The seal matters less than the diary.

Economic assurance complements the technical and social layers. Bug bounty programmes with meaningful rewards, insurance funds sized to historical loss plus a stress multiplier, and over-collateralisation in lending markets all turn promises into stakes. When a lending platform publishes how auctions work, who can bid, and how keeper incentives behave under stress, it provides a rare commodity: ex-ante verifiability. Users can simulate likely outcomes. That behaviour—simulation before commitment—beats glossy badges every time.

Two named examples trace these layers in practice. First, MakerDAO's "Black Thursday" (12 March 2020) saw collateral auctions misfire during a market collapse and oracle delays. Audits existed; code largely performed; still, bids landed at zero in thin conditions. The remedy afterwards was layered: oracle procedures tightened, keeper incentives adjusted, risk parameters revisited, and governance processes clarified. The lesson was not that audits failed but that audits sat inside a larger assurance stack that needed strengthening. Second, after FTX collapsed in November 2022, several centralised exchanges rushed to publish "proof-of-reserves" attestations. Some engaged reputable firms to attest snapshot liabilities; some produced Merkle proofs of assets without credible liability accounting. The better examples admitted limitations and published follow-on procedures; the worse played theatre. The reader's job is to distinguish accounting with ballast from optics with hash trees.

A credible counter-example tempers zeal. Kraken, years before the FTX scandal, commissioned third-party attestations of client asset holdings and published methodologies that allowed users to verify inclusion via privacy-preserving proofs. This improved transparency. Yet even well-constructed attestations remain periodic, not continuous; they still rely on governance over off-chain liabilities. Reconcile the limitation with proportion: a good attestation is a useful brick in a wall that still needs mortar—segregated accounts, jurisdictional clarity, audits of controls, and operational runbooks for freezes and exits. Assurance is additive. No single document carries the cathedral.

Across all of this runs a quiet motif: *the seal*. Auditors affix seals; firms brand them; users seek them. But the seal's power is performative. It moves markets only insofar as a community believes that a named auditor with a named method applied to a named codebase within a named time actually constrains behaviour. Strip away names or time or method and the seal becomes decoration. Precision sustains belief.

How, then, should an intelligent reader audit an audit? Begin with *scope discipline*. Does the report bind itself to a specific commit and list exclusions without euphemism? "Economic attacks out of scope" deserves a red flag. So does a report that collapses remediation into vague assurances. Next, look for *method pluralism*. Do you see static and dynamic techniques, property-based tests that encode invariants ("collateral ratio never falls below X unless Y"), and, where appropriate, formal proofs of critical properties? Single-method reviews invite single-point failure. Finally, inspect *response hygiene*. Are fixes linked to issues, issues linked to code, and code linked to release notes? Do dates move from draft to merge in a rhythm that suggests a living process rather than a hurried performance? The best reports read like correspondence between grown-ups.

Assurance ≠ audit. Consider four complementary channels. Technical assurance (reviews, tests, proofs). Economic assurance (bounties, insurance, over-collateralisation, fee-backed reserves). Operational assurance (key custody, timelocks, emergency drills). Social assurance (reputation, governance transparency, credible post-mortems). None alone determines safety. All together tilt odds. Where a project refuses one channel, ask why. A refusal may be principled (immutable contracts that truly cannot change) or evasive (no appetite for external scrutiny). The difference appears in behaviour: immutable systems publish risk warnings and wrappers for cautious users; evasive ones publish slogans.

We should also confront the psychology of disclosures. Marketing turns hard-won nuance into gloss. "Audited by X" compresses months of work into a sticker. Resist the sticker. Read the appendix before the headline. Where numbers appear, interrogate their meaning. A "99% coverage" claim in tests can be as meaningless as a single perfect uptime figure: coverage of unimportant lines, uptime during trivial loads. The ethical reader practices *sceptical empathy*: assume most teams want to ship something good; assume also that incentives nudge them to over-claim. Empathy keeps you from cynicism; scepticism keeps you from credulity.

Nor can we ignore the auditors. They are human institutions with incentives and conflicts. Good ones publish methodologies, rotate teams, recuse when necessary, and maintain public registries of past findings and severities. They welcome reproduction: a competing firm rerunning a subset of tests is not an insult but a service. Weak firms lean on brand, not method; they over-extend scope, under-specify techniques, and disappear after handover. The signal is whether an auditor writes as if a peer will check their work or as if a marketer will quote it. The better houses write for peers.

Where proof-of-reserves or attestations are concerned, vocabulary matters. Audit, review, attestation, agreed-upon procedures—these are not synonyms. An *audit* of financial statements follows rigorous standards, tests controls, and expresses an opinion. An *attestation* confirms facts provided by management under a specified method. *Agreed-upon procedures* simply report findings from steps both sides defined in advance. Confusing these terms is not a harmless mistake: it inflates confidence where care is required. Read the opinion language line by line. If the word "limited" appears, treat it as a scope cue, not legalese to skip.

Some things cannot be proven—and naming them is a form of assurance too. You cannot prove that a keyholder will not collude next month; you cannot prove that a backdoor does not exist in firmware you did not build; you cannot prove that oracles will be honest in a political crisis. You can, however, reduce the cost of betrayal (threshold signatures, jurisdictional distribution), slow the speed of catastrophe (timelocks, staged rollouts), and make silence expensive (public incident ledgers, mandatory post-mortems). Here, assurance becomes constitutional: it shapes the powers and pauses that stand between error and ruin.

A counter-intuition deserves space: sometimes less automation increases assurance. Systems that leave a small, well-governed human checkpoint—say, a two-of-three committee for emergency halts with strict logging and time-bounded authority—may prevent more harm than systems that insist on purity while lacking repair paths. The reconciliation is not to idolise discretion but to instrument it: every use of human power must create a trace and trigger review. A good seal needs a witness.

We return to the motif. The seal endures when surrounded by process: layered methods, candid scope, rehearsed operations, economic stakes, and public diaries. It fails when isolated on a splash page. The reader's task is to calibrate belief to evidence. Ask: what, precisely, did this document examine; what changes did it provoke; what still lies outside its frame; and who will pay if that outside world intrudes? Confidence, properly achieved, feels narrow and earned. It resists the two cheapest temptations—paranoia and hype.

The unresolved tension is not semantic but civic. How much proof do we require before we entrust common goods to code? How frequently should we demand renewed assurance, knowing each check costs money and time? And when a seal, honestly crafted, fails in the wild, how do we apportion blame among authors, auditors, and users without driving everyone back to opacity? A mature polity will answer by habit, not slogan: specify what can be proven, admit what cannot, and keep the diaries that let us learn without burning the commons twice.

Ethics of Irreversibility

In December 2010, after WikiLeaks published U.S. diplomatic cables, Visa, MasterCard, and PayPal cut off donations to the organisation. Bank accounts stayed open; payment pipes did not. Yet money kept moving. Supporters routed funds through Bitcoin when it was barely a curiosity, its blocks small and its price volatile. No bank manager could reverse those transactions, no chargeback could claw them back, no payment processor could freeze the flow. The ledger recorded transfers; the transfers stayed. Censorship met finality and lost. For dissidents and publishers, that permanence felt like dignity made programmable. Finality disciplines. It also bites. The brake must be credible.

Seven years later, in November 2017, a user interacting with Parity's multi-signature wallet library triggered a flaw that "killed" the library and froze more than half a million ether. There was no fraud, only a bug and a set of contracts that could not be mended without rewriting history. Funds were locked, perhaps forever. Here, finality looked less like justice and more like a trapdoor. The same property that had shielded donations from political pressure had punished honest error without mercy. The tool had not changed; the ethics had. The motif of this subchapter is the *brake*: where it exists, how and when it may be pulled, and who bears the risk when it isn't.

Show, name, explain, imply. The WikiLeaks episode shows *finality as refuge*. When centralised rails enforce an extrajudicial blockade, a permissionless ledger grants continuity of association. The implication is civic: irreversible transfers can be a shield for lawful dissent against arbitrary deplatforming. The Parity freeze shows *finality as penalty*. When logic fails or humans misclick, an irreversible system imposes absolute loss. The implication is moral: as we design cryptographic institutions, we must decide where to place compassion without reintroducing capture. The question is not whether to allow reversals, but *how to architect mercy*.

Finality is not a single switch; it is layered and contingent. Bitcoin's confirmations, Ethereum's checkpoints, and proof-of-stake finality all aim to make history hard to rewrite. They succeed by aligning incentives against rollback. This makes censorship costly. It also makes repair costly. A mature design acknowledges both. It separates *base-layer finality*, which underwrites political rights, from *application-layer grace*, which can mitigate human mistakes under strict, pre-agreed rules. Failing to separate them tempts either tyranny—arbitrary reversals at the base—or cruelty—unfixable harms at the edge. The brake belongs on the vehicle, not on the road.

Reversible *wrappers* have emerged as a candidate middle path. The idea is straightforward: users opt into a token form that carries an embedded, narrow reversal process. In September 2022, a group of Stanford researchers proposed ERC-20R and ERC-721R, standards that allow frozen funds to be returned upon a showing of theft to a decentralised court within a short window. Show: a stolen wrapped token can be flagged, adjudicated, and reissued by a court that meets pre-published evidentiary thresholds. Name: *opt-in reversibility*. Explain: no one can rewrite the base chain; users who prefer recourse choose an asset whose contract codifies it. Implication: mercy becomes a product choice rather than a constitutional amendment.

Design lives in the details. A wrapper that can reverse anything for any reason at any time is a custodial promise by another name. A wrapper that can reverse only theft reported within, say, seven days and approved by a supermajority of randomly selected jurors after a posted bond behaves differently. You can measure it. False-positive rates are public. Median *time-to-resolution* is public. Appeal thresholds and costs are public. The court's members can be rotated; conflicts of interest can be declared and punished. The brake is visible, heavy, and slow. This is a *mercy with frictions* rather than a hotline to favour.

Real cases illuminate the stakes. Consider the July 2016 Ethereum fork after *The DAO* exploit. The community chose an exceptional, one-time state change to return funds. That was mercy at the base layer, justified as extraordinary equity. It worked and it burned. The precedent still divides. A second example points the other way. In August 2022, shortly after the U.S. Treasury sanctioned Tornado Cash addresses, Circle blacklisted sanctioned addresses at the USDC contract level, instantly freezing tokens. That was reversibility without due process on a private asset: fast, compliant, and frightening. The implication from both examples is blunt. If the brake sits too low (in the base protocol), every pothole invites a constitutional crisis; if it sits too high (in a single issuer's contract), one actor can decide whose money moves.

The counter-example is deliberate restraint. Bitcoin's refusal to reverse transactions since its launch is not merely technical conservatism; it is a political stance that places all mercy above the protocol. The cost is borne by users who must build their own recovery structures: multisig with timelocks, social recovery graphs, and spending limits that prevent catastrophic error. The benefit is a base you can depend on in a storm. Reconciling this with the appetite for recourse means pushing reversibility up into *consensual mechanisms*—insurance funds, community courts, and opt-in wrappers—rather than down into ledger edits.

To keep mercy from becoming moral hazard, criteria must be hard and legible. First, *opt-in only*: no asset should be silently reversible. Second, *narrow triggers*: theft or demonstrable coercion, not buyer's remorse or price collapse. Third, *tight windows*: claims expire quickly to prevent chilled commerce. Fourth, *stake and skin*: claimants post bonds; adjudicators stake reputation and capital; frivolous claims are costly. Fifth, *transparent evidence*: signed messages, transaction traces, and device forensic reports form the evidential core; hearsay does not. Sixth, *slow brakes*: reversals require layered confirmations—initial freeze, deliberation, final action—with alerts in between to allow counter-evidence. These criteria do not eliminate abuse; they price it and expose it.

Ethics arrives in the *distribution of pain*. In a wrapper regime, honest errors can be partly mitigated while preserving adverse selection. A hot-wallet mistake becomes survivable; a repeated pattern of recklessness becomes expensive. You can encode this by tying insurance premiums to historical behaviour: wallets that pass quarterly recovery drills pay less; treasuries that practise staged deployments pay less. The brake is priced like a safety feature: cheaper when you maintain it, costlier when you ignore it.

We can also anchor mercy in market structure. Batch auctions and delayed settlement for large transfers already impose temporal buffers that let fraud signals arrive before funds land beyond reach. Exchanges that delay first withdrawals to new addresses by 24 hours prevent a class of irreversible errors. Wallets that simulate transactions and cap velocity by default reduce fat-finger disasters. These are *soft brakes*—defences that make reversals less necessary by catching error upstream. Measurably so: track *first-withdrawal reversal requests prevented*, *median confirmation-to-transfer delay*, and *velocity cap overrides*. If those numbers improve, you are saving futures.

Still, the politics of mercy will not disappear. Sanctions, court orders, and cross-border crimes will intersect with wrapped assets and community courts. One jurisdiction's due process may be another's persecution. That is why any reversible wrapper must embed *jurisdictional plurality*: multiple courts, multiple appeal venues, and explicit choice of law at the time of wrapping. The user chooses not just a token but a *remedy stack*: legal forum A, arbitration forum B, or purely on-chain juries C. Diversity here is not chaos; it is insurance against capture. The brake should never be monopolised.

A legitimate worry remains: won't reversible assets fragment liquidity and confuse users? Yes, unless interfaces do their job. Wallets can present asset lineage clearly: "wETH-R (reversible, 7-day window, court: Kleros), wETH-S (sovereign, irreversible)." Protocols can choose which assets to accept as collateral and at what haircut. Markets can price mercy: reversible tokens might trade at a slight discount or face stricter collateral ratios. This is not corruption of neutrality; it is the monetisation of risk. Visibility makes those prices honest.

Programme design must also account for asymmetric power. Wealthy actors will exploit any recourse channel if it is vague. So publish *use-of-brake ledgers*: every freeze, every adjudicator, every evidence bundle, every appeal, with dates and signatures. Make silence expensive. An institution that pulls the brake often should see its cost of capital rise. A court that reverses lightly should see litigants flee. The language of ethics becomes a table of figures: *false reversal rate, average adjudicator dissent, stake slashed per thousand cases, case-mix drift over time.* Raw numbers do not settle arguments, but they ground them.

A second motif threads back here—the *window.* Mercy must live within a window narrow enough to preserve predictability yet wide enough to catch real harm. Seven days could be too long for fast markets, too short for cross-border theft. The only honest answer is governance by hypothesis and revision: publish a window, publish a target *false negative* and *false positive* rate, adjust with evidence. The vocabulary shifts from absolutes to tolerances. A civilised system admits that it learns.

None of this obviates personal responsibility. Reversals cannot make good a wiped seed phrase, a key left on an airport bench, or a contract signed under sleep. They must not. A world that guarantees repair for all error abolishes prudence and invites fraud. Yet a world that never forgives honest mistake breeds timidity and needless ruin. Ethical design locates a middle: it honours the dignity of decisive action while keeping a small, visible brake for when humans trip. The base stays hard; the edge learns to bend.

Return to the two scenes. The WikiLeaks blockade taught that permanence can preserve a public good when private chokepoints collude. The Parity freeze taught that permanence can crystallise private tragedy. A just architecture refuses to choose absolutism for convenience. It designs recourse where consent exists, it measures mercy, and it leaves the foundation intact enough to shelter dissent tomorrow. Irreversibility, handled well, becomes a shared promise rather than a threat.

The unresolved tension is practical and constitutional. How wide should your mercy window be before counterparties refuse your asset? Which institutions do you trust to sit next to the brake without resting their hand on it? And when the next high-profile loss prompts pleas for reversal, will your polity defend base-layer hardness while allowing opt-in grace at the edge? The answers will not come from slogans. They will come from instruments—windows, brakes, and ledgers—that teach us how much mercy a free people can afford, and at what price they wish to buy it.

Chapter 6
Power Without Permission

In March 2023, a young Nigerian developer named Ijeoma watched her country's central bank restrict cash withdrawals amid a faltering naira. For weeks, long queues formed outside banks. Payment apps failed, point-of-sale networks froze, and small traders reverted to barter. Yet across Telegram channels and peer-to-peer markets, transactions continued—priced in USDT, settled through phones, confirmed by strangers thousands of miles apart. No licence, no bank, no permission. What began as a workaround looked, to many, like a quiet declaration: the power to transact had escaped the gatekeepers. Still, in those same weeks, millions of dollars' worth of "stable" tokens also vanished when intermediaries—bridges, issuers, exchanges—froze addresses or failed under pressure. Power had moved, not disappeared.

This is the paradox of crypto's second decade: technology disperses authority, but convenience recentralises it. Decentralisation promised exit; comfort rebuilds the gate. As wallets simplify and protocols interconnect, new chokepoints emerge at the front-end—the bridges that shuttle value across chains, the stablecoins that hinge on dollars, the DAOs that coordinate labour yet mirror corporate bureaucracy. Every time we make decentralisation easier to use, we risk returning to the very dependencies it sought to escape. The challenge now is not invention but discipline: designing systems that make *leaving* as credible as joining.

Power without permission is an ethic before it is an engineering feat. It means the ability to act, transact, and organise without appealing to a central authority for clearance. Yet history shows that exit, not voice, disciplines power. The capacity to walk away keeps institutions honest. Crypto's political wager rests on this principle: that credible exit—whether from banks, platforms, or protocols—can substitute for regulatory coercion and moral pleading. But credibility depends on friction. When switching costs rise, decentralisation rots from the user interface inward.

Consider how the web's architecture quietly re-centralised. The protocols of the 1990s—email, HTTP, RSS—were open, federated, interoperable. By 2010, those same functions had been captured by proprietary platforms: Gmail for mail, Facebook for social graphs, Apple for distribution. Users stayed not out of loyalty but inertia. The network effects that once favoured open standards now entrench closed ones. Crypto, for all its rhetoric, faces the same gravitational pull. Bridges consolidate liquidity, wallets consolidate users, stablecoins consolidate trust. Unless exit remains technically and economically viable, decentralisation becomes decorative.

The first section of this chapter interrogates those chokepoints: the platforms and protocols whose front-ends now mediate permissionless back-ends. It asks what "freedom to exit" truly means when most users rely on custodial bridges or black-box smart contracts. We will examine design patterns that lower switching costs—modular interfaces, portable identity, exit-to-community models—and assess whether they can resist the convenience trap. Readers will learn to evaluate systems not by slogans of openness but by how gracefully they let you leave.

The next section turns to *Stablecoins and the Dollar Hinge*. Here the paradox deepens. Most crypto economies, whatever their ideological posture, depend on fiat-pegged instruments for liquidity and accounting. USDT, USDC, and their kin give traders stability but tie decentralised finance to the geopolitical muscle of the dollar. The peg stabilises markets while silently exporting U.S. monetary and regulatory influence. A freeze order from a single jurisdiction can immobilise billions in purportedly global assets. Readers will trace how different designs—collateralised, algorithmic, hybrid—balance solvency, sovereignty, and censorship resistance. The dollar hinge is not just an engineering parameter; it is a foreign policy instrument.

From money we move to *DAOs as New Firms—or New Clubs*. Decentralised autonomous organisations promised to replace corporate hierarchy with transparent, tokenised participation. In practice, many have recreated familiar dysfunctions: voter apathy, opaque agendas, informal oligarchies. Yet some DAOs thrive precisely because they narrowed their scope and clarified rights: developer collectives funding open-source maintenance, art syndicates pooling resources, mutual-aid treasuries with explicit exit rules. By studying their failure patterns—where enthusiasm outran clarity—we uncover the conditions under which decentralised coordination works. This section restores a moral vocabulary to DAO design: cooperation is a craft, not a slogan.

Finally, the chapter descends to what may be the most powerful layer of all—the *Culture Layer*. Memes, rituals, and shared symbols coordinate faster than governance votes ever can. They seed identity and cohesion, yet they can also sanctify abuse or groupthink. Within crypto, cultural capital often precedes financial capital: a narrative gains traction, and liquidity follows. Culture can harden into orthodoxy or become a renewable commons. We will treat culture not as ornament but as infrastructure—the substrate on which meaning, legitimacy, and loyalty are built. How a community jokes reveals how it governs.

Threaded through these explorations is a recurring image: *the exit door*. Does it open, and for whom? For a Nigerian trader whose savings depend on a dollar-backed token? For a DAO contributor voting in a captured treasury? For a builder trapped behind an API key or bridge fee? The freedom to build alternatives must be matched by the freedom to depart. Without that, decentralisation becomes branding, not governance.

Power without permission is the promise that first drew people to crypto. Yet the last decade has shown how power, once decentralised, reforms itself in new shapes: custodial front-ends, regulatory choke points, cultural hierarchies masquerading as consensus. This chapter examines those transformations with both sympathy and scepticism. The goal is not to romanticise exit but to make it credible again—to build systems whose resilience does not depend on benevolence or hope.

As you turn the page, consider a simple test: if a community or protocol you use vanished tomorrow, how easily could you migrate—your assets, your data, your relationships—elsewhere? The distance between that answer and zero is your true measure of freedom. The rest of this chapter explores how close we can get, and what it will cost to stay there.

Platforms, Protocols, and the Politics of Exit

On 14 March 2023, when the Arbitrum bridge briefly halted withdrawals after a validator outage, traders across several exchanges froze mid-transfer. The pause lasted less than two hours, yet the effects rippled far beyond the blockchain: decentralised exchanges reliant on the bridge's liquidity spiked in slippage, market makers withdrew positions, and social media filled with frustration. The irony was plain. A system built to transcend chokepoints had recreated one. The problem was not in the code itself, but in the architecture of convenience. The more seamless the interface, the more opaque the dependencies beneath it. Finality may have been distributed, but exit was not.

The motif of this subchapter is *the gate*. Every open system builds one, even if it claims not to. Permissionless networks promise freedom of movement, but human habits and design incentives quietly favour centralisation. Most users access "decentralised" networks through a few dominant gateways—MetaMask, Binance, Coinbase, Infura. Each acts as a gatekeeper: they aggregate liquidity, simplify keys, abstract complexity. The result is paradoxical. As the technology for exit matures, the practice of it declines. Switching costs grow not because of cryptographic constraints but because the gate is comfortable.

The political philosopher Albert O. Hirschman, in *Exit, Voice, and Loyalty* (1970), described how institutions decay when members cannot credibly leave. Exit disciplines power; voice merely pleads with it. Protocols, like firms or states, rely on this same dynamic. A credible exit keeps the core honest. Without it, governance ossifies, convenience consolidates, and network effects become coercion. In the crypto economy, exit is expressed not in rhetoric but in *switchability*: the ability to migrate funds, data, and identity without friction or loss.

We can see this principle unfold through two emblematic cases. First, the saga of Uniswap's evolution between 2019 and 2021. Version 3 introduced concentrated liquidity—an elegant technical improvement that made markets more efficient. Yet it also entrenched a front-end monopoly: the Uniswap interface, hosted and branded, became the default entry point for millions of users. Forks like Sushiswap attempted to compete by copying the code and adjusting incentives. In theory, permissionless competition thrived. In practice, the convenience of the canonical interface won. The protocol remained decentralised; the experience did not. Show, name, explain, imply: Uniswap demonstrated that open infrastructure can still form behavioural monopolies. The implication is sobering—open code is not enough when exit requires effort.

A contrasting case emerged in 2022 with the migration of users from Tornado Cash to smaller privacy mixers after U.S. sanctions. Tornado's contracts were immutable; its interface was not. Once the front-end disappeared under regulatory pressure, few users accessed the smart contracts directly. Usage fell over 70% in a week. Those with technical skill exited; most simply stopped transacting. Here, design itself determined who could exercise exit. A right unexercised becomes an ornament.

The bridge and the gate repeat across domains. MetaMask routes billions in daily value yet depends on Infura, a centralised API provider owned by ConsenSys. When Infura suffered an outage in November 2020, users worldwide found themselves unable to broadcast transactions—on "decentralised" networks. Infura has since added redundancy, yet the architecture remains structurally similar: the convenience layer sits atop the permissionless one, holding disproportionate leverage. In essence, the power to provide a good default is the power to define participation.

Design, then, is political. Defaults shape freedom. Apple's App Store rules, PayPal's content policies, and Meta's algorithmic recommendations all illustrate how front-ends evolve into regimes. The crypto world inherits the same pattern. What begins as interface design ends as governance. To discipline those regimes, systems must embed *credible exit paths*—technical, economic, and social mechanisms that make switching feasible without heroic effort.

Technically, this means composability and portability. A user's funds, credentials, and social graphs must migrate as easily as their browser bookmarks. The Ethereum Name Service (ENS) and Sign-In with Ethereum protocols hint at this possibility. A developer can port a user's identity across dApps without re-registration. Similarly, LayerZero and IBC aim to make cross-chain transfers trust-minimised, allowing users to move capital without surrendering custody. But each new bridge or interoperability layer introduces both complexity and a new gate. The exit door multiplies, but so do its locks.

Economically, credible exit requires symmetrical liquidity. Users stay trapped when the cost of moving outweighs the benefit. Liquidity mining schemes can bribe entry but rarely sustain migration. More durable mechanisms—fee sharing, revenue redistribution, community airdrops—reward migration itself rather than lock-in. An instructive metric is *liquidity stickiness*: the percentage of volume retained after incentives end. Protocols with lower stickiness paradoxically indicate healthier competition: users actually exercise exit.

Socially, exit demands continuity of meaning. A community can only move if its culture travels. Bitcoin's forks—Bitcoin Cash in 2017, Bitcoin SV in 2018—showed how technical divergence without cultural continuity yields fragmentation, not freedom. Ethereum's own fork after *The DAO* exploit survived because the narrative of "code with conscience" held moral traction. Exit, to be credible, needs a story as much as a script. The story binds people across the bridge.

A counter-example grounds the argument. Consider the stubborn persistence of Twitter—even after Elon Musk's 2022 takeover sparked migration drives to Mastodon, Bluesky, and Nostr. Each alternative offered technical freedom and ideological purity. Yet few users left. Network effects, inertia, and the friction of rebuilding social graphs kept the majority within the gate. The limitation is clear: exit must be not only possible but *coordinated*. One person leaving achieves little. Mass migration requires synchronised tooling, bridges for reputation, and shared incentives to move together. Without them, the gate stands open but empty.

Protocols that design for exit, therefore, must design for coordination. One promising pattern is *exit to community*: a transition in which users, developers, and early investors collectively acquire control from founders, as seen in cases like Handshake (2020) and Friends With Benefits DAO (2021). These experiments illustrate how governance and ownership can decentralise without collapse when exit is framed as succession rather than rebellion. The door opens, but the house remains inhabited.

The motif returns. A gate is not inherently evil; it becomes dangerous when it locks both ways. A healthy system distinguishes *entry control* (who may come in) from *exit friction* (who can leave). Many "Web3" projects conflate the two, designing elaborate onboarding funnels while ignoring the off-ramps. The result is a network of ornate gates with no hinges.

To lower switching costs, certain design heuristics now appear repeatedly across credible projects. First, *open state*: data structures exposed via public APIs or IPFS storage allow independent clients to reconstruct user history. Second, *modular front-ends*: multiple competing interfaces drawing from a shared protocol back-end, as with Zapper and Zerion for DeFi portfolios, distribute power horizontally. Third, *standards-first culture*: ERC conventions, open SDKs, and reproducible builds prevent rent-seeking via proprietary glue. These are not aesthetic choices—they are constitutional ones.

Yet each success brings a paradox. The more standardised the exit path, the more predictable and profitable it becomes to build businesses atop it. Convenience returns, wearing new clothes. Decentralisation is not a destination but a rhythm—a continual reassertion of user agency against entropy. Every generation of technology faces the same slope. The mainframe begot the PC, which begot the cloud, which begot the token network. Each wave promises liberation and ends with a gate.

The politics of exit, then, is the politics of discipline. Users who demand switchability impose constraints that preserve pluralism. Developers who measure migration costs rather than market share create systems that resist capture. A functioning commons needs friction where greed gathers, and grease where users stall. The architecture of freedom is not invisible; it is engineered.

The unresolved tension is not whether centralisation will return—it will—but how often and how easily we can leave when it does. The final diagnostic question, then, is brutally simple: if your chosen bridge, wallet, or platform vanished tomorrow, could you reconstruct your digital life elsewhere by design, not miracle? If not, the gate you stand before may already be locked.

Stablecoins and the Dollar Hinge

On 10 March 2023 in Santa Clara, California, Silicon Valley Bank entered receivership. Over the next forty-eight hours, a $1:1 dollar-pegged crypto token—USDC—traded below par after its issuer, Circle, acknowledged that a portion of its reserves sat at the failed bank. Central bankers were asleep; on-chain markets were wide awake. Arbitrageurs, treasurers, and ordinary users watched a simple truth reassert itself: every stablecoin is a promise chained to a balance sheet. When the bank reopened and guarantees were extended, the peg recovered. The lesson endured. Stability in crypto frequently depends on the solvency and policy of institutions far outside the chain. The hinge creaked; the door held.

Stablecoins are marketed as neutral pipes. They are not. They embed legal claims, redemption terms, censorability, and, most consequentially, a currency choice that carries geopolitical weight. Dollar-linked tokens have become the unit of account for much of decentralised finance, and for a growing slice of peer-to-peer commerce from Buenos Aires to Lagos. The dollar's reach thus extends through code. This stabilises pricing and lowers volatility. It also exports the constraints of a monetary regime that most users did not vote for. The hinge holds the system steady; it also sets its angle.

Start with what the dollar hinge enables. Pricing in a widely recognised unit compresses information. Traders can compare assets; merchants can set costs; households can budget. A unit of account is a public good. In crypto, dollar tokens deliver that good without the bureaucracy of bank accounts. The rails are fast and global. Yet the price of convenience is exposure to policy levers originally designed for domestic banking. When issuers hold reserves in U.S. treasuries and banks, they inherit U.S. jurisdiction, sanctions rules, and supervisory expectations. A freeze order travels further than a market shock. A single signature can immobilise value across thousands of wallets. Neutrality, in practice, is a story told by those who control the blacklist.

Designs matter because they distribute power differently. Fiat-backed stablecoins—USDC, USDT, Paxos-issued tokens—promise 1:1 redemption for dollars held in cash and short-dated securities. Their strengths are clear: straightforward redemption, low volatility, and legal recourse. Their weaknesses are equally clear: censorability at the contract level, exposure to banking crises, and dependence on auditors, custodians, and regulators. Crypto-collateralised stablecoins—most prominently DAI—lean on over-collateralisation, liquidations, and open governance. They are harder to censor at the asset level but can drift towards the very fiat rails they hoped to escape when they accept tokenised treasuries or custodial stablecoins as collateral. Algorithmic designs—such as Terra's UST before its May 2022 collapse—attempt to replace reserves with reflexive market mechanisms. They can work in small, sleepy markets; they tend to fail under stress. The door swings freely—until it does not.

Two named episodes make the contrasts vivid. First, Terra's unravelling in May 2022, following sustained redemptions and loss of confidence, erased tens of billions in paper value and cratered trust in "algorithmic" stability. The mechanism—minting and burning between UST and LUNA—relied on arbitrage that evaporated under pressure. Liquidity fled faster than governance could respond. The coin's promise of sovereignty proved empty because its guarantees had no external anchor. Exit accelerated ruin. Second, in August 2022, after the U.S. Treasury sanctioned Tornado Cash addresses, several issuers—most prominently Circle—added sanctioned addresses to their blocklists, freezing token balances at the contract level. That action was lawful, prompt, and politically legible. It also demonstrated that some "decentralised" dollars carry a kill switch. Stability, here, included obedience.

A credible counter-example is MakerDAO's gradual recalibration after 2020. Initially backed mostly by crypto collateral such as ether, DAI later introduced real-world assets and custodial stablecoins to dampen volatility and support growth. Critics argued that the protocol had "dollarised" itself and imported censorability. Supporters countered that measured exposure to treasuries improved resilience and allowed conscious governance of risk. Both claims have merit. The reconciliation is design discipline: Maker's public debates, risk frameworks, and collateral caps made trade-offs visible. Users could see the hinge, measure the angle, and decide whether to walk through.

The hinge metaphor helps organise the evaluation of stability claims. A hinge joins two structures—the chain and the state—and allows movement between them. Strong hinges are *transparent*: they reveal legal structure (who holds what, where), reserve composition (cash, T-bills, repos), custody arrangements, and audit or attestation cadence. Strong hinges are *predictable*: they publish redemption terms (who can redeem, minimums, cut-off times), settlement lags, and stress procedures for halts. Strong hinges are *bounded*: they disclose blacklist criteria, due-process pathways, and the scope of discretionary freezes. Weak hinges conceal, improvise, and widen discretion when the weather turns foul. Users cannot see the angle until the door is already moving.

Geopolitically, the spread of dollar tokens deepens a long American project: dollar primacy as the operating system of world trade. In one reading, stablecoins extend financial inclusion—anyone with a smartphone can hold a near-dollar. In another, they amplify extraterritorial enforcement—policy set in Washington can reach wallets in Nairobi with a message to a Delaware issuer. The contradiction is real. A Nigerian merchant can price goods in USDT and escape domestic currency chaos. The same merchant can wake to find balances frozen because an upstream exchange or issuer received a compliance notice. Dollar stability and dollar sovereignty are an inseparable pair. To hold one is to hold the other.

For designers and citizens, the question is not "dollars or not". It is *how much dollar, where*, and *under whose governance*. A portfolio approach is plausible: use fiat-backed tokens for high-velocity payments and treasury operations; use crypto-collateralised tokens for censorship-sensitive savings; avoid reflexive mechanisms that rely on goodwill or perpetual bull markets. More importantly, embed *exit* into choices. If a community can switch from a custodial coin to a more neutral one with manageable effort, issuers face discipline. Switchability is not ideology; it is insurance.

Evaluation, then, becomes a craft. Test claims against behaviours rather than brochures. If an issuer promises "1:1 redemption", measure whether small holders can redeem directly or must route through market makers. If attestations are monthly, ask why not weekly. If reserves include commercial paper, ask for maturities and counterparties. If blacklisting exists, ask for a transcript of policy: what triggers action, what evidence is required, who signs, how appeals work. The vocabulary of stability should be specific: T+1 or T+3 redemption; percentage of reserves in cash versus bills; number of custodial banks; concentration limits; frequency of freeze actions and the process for unfreezing. Where numbers are absent, so is trust.

Not all dependence is malign. The monetary base of a state exists for reasons beyond hegemony: lender-of-last-resort functions, payments standards, prudential supervision. Tying a token to that base can import useful discipline. The Monetary Authority of Singapore's 2023 framework for single-currency stablecoins, for example, emphasised high-quality reserves, timely redemption, and clear disclosure—rules that make failures rarer and reversals orderly. The European Union's MiCA took a similar path by demanding authorisation and reserve governance. Such regimes narrow moral hazard and protect small users from the worst predations, while inevitably constraining absolute censorship-resistance. The hinge is strengthened, but the door swings within a frame set by law.

There is, however, a ceiling to how far regulatory clarity can go without re-centralising everything. If safety demands direct issuer oversight of every address, the token becomes a bank account with better UX. If stability requires reserves solely in government paper, monetary policy can indirectly throttle a decentralised economy. The question is not whether law should matter; it is how much of the decentralised stack should be designed to survive legal shocks without collapsing. That implies at least one censorship-resistant reserve asset—ether, bitcoin, or similar—supporting a parallel monetary layer for those moments when policy itself becomes the risk.

Culture shapes all of this. Communities habituated to compliance will seek stablecoins that behave like regulated money. Communities preoccupied with resistance will prefer instruments that sacrifice convenience for autonomy. Many will try to mix both, and the mixing will fail in moments of stress unless the interfaces are explicit. A wallet that lets users label balances "freezable" and "sovereign", and shows the associated redemption rights, teaches prudence by design. It replaces slogans with affordances. Ethics becomes a toggle that users can see.

The hinge metaphor applies to bridges too—the infrastructural crossings where stablecoins move among chains. Bridges concentrate control and are prime targets for policy and attack. A censored bridge can be as paralyzing as a seized bank account. Design responses include light-client verification, multiple independent relayers, and escape hatches that let users withdraw to Layer 1 when intermediaries fail. Again, stability is not a feeling; it is a sequence of behaviours under stress. The question to ask of any hinge or bridge is simple: who can stop me, how quickly, and what must they prove?

A final counterpoint deserves respect: purely crypto-collateralised systems rarely scale to consumer prices without importing fiat exposure somewhere—through oracles, wrapped assets, or liquidity providers who keep their own books in dollars. Attempting to float an entire economy on volatile collateral can turn a currency into a speculative asset by stealth. This is not a call to surrender; it is a call to specify ambitions. Use crypto-money where censorship-resistance or credibly neutral settlement is paramount; use fiat-backed money where price stability and smooth redemption dominate. The hinge is not a betrayal. It is a choice of load path.

What, then, should a careful reader carry forward? First, that "stable" is a property of systems, not tickers. Price stability without redemption discipline is theatre. Second, that sovereignty is not a flag but a budget—how much you are willing to pay, in volatility and friction, to avoid external control. Third, that evaluation must privilege behaviours you can time, count, and audit over language that flatters. A system that can freeze must say so, loudly. A system that cannot must show you how it fails safely. Both can be ethical. Neither should be coy.

The unresolved tension is deliberate. How much dollar should a decentralised economy import before it ceases to be decentralised in any meaningful sense? Which hinge settings—reserve mix, redemption terms, censorship powers—maximise public benefit without handing a veto to distant offices? And when the next banking shock or sanctions wave arrives, will your community discover that its stability was rented or that its hinge, tested under load, bends without breaking? The answers will be measured in redemption windows and freeze logs, not rhetoric. The door will swing. The hinge you chose will decide whether it returns.

DAOs as New Firms—or New Clubs

On 18 November 2021 at Sotheby's in New York, a pseudonymous collective calling itself ConstitutionDAO bid for a first printing of the United States Constitution. They had raised the money—tens of millions of dollars crowdfunded in a week—and they had the plan: to place the document on public display, stewarded by token-holders through on-chain votes. When the final paddle fell, the DAO lost to a higher bid. The bidder was later named as Kenneth Griffin of Citadel. The room fell quiet. What remained, however, was not a failed purchase but a public experiment. A group with no legal charter, board, or office had coordinated capital at speed, then dissolved its purpose with comparable speed. Show the feat; name the form. A DAO can act like a firm for a week or a club for a lifetime. The difference lies in scope and rights.

ConstitutionDAO did one thing, very quickly, then stopped. That narrow scope—acquire or fail—meant rights could be crisp. Donors received governance tokens with clear limits; there would be no mission creep, no endless obligation. The implication is structural. DAOs work when they define a bounded object—infrastructure grants, a software client, a gallery, a recurring auction—and give members unambiguous powers relative to that object. The trouble begins when "community" is asked to be company, parliament, and fandom at once. A club survives that confusion through culture; a firm does not.

Consider the other end of the spectrum. Nouns DAO, launched in August 2021, auctions a single NFT each day and directs proceeds to a treasury controlled by token-holders. It has funded public goods, art installations, and software experiments. Show the rhythm: one auction, one vote-stream, one treasury. Name the pattern: *bounded abundance*. Explain:

the scope is broad in spending but narrow in machinery; membership equals one token, one vote; rights are legible—propose, deliberate, fund. Implication: where the object is continuous and the procedure simple, a DAO behaves like a patient club with a standing endowment. Narrow powers, long horizon.

Now the counterpoint. In 2022–2023, several general-purpose DAOs attempted to "do everything": invest, incubate, lobby, curate, entertain. Forum posts bloated; proposals bundled unrelated decisions; working groups multiplied. The effect was predictable—agenda control concentrated among a few delegates, and ordinary members learned to disengage. Name the failure: *committee creep*. Explain: when a DAO's scope expands faster than its capacity to specify rights, the club loses its intimacy while the firm never gains execution. Implication: unless you can identify the concrete outputs a DAO is responsible for—and tie membership rights directly to those outputs—your structure will default to theatre. A decent test is brutal in its simplicity: list the two verbs the DAO actually performs. If you cannot, you are writing slogans, not a charter.

The motif of this subchapter is the *key*. Membership should feel like holding a key: it opens certain doors, not all; it confers clear privileges and defined duties; it has a lock that can be changed without burning the house down. In MolochDAO (launched in 2019), the *ragequit* mechanism allowed members to exit with their share of uncommitted funds when they disagreed with the direction of spending. Show the behaviour; name the right: *exit-as-right*. Explain: by making exit cheap and explicit, MolochDAO reduced internal blackmail and kept deliberation honest. Implication: DAOs that specify exit procedures in advance can afford sharper debates because power does not hinge on persuasion alone. A key that also opens an exit door disciplines the room.

Membership templates signal whether you are building a firm or a club. In a firm-like DAO, rights map to labour: propose a change, perform work, receive tokens or cash, and be reviewed against a scope. MakerDAO's "core units" (2021–2023) exemplified this arrangement: teams with charters, budgets, and performance reporting. Show the machinery; name the form: *work units*. Explain: by separating policy from delivery, Maker turned token votes into budget approvals and milestones into accountability. Implication: where labour is the point, membership must be conditional and revocable with due process. Keys here have expiry dates and renewal rituals.

In club-like DAOs, rights map to belonging: access to spaces, participation in events, stewardship of a treasury for shared pursuits. Friends With Benefits (from 2021) tied entry to holding a threshold of tokens and combined cultural programming with grants. As token prices whipsawed, membership briefly became prohibitively expensive for the very people the club hoped to include. Name the limitation: *price-gated belonging*. Explain: financialised keys inherit market volatility; if membership is purely a balance, the door swings with the market. Implication: club DAOs need dual keys—one signalling commitment (time, contributions, reputation), another signalling stake—so that culture is not priced out by its own asset. Several DAOs have since introduced non-transferable credentials or contribution-based allowlists to stabilise membership without freezing fluidity.

Labour templates likewise need clarity. In a firm, a job is a contract. In a DAO, a job often starts as a proposal and turns into a grant or stream. Without scopes, grants expand until they fail. Gitcoin DAO's transition from a central team to a grants-based, workstream model (2021–2022) exposed both strengths and weaknesses. Show the shift: open calls, quadratic funding, public roadmaps. Name the friction: *diffuse accountability*. Explain: when everyone is a contractor, no one owns the boring tasks—documentation, incident response, maintenance. Implication: DAOs should specify a layer of *civil service*—small, dull, indispensable roles with tenure-like protection and periodic review—so that the continuity of the commons does not depend on charisma. Keys must also open the utility cupboard.

Incentives often tip clubs into committees. Liquidity mining and governance bribes can mobilise voters quickly; they also convert deliberation into income. Convex and Curve's vote markets (since 2021) showed how rational parties rent voting power to direct emissions. Show the outcome: productive for liquidity, corrosive for legitimacy. Name the trade-off: *efficiency without dignity*. Explain: if a DAO ties its most consequential votes to immediate cashflows, members will evaluate proposals on short-term yield rather than long-term health. Implication: cordon the money. Place the richest emission decisions behind slower, higher-quorum procedures, and keep day-to-day parameter-tuning in smaller, expert councils with tight mandates and revocation. The key must sometimes turn two locks.

Failure patterns repeat with numbing regularity. *Bikeshedding*—protracted debate on trivial matters—consumes the forum while hard questions languish. *Quorum games*—timing votes when opposition sleeps—produce "legitimate" decisions that no one respects. *Working group feudalism* emerges when contributors control information flow and starve rivals of attention. Show one, name it, explain its mechanics, then draw the implication: design is the remedy. Agenda-setting by rotation, minimum discussion periods, and proposal hygiene (single-purpose, fully scoped, with rollback plans) prevent abuse. A club that keeps minutes and rotates chairs stays a club. A firm that publishes implementation diaries and reversal envelopes stays a firm. Keys and calendars share a root.

Two additional examples, concrete and contrasting, sharpen the distinction. In November 2020, Yearn Finance merged with several DeFi projects, informally combining treasuries and teams. The "mergers" were, in truth, interlocking working agreements ratified by token-holders, with committees managing integration. Show the process; name the shape: *federation by consent*. Explain: Yearn behaved like a firm—coordinating labour, budgets, and roadmaps—while retaining token governance for high-level approvals. Implication: complex production favours firm-like DAOs that wall off execution from open debate. By contrast, Krause House (2021) sought to buy a stake in an NBA team to democratise club culture. It did not. But the club still funds basketball courts and community events with small, transparent grants. Name the form: *club with a banner dream*. Explain: even when the headline fails, the club's bounded acts survive. Implication: keep the dream; shrink the scope. The key still opens a door people actually use.

Legal wrappers and off-chain interfaces are not trivialities; they are constitutions. Wyoming's 2021 DAO LLC legislation and the use of foundations in the Cayman Islands or Switzerland attempt to reconcile on-chain votes with off-chain enforcement. Show the anchor; name the function: *legal hinge*. Explain: a DAO that signs contracts, hires, or holds IP needs a human-readable body to be sued, to sue, and to hold licences. Implication: a firm-like DAO should likely adopt a legal wrapper; a club-like DAO can often avoid it, provided it keeps spending small and scope narrow. Keys that also open courtrooms must be issued judiciously.

Culture completes the picture. A DAO with ambiguous values cannot adjudicate edge cases without tearing itself apart. MakerDAO's "Endgame" debates (2022–2023) were not just technical; they were cultural—about risk appetite, regulatory exposure, and time preference. Show the vocabulary: *mandates, scopes, sunset clauses*. Name the binding agent: *shared language*. Explain: when terms are defined and recited, coordination accelerates; when words are vibes, proposals become Rorschach tests. Implication: clubs need rituals that reinforce norms; firms need templates that encode them. In both, the key is semiotic as well as cryptographic.

How should a reader evaluate a DAO's claim to be a new firm rather than a new committee—or a new club rather than a new clique? Not with vibes, but with behaviour. Measure *proposal-to-implementation time* across quarters; track *reversal rate* of passed proposals; examine *member churn* and *participation dispersion* (how many unique proposers authored the last twenty items). If you can, observe *funding cadence*—predictable streams correlate with sustained outputs. These are not academic niceties; they are the diary entries by which institutions prove they exist. A DAO without a diary is a chatroom with a treasury.

The *key* returns for the last time. A good key opens a door that leads somewhere useful; it also locks when needed. For DAOs, this means *rights with remedies*. Membership should come with explicit exit (how to leave with dignity), explicit voice (how to place items on the agenda), and explicit boundaries (what this group does not do). Labour should come with clear scopes and anti-burnout cadence. Incentives should reward maintenance as surely as marquee launches. These features are not ornaments. They are the difference between cooperation and drift.

The unresolved tension is productive. When should a DAO behave like a firm—tight scopes, hire-and-fire, budgets with teeth—and when should it behave like a club—open membership, soft power, funds for culture? How much law should wrap the contract before the contract becomes law's appendage? And when a token soars, will membership become exclusionary by accident, or will the group remember that keys are for people, not just for prices? The next time you encounter a DAO, ask three questions that no branding can dodge: what is the object; what does my key open; and how easily can I return it? The answers will tell you whether you have found a co-op with a constitution—or a committee looking for a quorum.

The Culture Layer

On 27 January 2021, a joke became an order. The joke was a collage of rocket emojis and "diamond hands" posted across Reddit's r/WallStreetBets; the order was to buy and hold shares of GameStop in defiance of hedge funds shorting the stock. Within forty-eight hours, trading volumes spiked, Robinhood restricted purchases, and a midwinter meme wrote itself into market history. The slogans were absurd by design. They were also executable. The meme moved markets. What looked like noise revealed an old truth: culture is a coordination technology dressed as humour. Where blockchains promise "rules without rulers", cultures deliver "moves without meetings".

Memes compress strategy into shareable signals. Rituals give those signals a clock. In crypto, both have become governance primitives: they mobilise liquidity, harden norms, and assign reputations before any formal vote. Consider 8 May 2021, when Elon Musk hosted *Saturday Night Live* and riffed about Dogecoin. Price surged before the broadcast, then fell during it. Jokes were trades. The spectacle was financial. If you found the episode distasteful, you are already facing the point of this subchapter: culture can coordinate at speed, but speed can erase caution. Coordination without reflection can become a stampede.

To treat culture as infrastructure, not ornament, we need to name the parts we can measure and the parts we can only steward. Show, name, explain, imply. Start with memes. A meme is a compact script for action: "gm" signals presence; "WAGMI" signals optimism; "rekt" signals risk realised. These fragments carry instructions. They accelerate onboarding by shrinking complex ideas into in-jokes. They also narrow attention. When "number go up" becomes the lingua franca, maintenance work struggles for air. The implication is obvious. Communities thrive when their fastest memes point towards their slowest needs.

Rituals lock tempo. The Nouns DAO, since August 2021, has auctioned one NFT per day; each auction feeds a treasury; each day resets a rhythm. The ritual is boring. That is the point. Its predictability has funded public goods, art, and software across years rather than weeks. The cadence—one auction, one proposal stream, one treasury—makes culture legible as a calendar. Contrast that with the adrenaline of token launches timed around "TGE day" and breathless "24-hour community calls". Those rituals select for hype, not stewardship. A culture chooses its seasons. A culture chooses its weather.

A second example, less financial but equally instructive, is Reddit's r/place canvases (April 2017; April 2022). Millions of users placed pixels on a shared board with cooldown timers; coalitions formed to defend flags and artwork; borders were negotiated in memes and truce pacts, not in charters. The behaviour showed how rituals and symbols harden norms quickly. It also showed fragility. Alliances frayed when timezones shifted; coalitions collapsed when leadership left. The implication for crypto is clear: if your culture depends on permanent mobilisation, it will exhaust itself. Rituals must be sustainable. Design them like breathing, not like battle.

Culture is not always benign. In January 2018, after months of gaudy rallies and YouTube chants, Bitconnect was ordered to cease operations by U.S. and Texas regulators. Its "community" had supplied more than capital. It supplied theological certainty: critics were "FUD"; leaders were saints; disbelief was treason. Years later, Terra's "LUNAtics" slogan and meme-fied defences of algorithmic stability (early 2022) rehearsed the same pattern at institutional scale: rhetoric of destiny, disdain for risk warnings, and ritualised mockery of caution. Show the pattern; name the hazard: *memetic absolutism*.

Explain: when culture punishes doubt, it incubates fraud and error. Implication: communities must plan for dissent as carefully as they plan for growth. A healthy culture protects heretics.

If culture coordinates, we need tools to steward it deliberately. Treat the community's lexicon like an API. Define terms in public handbooks; retire slogans that mislead. Replace "decentralised" with the specific: "two client teams, four relayers, seven signers, 48-hour pauses". Language calibrates risk. Similarly, treat rituals like product surfaces. If you hold weekly calls, publish minutes and action lists; rotate facilitation; annotate decisions with when and who. The point is not bureaucracy. The point is to leave a trail so the culture remembers rather than repeats. A culture without a diary is theatre.

Narratives matter because they decide who belongs. ConstitutionDAO's "We the People" frame (November 2021) invited a particular kind of participation—small contributions for a symbolic bid. It worked for seven days, then disbanded. A narrow story produced bounded action. That is a success. By contrast, "we are the future of finance" invites everything and therefore nothing. The implication is operational: pick a story that constrains, not inflates, your scope. Plant a banner you can actually defend.

We should also acknowledge the politics of fun. Parties, conferences, merchandise, and "vibes" do work. They convert weak ties into stronger ones; they reward contributors with status beyond tokens. But fun can become feudal. When access to parties confers influence, culture becomes a toll gate. The metric here is subtle: watch who gets the microphone after markets fall. If the same four names, the same private dinners, the same "alpha" rooms persist, you're looking at a hierarchy in costume. Culture that never rotates stewards will eventually protect stewards rather than norms.

How, then, to measure cultural health without killing it in spreadsheets? Three behaviours travel. First, *retention through drought*: after a 50 per cent price drawdown, does contributor activity recover within a quarter? Second, *distributed authorship*: across the last twenty proposals, how many unique voices drafted the text? Third, *dissent bandwidth*: do negative votes and minority reports recur without triggering exile? These are not academic metrics. They are early warnings. A culture that cannot survive a bear market, share authorship, or hear no will not govern.

Memes can also discipline power. "Not your keys, not your coins"—first popularised by Andreas Antonopoulos around 2014—stubbornly encoded a custody norm that saved fortunes in 2022 when centralised exchanges failed or froze withdrawals. The phrase is crude and incomplete; it is also lifesaving advice compressed to five words. Rituals like "proof-of-keys day" on 3 January, encouraging withdrawals to self-custody, make the proverb tactile. This is culture at its best: a story that becomes a habit that becomes safety.

A counter-example tempers exuberance. In 2020–2021, "vampire attacks" became a celebrated meme in DeFi: a new protocol offered token incentives to suck liquidity away from incumbents. Some attacks improved fees and composition; many simply reshuffled deposits while degrading trust. Memes motivated action; rituals (liquidity mining cycles) gave it a clock; the public good—credible neutrality—lost ground. The reconciliation is discipline. Celebrate competition; memorialise maintenance. Build rituals that reward documentation and audits as much as launches. If your calendar only honours bravado, your culture will select for arsonists.

Stewardship starts with roles. Appoint culture editors as deliberately as you appoint protocol engineers. Their job is not to police jokes. It is to manage memory: keep a living glossary; curate a canon of post-mortems; interview elders before they leave; seed onboarding kits that teach values without decrees. Tools exist. A "lore repository" in a public repo; a quarterly *State of the Culture* note covering rituals, language shifts, and contested norms; a calendar of recurring civic acts—cleanup sprints, documentation weeks, public retrospectives with named owners and dated commitments. Bit by bit, the soft becomes hard. Culture writes to disk.

Because culture can excuse abuse, it needs watchdogs. Anonymous whistleblowing portals with clear triage; ombudspersons elected on fixed terms; moderation logs that show when and why posts were removed; a visible *cooling-off* policy for leaders—no proposal sponsorship for a cycle after a failed vote, no emergency power without a post-mortem within seven days. These are not panaceas. They are speed bumps. They force a pause when charisma outruns caution. They slow the crowd without insulting it.

Geography matters too. Crypto culture claims to be global; it often defaults to Anglophone, male, and chronologically US-centred. Rituals are time-zoned; memes are linguistic; humour is cultural. If all your calls cluster around San Francisco and Berlin, you have already narrowed your collective mind. Rotate time slots. Commission translations. Fund local stewards to run parallel rituals and report back. The metric here is presence: count how often voices from Nairobi, Bangalore, or São Paulo propose, not merely attend. Coordination power that never leaves familiar rooms is not power. It is preference.

A recurring motif threads this chapter: *the drum*. Memes are the call; rituals are the beat. If the drum only speeds up, participants fall. If it never varies, participants drift. The craft lies in composing rhythms that widen the circle without dropping the tempo that keeps a group together. You modulate. You slow for audits and upgrades. You quicken for crises, then slow again. Governance lives in that tempo.

Culture is path dependent. Early jokes cast long shadows. Ethereum's "rough consensus and running code" ethos licensed patience with research; Bitcoin's suspicion of change licences conservatism. Neither is wrong. Each has costs. The right question is not which culture is superior but which risks each selects by default. A conservative culture will miss opportunities and avoid disasters; a high-velocity culture will catch opportunities and court disasters. Naming that trade-off aloud is itself governance. It lets members choose the ship they can stomach.

What should a reader do with this? Treat culture as the first layer, not the frosting. When evaluating a project, read the memes and rituals as attentively as the whitepaper. Who gets celebrated? Who gets thanked? What gets calendar time? Which words are sacred, and can they be challenged? If you cannot answer, you lack due diligence on the only layer that moves faster than code. Culture frames risk. Culture prices time.

The unresolved tension is durable. How do you keep memes sharp enough to mobilise without turning them into dogma? How do you design rituals that reward care without turning care into delay? Who should be trusted to hold the drum, and how often must that role rotate before rhythm becomes theatre? The next coordination surge will not arrive on a roadmap. It will arrive as a joke, a chant, a day on the calendar. The question is whether your culture has built enough humility to laugh, march, and pause on cue—and enough memory to remember why.

Chapter 7
Global Frictions, Local Lives

In December 2022, as inflation ravaged Argentina's peso and cash withdrawals were rationed, a café owner in Buenos Aires began accepting USDT—a dollar-pegged crypto token—through a QR code on the counter. She was not a zealot, nor a speculator. She wanted her morning suppliers to be paid by noon, and her customers to avoid carrying paper money that melted by the day. Each payment took seconds, not hours. Yet every few months, the bridge she used changed terms, fees climbed, and once—after a government notice—the service froze. The rails promised autonomy; the terms rewrote themselves elsewhere. Global money had arrived without a local covenant.

That small café could stand anywhere. In Lagos, freelancers invoice in stablecoins because banks throttle transfers. In Beirut, families save on-chain because depositors have been locked out of their own accounts since 2019. In Manila, millions of migrant workers move wages through crypto corridors to dodge remittance gouges. Each story opens with empowerment and ends in ambiguity. Access is not the same as agency. A tool that can bypass gatekeepers can also bypass recourse. As digital finance crosses borders, the central tension of this chapter surfaces: when global protocols meet local lives, whose values travel with the code?

Blockchain rhetoric often speaks of liberation. Yet freedom with fees, scams, and volatility can disguise extraction under new names. The frictionless world still rubs hardest against those with least margin for error. The promise of "financial inclusion" becomes credible only when we can separate empowerment from displacement—when we can tell who gains resilience and who inherits someone else's risk. That is why the first section of this chapter returns to the ground: remittance stalls, micro-merchants, informal cooperatives, and the ethics of making finance borderless but not faceless. It traces how new rails extend dignity in one transaction and impose dependency in the next, offering criteria for honesty rather than comfort.

From inclusion we move to power. Authoritarianism and sanctions are not abstractions for those who depend on permissionless rails to survive. In 2021, Belarusian activists used Bitcoin to fund legal aid during mass arrests. The same year, ransomware networks laundered crypto through similar channels. Both exploited the same affordances: censorship resistance, pseudonymity, transnational liquidity. The question, then, is not whether such tools are neutral, but how design can bias their use toward freedom rather than predation. Governance, defaults, and documentation matter as much as code. Readers will meet dissidents, developers, and compliance officers each wrestling with the same paradox: how to keep the door open for rescue without leaving it ajar for abuse.

Then comes labour. Programmable contracts, the so-called "future of work", promise to strip out intermediaries and deliver direct ownership. Yet disintermediation rarely abolishes power; it merely relocates it. A marketplace governed by tokens can reproduce gig-economy asymmetries under decentralised branding. The worker still faces the algorithm—only now it lives on-chain. But not all paths lead to precarity. In music and design collectives, smart contracts have begun to codify attribution, royalties, and shareable ownership without requiring corporate custodians. This section asks a sharper question than "will we own our work?" It asks, "can the rails that carry our labour also protect our bargaining power?"

Culture and education close the loop. If decentralisation is to mean self-rule rather than self-service, citizens must be literate in its grammar: how keys function, how threats emerge, how governance proposals are read. Civic education once meant knowing how to vote and how to read a budget; it now must include knowing how to verify a contract and spot a rug-pull. The final section of this chapter turns toward habit formation—curricula, community schools, and small, teachable practices that scale autonomy from the individual to the collective. The point is not to romanticise self-reliance but to cultivate competence: to replace slogans with skills.

Across these four movements runs a single motif: *friction*. Friction slows, protects, exposes. When global systems erase it entirely, local agency evaporates. When they preserve just enough, communities gain traction. The chapter's stories—from border remittances to blacklisted addresses, from labour DAOs to digital civics—reveal how freedom depends not on speed but on the right kinds of drag: transparency, deliberation, accountability. The friction that keeps us grounded also keeps us free.

Readers will meet lives shaped by these tensions—entrepreneurs, artists, engineers, migrants—each balancing the promise of borderless coordination against the pull of local reality. Their experiences show that global systems, no matter how decentralised, land somewhere: on a street, a screen, a phone, a hand. The ethics of design become the ethics of daily survival. And so, the question that threads through this chapter remains unfinished by design: how do we build technologies that can cross every border without erasing the people who live within them? The answer, as you will see, depends less on code than on conscience—and on the frictions we choose to keep.

Financial Inclusion Without Extraction

In February 2021, the Bangko Sentral ng Pilipinas recorded that overseas Filipino workers remitted over 2.6 billion US dollars back home. A third of those transfers passed through informal channels—friends carrying envelopes, traders routing digital vouchers, couriers operating off WhatsApp. Official remittance fees averaged nearly 6 per cent. Informal ones varied from 1 per cent to 10 per cent, depending on risk. Then came the crypto corridor: Binance's peer-to-peer marketplace promised settlement in minutes, at almost no cost. Within a year, remittances via stablecoins surged. Yet a local cooperative in Quezon City reported an unanticipated pattern: when prices dipped, families withdrew less, vendors refused tokens, and payday cycles broke. Inclusion, it turned out, was not a switch—it was a series of fragile bargains.

That bargain is the motif of this subchapter: the *bridge*. Every tool that claims to bridge exclusion must be judged by what it carries across, and what it leaves behind. Financial inclusion, when measured solely by access, flatters itself. The more honest question is whether the bridge delivers autonomy or dependency. Crypto's strongest case for inclusion lies in removing intermediaries; its weakest lies in reproducing new ones—exchanges, liquidity providers, wallet apps—that tax trust instead of credit.

Consider El Salvador, where Bitcoin became legal tender in September 2021. Government-sponsored adoption brought global headlines, lightning payments, and, briefly, tourist enthusiasm. For micro-retailers, though, the arithmetic changed little. A coffee seller in San Salvador still paid network fees to convert sales into dollars; outages froze transactions; volatility wiped margins overnight. Studies by the National Bureau of Economic Research (April 2022) found that only 20 per cent of businesses reported ongoing use of the Chivo wallet. The showpiece of inclusion had become a state wallet—centralised, data-collecting, subsidy-dependent. The bridge stood, but tolls and cameras lined the span.

Now shift to Nigeria, 2022, when the Central Bank restricted cash withdrawals and capped foreign exchange. Peer-to-peer crypto trades rose sharply. Informal traders in Lagos and Kano began quoting stablecoin prices in Naira per USDT. For cross-border freelancers, this was salvation; for others, it was exposure. Scams multiplied, fake escrow accounts proliferated, and regulators launched sting operations. The same rails that empowered the excluded offered new surface area for predation. This pattern—empowerment followed by displacement—is not a footnote but a design flaw. When volatility and fraud become routine costs of access, inclusion slides toward extraction.

To separate genuine empowerment from disguised exploitation, we can trace three coordinates: *friction, literacy, and reciprocity.* Friction first. True inclusion preserves some resistance—the right to slow down, verify, and contest. When everything is instant, errors compound silently. Micro-finance cooperatives understand this; they stage lending decisions over weeks precisely to surface community checks. By contrast, instant remittance platforms prize throughput. Their dashboards display velocity, not retention. A more responsible design would highlight *recovery rate*—how much value recipients still hold after a quarter. Access without durability is merely transaction volume.

Second, literacy. Financial tools that demand constant vigilance from the poor are not inclusion but outsourcing of risk. The success of Kenya's M-Pesa since 2007 rests less on cryptography than on social pedagogy: ubiquitous agents, transparent balances, and collective trust. Compare this to decentralised exchanges, where phishing, private-key loss, and smart-contract exploits transfer operational risk onto individuals least equipped to bear it. Education can close part of that gap, but architecture matters more. Interfaces that translate volatility into understandable ranges, or wallets that sandbox speculative features from essential transfers, convert complexity into safety. Literacy thrives when the system respects attention as a scarce resource.

Third, reciprocity. Inclusion that does not circulate value back into the communities it serves eventually hollows them out. In Colombia's Catatumbo region, remittance flows stabilised household income during 2020–2021 but also inflated rents and reduced labour availability for local farms. Digital liquidity outpaced physical production. When money flows faster than trust, the bridge collapses. Responsible inclusion therefore ties rails to re-investment: local stablecoin treasuries pegged to community projects, cooperatives issuing tokenised shares redeemable only for local goods, diaspora remittances routed through verified savings pools rather than speculative exchanges. The principle is simple: build rails that circle back.

A counter-example tempers the optimism. During 2021's bull market, Venezuelan families used crypto wallets to hedge against bolívar hyperinflation. For a season, purchasing power improved. Yet as stablecoin issuers tightened compliance, local on-ramps were delisted, and liquidity shrank. Informal exchangers returned, charging premiums up to 15 per cent. The cycle reverted. Inclusion faded into dependency on faraway policy decisions. What this reveals is structural: global tokens are still tethered to central infrastructures—the dollar banking system, US Treasury licences, exchange KYC regimes. The excluded remain one compliance update away from renewed exclusion.

The extraction risk is not only economic. Data is currency, too. Wallet analytics firms map transaction graphs with forensic precision. A migrant worker's remittance, once public on-chain, becomes marketable insight for advertisers and surveillance agencies. Privacy—integral to dignity—has become a luxury feature. The paradox is brutal: the poorer the user, the more traceable their trail. Technological inclusion without informational protection reinforces asymmetry. Efforts such as zero-knowledge proofs and selective disclosure wallets hint at remedies, but implementation remains thin. Until privacy is embedded as default, inclusion will mean exposure.

To make the bridge hold, criteria must tighten. A financial inclusion initiative should meet three tests before claiming virtue. First, *cost transparency:* can users compute total fees—exchange spreads, bridge costs, volatility slippage—without expert help? Second, *exit autonomy:* can they withdraw to self-custody or alternative networks at any time without punitive penalties? Third, *local relevance:* does the system anchor value in the currencies, goods, or obligations people actually use? Anything failing these is not inclusion; it is colonialism in digital form.

Pragmatic models exist. In rural India, the Self-Employed Women's Association (SEWA) tested blockchain-based savings groups in 2020 with assistance from the International Labour Organization. Transactions were recorded locally, mirrored to an immutable ledger, but disbursements remained cash-anchored. Members could audit without surrendering privacy. The pilot reduced ledger tampering and improved transparency in profit sharing. Importantly, governance stayed community-based. Here, the bridge touched both shores. Similarly, in Brazil, Instituto Locomotiva's 2022 research on digital payment adoption among informal vendors showed that when platforms reduced chargeback risks and offered local customer support, merchant retention doubled. Design, not hype, drives resilience.

The limitation, however, persists: volatility externalities. When a stablecoin loses peg—as TerraUSD did in May 2022, erasing $40 billion—those least diversified suffer most. For them, "algorithmic" stability meant unsupervised exposure. Even dollar-backed tokens inherit geopolitical fragility; Circle's USDC froze sanctioned addresses in 2022, demonstrating how political filters re-enter supposedly neutral systems. The honest conclusion is that no inclusion is unconditional. It is always conditional on who can press *pause.*

Across these cases, a quiet motif returns: *weight.* Real inclusion feels heavier, not lighter. It carries accountability, comprehension, and continuity. The lighter versions—instant apps, yield promises, "zero-fee" slogans—float away at the first gust of volatility. When we speak of building bridges, we must choose the materials: steel of governance, not paper of slogans.

The unresolved question remains: how much friction, oversight, and locality can a global network bear before it ceases to be "borderless"? And conversely, how much convenience can we add before inclusion collapses into extraction by another name? Each new rail must answer this test in practice, not pitch decks. For the café owner in Quezon City, for the worker in Lagos, for the saver in Beirut, the bridge matters only if it holds their weight.

Authoritarianism, Sanctions, and Safe Havens

On 9 August 2020, Belarus went dark. As protests spread across Minsk following Alexander Lukashenko's disputed re-election, the government ordered a nationwide internet blackout. Bank transfers froze. ATMs emptied. The Coordination Council, a loose network of activists and lawyers, suddenly found itself without infrastructure—no reliable banking, no communications, no channels to fund legal aid for detainees. Within forty-eight hours, a volunteer group began routing Bitcoin donations through a Telegram bot. By the end of that week, the Belarus Solidarity Foundation had distributed more than $2 million in crypto to families of arrested protesters. They bypassed state-controlled banks, avoided censors, and turned code into lifeline. The same properties that once sounded theoretical—permissionless, borderless, immutable—became tangible acts of resistance.

The rails that rescue can also corrupt. In the same year, blockchain analytics firms traced hundreds of millions of dollars in ransomware proceeds—Colonial Pipeline (May 2021), JBS Foods (June 2021), and others—through the very same networks. What empowered dissidents also enriched criminals. This is the paradox at the heart of digital money under pressure: neutrality, while elegant in code, is morally ambivalent in practice. Networks that cannot discriminate must rely on design, defaults, and culture to tilt toward virtue. The question is not whether decentralised rails will be used under authoritarianism or sanctions—they already are—but whether their architecture can protect human rights without providing cover for abuse.

Show, name, explain, imply. Consider the humanitarian corridor first. During Russia's invasion of Ukraine (February 2022), the Ukrainian government published official crypto addresses for donations. Within a fortnight, more than $100 million had flowed in, much of it converted to equipment and aid. The rails worked precisely because no bank or clearinghouse could veto them. Yet these same features made neighbouring states wary: as early as March, reports surfaced of Russian entities attempting to use crypto to skirt sanctions. Exchanges including Binance, Coinbase, and Kraken faced political pressure to block users from entire jurisdictions. Their responses diverged. Kraken's CEO, Jesse Powell, publicly refused to impose unilateral restrictions without legal requirement, arguing that "Bitcoin embodies the very values Ukraine is fighting for." The implication was clear: selective censorship cannot be outsourced to platforms without eroding the principle of equal access that underpins their legitimacy.

Design choices, then, become ethical choices. Protocols can bias toward rights-preserving outcomes by embedding transparency, verifiability, and optional privacy rather than indiscriminate opacity. Tornado Cash, the Ethereum mixer sanctioned by the US Treasury's Office of Foreign Assets Control (August 2022), tested that boundary. Built to enhance transactional privacy, it became a laundering conduit for the North Korean Lazarus Group. In response, developers began exploring "view keys"—tools allowing users to prove innocence without revealing everything. The technical idea is subtle but profound: privacy should shield citizens from coercion, not shield coercion from scrutiny. True safe havens must be private for the weak, not secret for the powerful.

To see why this distinction matters, recall the Arab Spring. In January 2011, as Hosni Mubarak's regime cut Egypt's internet, activists smuggled footage and funds through dial-up and foreign VPNs. Had robust decentralised payment rails existed, they could have financed resistance without reliance on foreign NGOs or compromised intermediaries. But decentralisation alone would not have sufficed. Without discoverability, without trust, and without ways to authenticate legitimate actors, disinformation would have overwhelmed them. The lesson applies still: dissidents need more than anonymity—they need credible identity without exposure. Mechanisms like digital signatures, reputation proofs, and selective attestations make this possible. Tools must support accountability by consent, not by coercion.

A contrasting case shows the cost of indifference. Between 2017 and 2021, Venezuelan officials used the Petro—a state-issued cryptocurrency supposedly backed by oil reserves—to circumvent financial sanctions. The project, endorsed by Nicolás Maduro's government, promised inclusion and sovereignty. In practice, it consolidated surveillance and extracted hard currency from citizens compelled to transact in it. The Petro's ledger was opaque, its conversion controlled by state agencies. Here, "blockchain" became theatre: the language of decentralisation wrapped around a centralised apparatus. It illustrates how authoritarian regimes co-opt innovation while preaching autonomy. Technology without civic design becomes decoration for power.

The motif threading through these cases is *the corridor.* A corridor connects two spaces while constraining movement. Its design decides who passes freely and who is stopped. Digital payment rails are the corridors of twenty-first century geopolitics. When built with public verifiability, they illuminate abuses; when captured by private intermediaries or compromised protocols, they conceal them. Rights-preserving architecture therefore demands constraints that frustrate both state censorship and criminal opacity—time delays, public audits, zero-knowledge disclosures, multi-signature withdrawals requiring human oversight. Friction, not frictionlessness, preserves ethics.

Ethical bias is not neutrality betrayed; it is neutrality informed. The myth that open systems must remain value-blind is untenable in the face of real harm. The practical question is where to draw the line. Exchanges that freeze assets under formal sanction lists act within the rule of law; those that pre-emptively deplatform entire populations enforce geopolitics through code. Between those poles lies a governance design space: selective compliance, jurisdictional diversity, and open-source verification of enforcement logic. The goal is not an impossible purity but transparent criteria. Dissidents must know the rules before they break them.

A counter-example illuminates the tension. The "Freedom Convoy" protests in Canada (February 2022) saw donors' accounts frozen under the Emergencies Act; organisers pivoted to Bitcoin and Tether. Some funds supported lawful assembly; others financed property damage. Law enforcement obtained court orders to blacklist wallet addresses. Critics decried this as financial repression; others hailed it as rule-of-law restraint. Both sides missed the deeper issue: the absence of a predictable protocol for adjudicating such conflicts. Ad hoc censorship breeds mistrust, but so does impunity. The reconciliation lies in procedural clarity—open warrants, verifiable freezes, time-bound restrictions—so that power, even when exercised, leaves a public footprint.

Metrics of virtue can help calibrate these systems. One is *reversibility index*: the proportion of assets recoverable after proven coercion or fraud. Another is *jurisdictional diversity ratio*: how many independent entities hold control keys or run relay nodes across political blocs. A third is *transparency delta*:

the difference between what users can audit and what regulators can secretly override. These are not perfect numbers, but they quantify moral posture in infrastructure. They translate rights into code reviews.

Rights-preserving tactics extend beyond design. Advocacy matters. In authoritarian contexts, local crypto communities often serve as informal ombudsmen—verifying aid distribution, warning of scams, maintaining bridges between anonymity and accountability. In Myanmar after the 2021 coup, such networks used stablecoins to fund exiled journalists while documenting misuse of funds in public ledgers. Their strength lay not in technology alone but in culture: norms of disclosure, shared risk, and a collective refusal to monetise suffering. This blend of cryptographic integrity and civic ethics forms the backbone of credible safe havens.

Still, every corridor faces capture. Surveillance firms expand visibility faster than privacy tools evolve. States learn to exploit on-chain analysis to target activists. Criminals adapt faster than compliance manuals. No protocol can freeze this dynamic. What can evolve is posture: a discipline of principled advocacy. It begins with bias—toward speech, toward transparency, toward the vulnerable. It continues through institutional redundancy: multiple bridges, multiple stewards, none omnipotent. And it endures through public memory: case studies, not slogans, as the basis for design.

The unresolved question lingers at the threshold of this subchapter. How do we code compassion into indifferent protocols? Should censorship resistance remain absolute when evidence of harm is overwhelming? And when the next blackout falls—whether in Tehran, Havana, or Hong Kong—will the rails remember their purpose as corridors for freedom or repeat the pattern of escape and exploitation entwined? The answer will not emerge from markets or ministries but from the daily, deliberate choice of designers, validators, and users: to build systems that remember who they are for, even when no one is watching.

Labour, Creativity, and Ownership

In May 2021, the musician 3LAU auctioned 33 NFTs linked to his album *Ultraviolet*, generating $11.6 million in a single weekend. Each token encoded not just a collectible but a share of future royalties. Holders could verify ownership and claim revenue automatically through smart contracts. No label, no lawyer, no quarterly statements—just code mediating trust. The experiment captured a broader question that has since unsettled every creative industry: when contracts can execute themselves, who becomes the boss?

Programmable money promised to flatten hierarchies. Yet, as with most technologies that claim emancipation, the distribution of power reconstitutes itself in subtler forms. Tokenised platforms still rely on infrastructure—marketplaces, wallets, oracles—whose operators extract rents through fees and visibility algorithms. For every 3LAU who gains independence, thousands of creators find themselves chasing speculative buyers or platform attention. What changed was not intermediation itself but its vocabulary: "protocol" replacing "publisher," "community" replacing "client." Decentralisation, misapplied, can rebrand the very asymmetries it set out to abolish.

Consider Ethereum's rise as the backbone of creative labour markets. Since its 2015 launch, it has enabled programmable contracts for digital art, freelance work, and collective funding. Smart contracts such as EIP-2981 (finalised 2021) standardised royalty enforcement, guaranteeing creators a share each time their work resold. Yet enforcement still depends on marketplaces choosing to honour that code. When OpenSea—by far the largest NFT exchange—disabled mandatory royalties in late 2023, citing competitive pressure, the mechanism collapsed. The promise of perpetual income reverted to optional courtesy. The protocol remained neutral; the platform, not the artist, dictated the rule.

This reveals the first structural truth: ownership in decentralised systems is only as sovereign as the interfaces that mediate it. Workers and creators can hold cryptographic keys but lose economic power if discovery and liquidity cluster elsewhere. To make labour truly programmable, exit must be credible—artists must be able to migrate contracts, reputations, and audiences without forfeiting livelihoods. Design patterns such as decentralised identity registries and portable provenance records aim to achieve this. Whether they can scale without re-centralising remains an open experiment.

A contrasting case from outside the art world clarifies the dynamics. In 2020, Gitcoin launched quadratic funding rounds for open-source developers, allowing thousands of small donors to pool resources efficiently. Payments were transparent, automated, and bias-minimised. Over $60 million has since flowed to maintainers of public software. Yet governance disputes erupted over who set matching formulas and eligibility criteria. The moment labour became programmable, policy became code. And once again, those who wrote the parameters—foundation members, not contributors—controlled distribution. Automation reduced administrative overhead but condensed decision-making power. The lesson echoes through every decentralised workplace: software cannot neutralise politics; it merely translates it.

To anchor abstraction, we return to the visible act of work. A designer contributing to a DAO might sign a contract specifying token compensation tied to milestones. The code escrows funds until the community approves deliverables. This appears meritocratic, yet approval votes often mirror popularity rather than output. Empirical studies by the Blockchain Governance Initiative (2022) found that participation rates in DAO voting averaged below 10 per cent; most outcomes were steered by whales—large token holders—with vested interests. The gig worker of Web3, like her Web2 predecessor, depends on unseen hierarchies. Labour markets, even automated, reproduce the incentives of their issuers.

A counter-example illustrates partial redemption. The collective known as Friends With Benefits (FWB), launched 2020, restricted membership through social and financial stakes. Members contributed cultural labour—writing, events, design—and were compensated in the same token that granted governance rights. The scope was narrow, incentives clear, and participation identity-based rather than purely financial. Where most DAOs drift toward speculation, FWB stabilised around shared purpose. Its model suggests that programmable contracts work best when domains are bounded and community norms pre-exist automation. Technology amplified trust rather than substituting for it.

The motif threading through these stories is *the ledger as mirror.* Code reflects rather than reforms moral economies. Every time we translate creative or cognitive effort into tokens, we choose what counts as value and who certifies it. In decentralised music, one can audit revenue splits but not emotional labour—the unpaid curation, mentoring, or community maintenance that sustains ecosystems. In decentralised journalism, writers may receive micro-tips through readers' wallets, yet algorithmic feeds still govern visibility. Transparency solves accounting, not attention. The ledger is fair only to what it can measure.

The same dilemma shadows collective bargaining. Traditional unions rely on shared identity and enforceable contracts; DAOs rely on open membership and code. The two logics clash. Smart contracts can automate payment distribution but cannot strike, negotiate, or express dissent. Attempts to unionise digital creators—such as the 2022 Writers DAO initiative—foundered when governance tokens became speculative assets, diluting solidarity into trading. This reveals the second structural truth: labour solidarity struggles in environments where ownership itself is liquid. When every share can be sold, shared interests erode.

Some designers are re-engineering around this. The protocol Mirror, launched in 2021 as a decentralised publishing platform, introduced "crowdfunds" that issue non-transferable tokens for backers—proofs of patronage rather than speculative assets. These "soulbound" models, proposed by Ethereum co-founder Vitalik Buterin (May 2022), restrict transferability to preserve community identity. While imperfect, they hint at a way to couple economic participation with social coherence. Programmability need not mean perpetual liquidity; sometimes the ethical boundary lies in making ownership less tradable, not more.

Yet automation cuts both ways. For freelance coders in developing economies, programmable escrow contracts offer protection once impossible through legacy platforms. A Kenyan developer completing a project for a European DAO can receive payment without currency conversion or third-party arbitration. No intermediary can delay or reverse funds. This tangible gain—predictability—remains decentralisation's strongest defence. Still, volatility in token value or governance disputes can erode those gains overnight. The system grants agency but demands vigilance. Agency without insulation is simply liability renamed.

The counterweight to this volatility is *collective intelligibility*—the ability of participants to read and understand the systems that govern them. Open-source documentation, plain-language summaries of contracts, and public disclosure of keyholder privileges convert technical complexity into civic knowledge. The open-source movement learned this decades ago; crypto labour markets are only beginning to absorb it. When creators understand how their revenue flows and can trace the conditions of its distribution, they regain negotiation power. Transparency without pedagogy, however, breeds fatigue, not empowerment.

A philosophical undercurrent shapes all this. Since the seventeenth century, labour has been the moral foundation of ownership: Locke's dictum that mixing one's labour with nature grants property. In digital economies, the material substrate is no longer land or resource but code—infinitely replicable, frictionless, borderless. When scarcity is synthetic, ownership must be justified anew. Programmable contracts shift that debate from law to logic: the terms of distribution are enforced not by courts but by compilers. Yet moral legitimacy still requires deliberation—collective agreement on what fairness means before it becomes executable. Without that, decentralised systems risk encoding yesterday's inequalities into tomorrow's ledgers.

The motif of the mirror returns. Automation reflects our biases faster than we can debate them. Platforms built to celebrate creativity now monetise engagement metrics; DAOs intended to democratise labour now mint governance oligarchies. But mirrors can also be instruments of correction. By observing which reflections distort most—whose work disappears, whose value inflates—we gain diagnostic clarity. The remedy lies not in rejecting programmability but in reclaiming authorship over its parameters.

The unresolved tension remains: can rails that promise "trustless" execution ever sustain trust between humans? Should creators embrace liquidity if it erodes the solidarity that once protected them? And when code becomes the contract, who writes the preamble of values it must obey? Each new generation of digital workers inherits not just tools but the task of deciding whether technology will continue to mirror old hierarchies—or finally, by deliberate design, refract them into something fairer.

Education for Self-Rule

In January 2015, in Taipei's Social Innovation Lab, hundreds of citizens, civil servants, and engineers opened laptops and logged into a public deliberation on how to handle Uber's arrival. The platform—vTaiwan—did not ask people what they liked in the abstract. It surfaced concrete trade-offs, mapped areas of consensus, and produced a set of recommendations that the ministry adopted within months. No lobbyist set the agenda. No closed room decided the terms. A civic ritual—read, discuss, commit—moved a policy. Self-rule is taught.

A second scene begins in Tallinn, December 2014. Estonia launched e-Residency, extending digital signatures and secure online services to anyone willing to be vetted. The state did not merely digitise forms; it trained a population in the habits that underwrite digital sovereignty: key custody, signature literacy, verifiable logs. What mattered was not the plastic card but the practice—learning to treat a private key like a passport, to check audit trails like receipts, to read a consent screen as if it were a contract. The lesson travels. Autonomy is not a posture. Autonomy is a curriculum.

To add decentralised rails to democratic life, civics must expand its syllabus. Show, name, explain, imply. Start with keys. A key is not a metaphor; it is a power. Losing it is not like forgetting a password; it is closer to granting power of attorney to a stranger. Name the competence: *key literacy*. Explain: people must learn generation, storage, rotation, and recovery the way earlier generations learned signatures and cheques. Implication: schools, unions, and libraries should teach keys at the level of drills, not lectures—time-boxed, repeated, scored. You do not "know" a recovery plan until you have rehearsed it with the clock running and the phone off.

Threats are the second pillar. Most citizens face phishing, device theft, and data brokers long before they encounter nation-state zero-days. Name the discipline: *civilian threat modelling*. Explain: map a day in a worker's life and list transactions that expose them—invoice approvals, chat links, exchange logins, grant signatures. Then pair each exposure with one deliberate friction: out-of-band verification for payments, hardware signers for large transfers, session compartmentalisation between work and savings. Implication: we scale safety not by scaring people but by teaching them where to slow down. The drill returns—pause, verify, proceed.

Governance reading forms the third pillar. In a world of tokens and votes, citizenship demands the ability to parse a proposal and ask who benefits, who pays, and where recourse lives. Call this *governance literacy*. It blends the habits of a budget committee with the scepticism of a good editor. What should people actually read? Commit hashes, quorum rules, timelocks, emergency powers, and reversal envelopes. How should they read? As if they might need to defend the decision publicly, ten months from now, under stress. Implication: literacy comes from repetition—monthly proposal clubs at co-working hubs; short, graded "governance briefs" that summarise a live vote in 200 words; public scorecards that reward clarity over hype.

Two examples show how teaching can reshape practice. Taiwan's vTaiwan, founded under Digital Minister Audrey Tang in 2015, ritualised participation with tools like Pol.is, which visualised patterns rather than counting noise. It taught citizens to disagree productively and authorities to accept bounded mandates. The design choice—surface consensus clusters, hide reply buttons—reduced performative flame wars and accelerated convergence. Estonia's digital signature regime, anchored by mandatory cryptographic ID and transparent logs, taught residents that every action leaves a trace that can be contested. Appeals are not a dark art; they are a workflow. The implication across cases is sharp:

institutions can train populations in self-rule by building platforms that make good behaviour easy and legible.

A credible counter-example tempers optimism. India's Aadhaar system—biometric identity at national scale—streamlined subsidy delivery and payments after 2010, yet produced exclusion where fingerprints failed or connectivity dropped. The Supreme Court's 2018 judgement narrowed its use in the private sector precisely because efficiency had outpaced consent and remedy. The lesson is not that digital civics should retreat. It is that speed without recourse converts citizens into supplicants. Reconcile by design: any system that binds welfare or work to a cryptographic claim must publish an *offline* exception path, an appeal process with human oversight, and a time-bounded window for correction. Drills should include failure.

The motif of *the drill* threads this subchapter for a reason. Democracies do not trust fire extinguishers that have never been checked. They should not trust recovery phrases that have never been tested or governance powers that have never been simulated. A curriculum for self-rule should schedule three recurring exercises. First, *key day*: rotate a sub-key, test a recovery from scratch, and measure the time to full restoration. Second, *consent audit*: review the last month's authorisations—OAuth tokens, smart contract approvals—and revoke those you cannot name. Third, *proposal rehearsal*: before a major vote, run a tabletop scenario—"what if the contract pauses?"—and assign response roles. Measure mean time to clarity. Publish the results. Normalise the diary.

Because autonomy is social, not solitary, the classroom must escape the classroom. Trade unions can adopt key custodianship for treasuries and publish open runbooks. Faith groups can host device clinics that install authenticators and practise emergency contacts. Public libraries can run governance reading circles where a librarian and a developer translate a live proposal line by line. Municipalities can publish their own "cryptographic civics" pages—how to sign documents, how to verify notices, how to recover accounts—like they once published bin collections and council minutes. The point is not glamour. The point is habit. Habits survive headlines.

We should also bring measurement into pedagogy. Without numbers, drills drift. Track *recovery success rate* in community workshops; track *median time to revoke a compromised approval*; track *proposal comprehension* by sampling plain-English summaries against the original. These do not reduce democracy to dashboards; they keep organisers honest about whether training works. If comprehension falls when markets rise, you have diagnosed a culture that confuses price for progress. If recovery times lengthen after new wallet features, you have found UX that flatters itself. Numbers redirect attention.

Curricula must name trade-offs aloud. Privacy defaults protect dissent but complicate fraud recovery; irreversible transfers protect against censorship but punish error. Teach both. Run paired drills that demonstrate each constraint. One week, simulate a donor mapping programme that respects anonymity using zero-knowledge proofs; the next, simulate a theft report routed through an opt-in reversible wrapper with strict evidence thresholds. Let students argue the ethics of each choice before they code it into a habit. Nothing hardens judgment like rehearsed disagreement.

This is also a cultural project. Memes and rituals coordinate faster than laws. Mark 3 January—the *proof-of-keys* tradition in Bitcoin circles—as a civic holiday for key literacy, stripped of tribalism and adapted for any wallet or chain. Mark a monthly *consent reset* where communities revoke stale approvals together. Replace "security awareness month" posters with quiet, useful rituals: two colleagues exchange sealed recovery fragments and file confirmations; a DAO publishes its emergency contact tree and tests a dry run at off-hours. The drill beats the slogan.

Education for self-rule must protect those who fail. That means embedding mercy into pedagogy: bursaries for victims of fraud who complete recovery training; insurance pools tied to proof of drills; ombudspersons who handle disclosures without public shaming. Responsibility sticks when forgiveness exists. A system that only punishes error breeds secrecy, not competence. And secrecy is captured quickly.

Finally, teaching autonomy means teaching when to delegate. Radical self-custody for everything is a recipe for exhaustion. A mature curriculum distinguishes between hot keys for daily spend, time-locked vaults for savings, and social-recovery guardians for catastrophe. It coaches students to choose *bounded delegation*: appoint three guardians across jurisdictions; set a 48-hour delay for large moves; require human-signed countersignatures for treasury changes. Humility is a civic virtue. Knowing when to slow down is part of knowing how to act.

The drill, the diary, the debate—these are the grammar of digital citizenship. They convert code into conduct. They ensure that when a community confronts a crisis—an exploit, a blackout, a sudden policy shock—it does not improvise rights it never learned to exercise. The unresolved test remains live: how much ritual can a free people tolerate before habit becomes hectoring, and how much freedom can a network afford before convenience dissolves it? We will find out by teaching, rehearsing, and measuring—by turning autonomy from a boast into a practice that even a teenager can run, count, and pass on.

Chapter 8
Designing for Dignity

In 1969, the Apollo 11 mission control room in Houston bristled with noise and telemetry. Every console was wired to redundancy. Every subsystem had a backup, yet decisions were made by a handful of humans staring at green screens. When Neil Armstrong's heartbeat spiked during descent—153 beats per minute at touchdown—the system did not override him. It trusted him. Behind the technology stood a compact institution: a thin constitution of roles, accountability, and procedure, light enough to move fast but heavy enough to hold meaning. The moon landing was not just a triumph of engineering; it was a triumph of dignity in design—machines subordinated to human judgment, authority dispersed but coordinated, responsibility indivisible.

Half a century later, most digital systems run the other way. They offload responsibility onto algorithms and bury discretion under dashboards. Users become operators of rules they did not write. Platforms and protocols, built to minimise friction, often strip away the slow grace of deliberation. Yet as decentralised networks evolve from code experiments into civic infrastructure, they face the same paradox NASA solved in analogue form: how to design systems that can act automatically without making humans disposable. Dignity, not efficiency, must become the measure of maturity.

To speak of *dignity* in design is to reintroduce the moral language that efficiency exiled. It means treating users not as endpoints or data points but as participants capable of error, growth, and appeal. A protocol without room for redemption is not sovereign; it is cruel. The challenge is practical: how to build minimal viable institutions—thin enough to avoid bureaucracy, thick enough to embody care. The next phase of decentralised architecture will not be measured by how little trust it needs, but by how much accountability it sustains.

The first movement in this chapter explores those minimal viable institutions. Many open networks begin with the fantasy of total automation, only to discover that even trustless systems need caretakers—key holders, moderators, dispute resolvers, and stewards of continuity. Bitcoin's code may be immutable, but its community norms and improvement process (BIP system, since 2011) reveal a social layer as vital as its cryptographic one. Ethereum's transition to proof-of-stake in 2022 required coordination among hundreds of clients and validators who rehearsed, debated, and enacted governance rituals that look suspiciously like a miniature parliament. Institutions reappear not as relics of bureaucracy but as stabilisers of meaning.

To design for dignity here means embedding proportional oversight—watchers who can be watched, powers that can be audited. The most resilient systems will treat governance not as a power struggle but as a rhythm: propose, verify, correct. This rhythm replaces hierarchy with choreography. Dignity is preserved when authority can be traced, not when it can be denied.

From there, the narrative turns to stewardship. After a decade of "move fast and break things," the new frontier is "move carefully and maintain." Stewardship reframes progress as care across time: ensuring that tools built for liberation do not become weapons of exclusion. The hype cycle of decentralisation, measured by token price or transaction throughput, must yield to metrics of safety, legibility, and reversibility. The ability to pause and repair should be as celebrated as the ability to scale. Dignity lives in reversibility—the space between the human impulse to correct and the system's permission to allow it.

Real stewardship also alters incentives. When investors measure success by resilience rather than speculation, they extend the time horizon of responsibility. When communities celebrate transparency and response speed over price spikes, they cultivate moral liquidity—the capacity to absorb shock without betrayal. In 2022, after the collapse of TerraUSD wiped out $60 billion in paper wealth, several stablecoin projects quietly introduced public stress dashboards, disclosing collateral and redemption ratios in real time. This shift from opacity to auditability was not driven by law but by shame and learning. It marked the first sign that decentralised economies could internalise civic lessons once reserved for states.

But ideals need metrics. The third movement of the chapter, *Measuring Legitimacy*, examines how legitimacy compounds when measured. Just as a market without accounting breeds fraud, a community without feedback breeds delusion. Indicators such as participation dispersion, remedy rates, and stress performance translate trust into data without cheapening it. Who votes, who speaks, who can recover losses—all become quantifiable reflections of moral health. Tracking them turns governance from a ceremony into a craft. Legitimacy, like interest, accrues through iteration.

Still, metrics alone can betray the very dignity they seek to honour if defaults mislead. The closing movement therefore interrogates *the ethics of default settings*. Defaults are invisible governors: they steer action before consent forms. A wallet that auto-connects to dApps may delight in usability but gamble with exposure; a voting interface that hides abstain options inflates consensus. To design ethically is to design default humility—requiring users to confirm, delay, and reconsider where stakes are high. The balance is delicate. Overprotective systems infantilise; indifferent ones abandon. The art lies in setting the curve of freedom, not the boundary of it.

Threaded through the chapter is a quiet motif: *the caretaker's hand*. Every network—whether codebase, community, or nation—depends on invisible caretakers who patch vulnerabilities, mediate conflicts, and archive memory. Their work resists glamour but defines survival. Designing for dignity means designing for them too: granting recognition, rotation, and rest. When maintenance becomes honourable, systems mature from movements into institutions.

This chapter thus invites a reordering of priorities. It suggests that credible commitment—not speed—is the true marker of innovation. That minimal institutions, well-scoped and humane, outperform maximal bureaucracies of code. That legitimacy must be measured to endure. And that every default we set, every reversal we permit, every safeguard we script expresses a stance on human worth.

The test ahead is quiet but decisive. Can decentralised systems grow up without growing cold? Can they institutionalise care without calcifying it? Can they prove that dignity, far from being an ornament of governance, is its most rigorous design constraint? The answers will not be found in the next protocol upgrade but in the patient choreography of oversight, mercy, and repair—the architecture of responsibility that remembers who it serves.

Minimal Viable Institutions

In November 2008, as Bitcoin's white paper circulated among cryptographers, it opened with a simple claim: "What is needed is an electronic payment system based on cryptographic proof instead of trust." Yet the irony was immediate. Within a year of its launch, the network's health depended not on code alone but on volunteers coordinating upgrades, managing forums, and mediating disputes. They were the *caretakers*—unpaid, unacknowledged, essential. By 2010, when Satoshi Nakamoto handed maintenance of the codebase to Gavin Andresen, the first institution of decentralisation was born: one person entrusted to hold a set of keys and a measure of moral responsibility. What began as an experiment in algorithmic order had already rediscovered a civic truth older than the internet: systems that last require stewardship.

The paradox endures. Every credible decentralised system—no matter how "trustless" its rhetoric—eventually erects thin constitutions and minimal hierarchies. The problem is not whether to have institutions, but how minimal they can be without collapsing into either chaos or bureaucracy. The idea of a *minimal viable institution* borrows the lean ethos of start-ups but applies it to governance. It asks: how little structure is enough to guarantee fairness, continuity, and dignity?

The first pattern is *credible commitment*. In economic history, institutions exist to make promises believable across time. The Magna Carta of 1215, for example, worked not because it created a government from scratch, but because it bound the sovereign with public procedure—charters, witnesses, and seals. The blockchain replays this insight in silicon. Smart contracts are procedural promises encoded in software. But they still need caretakers to update, interpret, and—when something goes wrong—decide. The Ethereum community's 2016 response to the DAO hack, when 3.6 million ether were drained from an experimental investment fund, exposed the limit of code. A hard fork reversed the theft but split the community. The question was no longer *can* we make irreversible systems; it was *should* we, and under what governance covenant.

Minimal viable institutions therefore hinge on proportional oversight. They need checks that match scale, not ceremonies that smother it. Take GitHub's open-source governance: small repositories rely on individual maintainers; mature projects adopt formal maintainers' councils or technical steering committees. Each layer adds accountability only when complexity demands it. Similarly, in 2022, the Uniswap DAO adopted a delegated voting framework—token holders appointed representatives who published periodic disclosures and faced re-election. Instead of adding bureaucracy, it added legibility: the public could trace influence and intervene. The institution remained thin but credible.

Yet proportional oversight must also account for exit. A minimal institution that cannot be left is merely a polite monopoly. The cooperative structure of the Swiss canton of Zug's "Crypto Valley," formalised in 2017, provides a contrasting model. Local foundations host protocols but bind themselves to transparent statutes, annual audits, and open membership registers. Should developers disagree, they can legally migrate assets or dissolve entities. The institution's lightness derives not from its absence of form but from its respect for departure. Dignity demands optionality.

The motif that threads through these cases is *the caretaker's hand*—visible enough to guide, light enough to release. Bitcoin's maintainers, Ethereum's coordinators, and GitHub's councils all embody this paradox. They are trusted precisely because their powers are limited, reversible, and documented. Their dignity lies in restraint. But restraint is a design, not an instinct.

Historical analogues remind us that minimal institutions are an ancient art. The Venetian Republic's governance model from 1297 to 1797 combined dispersed councils with term-limited officials. No single figure could dominate, yet decisions could still be made. Its constitution fit on a few pages, enforced through ritualised elections and rotation. Modern decentralised networks echo that principle through multi-signature wallets and rotating key custodians—cryptographic echoes of civic design. Thin constitutions, when credible, outlast thick bureaucracies because they trade volume for clarity.

There is, however, a danger in fetishising minimalism. When institutional scaffolding is too thin, exploitation fills the void. The collapse of FTX in November 2022 demonstrated this brutally. The exchange marketed itself as decentralised but operated through opaque internal structures and unverified reserves. Its "minimal" governance was, in truth, absence. The line between simplicity and irresponsibility is narrow. The correction must come from credible commitment patterns: separation of roles, published audits, time-locked decisions. In software as in law, restraint without record is not virtue but void.

How, then, do we design thin constitutions that sustain dignity rather than dilute it? The key lies in scope discipline—governance matching the problem's perimeter. For protocols handling assets, the perimeter is security; for social communities, it is discourse; for knowledge networks, it is accuracy. A DAO managing carbon credits, for example, may require a verification council and a dispute module, but not a full legislative apparatus. Overbuilding invites stagnation; underbuilding invites fraud. The art is calibration.

Calibration, in turn, depends on feedback. Institutions stay minimal by measuring their necessity. One promising method is *governance telemetry*—a dashboard of key indicators such as participation rate, proposal throughput, response latency, and recourse success. The Optimism Collective (2023) publishes such metrics quarterly, turning governance into a public experiment. When oversight becomes legible, it can shrink. Bureaucracy thrives in the dark.

Dignity enters here as both compass and constraint. A system that treats its participants as mere units of computation forfeits legitimacy. Dignity in institutional design means preserving space for dissent, error, and redemption. The open-source community's "code of conduct" movement—initiated by Coraline Ada Ehmke in 2014—demonstrates how small rules can transform culture. Projects that adopted transparent grievance procedures saw higher retention and collaboration quality. The procedure's purpose was not punishment but protection—the institutionalisation of respect. Minimal institutions succeed when they encode that ethos without excess.

There are credible counterpoints. Some argue that decentralised systems function better without formal institutions at all—that reputation, markets, and forks provide adequate discipline. The Bitcoin maximalist view, for instance, holds that governance should be entirely ossified, with evolution occurring through voluntary migration to new chains. Yet this radical minimalism produces a paradox of stagnation: without recognised channels for iteration, adaptation must masquerade as rebellion. Protocols that cannot reform peacefully invite schism. Minimal viability, not minimal interference, is the goal.

If the motif of the caretaker's hand implies moderation, the practical design question becomes: how do we maintain the hand's legitimacy? The answer lies in public accountability cycles. Caretakers must be both replaceable and remembered. Replaceability ensures humility; memory ensures continuity. Projects like Nomic DAO have begun recording steward actions immutably, so history becomes a governance resource, not a rumour. This codified memory prevents the institutional amnesia that kills many start-ups and collectives.

The paradox, then, is circular. To remain minimal, institutions must commit to periodic renewal—self-limiting charters, rotating stewards, expiring powers. Each cycle tests whether the structure still serves its purpose. When it fails, dissolution is not decay but discipline. The health of a decentralised system can be measured by how gracefully it retires obsolete functions.

As decentralised governance matures, the question is no longer whether we need institutions, but what shape of institution keeps dignity intact. A minimal viable institution must promise four things: continuity without hierarchy, accountability without suffocation, flexibility without volatility, and dignity without indulgence. It must choreograph care rather than command it.

The unresolved test remains simple yet profound. Can the next generation of decentralised systems institutionalise trust without freezing it? Can they make commitment credible while leaving space for mercy? Or will the pendulum swing once more—from code to chaos, from governance to capture—because we mistook minimalism for virtue rather than design? The answer will depend less on the brilliance of protocols than on the quiet competence of their caretakers, and whether the hand that guides them still knows when to let go.

From Hype to Stewardship

On 12 March 2020, as markets convulsed and ether's price halved in hours, MakerDAO's "Black Thursday" arrived. In Copenhagen and New York, risk teams watched liquidation auctions fail as network congestion spiked; some vaults were sold for zero bids. Losses hit participants who had believed they were over-collateralised. The protocol survived, but the narrative shifted. The lesson was not throughput. It was not "number go up". It was the craft of safety: circuit breakers, oracle hardening, and documented remedies for stressed markets. Hype would not have saved those accounts. Stewardship did, later.

A different scene, same year, opposite posture. On 15 September 2022, the Ethereum Merge executed after rehearsals on Ropsten, Goerli and Sepolia. Clients written in Berlin, Lisbon, Singapore and elsewhere switched a live economy to proof-of-stake with minutes of planned downtime: effectively none. It was a public systems upgrade measured not by slogans but by a checklist—shadow forks, testnets, client diversity targets, and kill-switch drills. Engineers did not crow about speed. They celebrated *lack of drama*. This is the crux of the chapter you are entering: the scoreboard for credible crypto is changing. Stewardship is slower. It sticks.

Stewardship begins with *safety*. Show, name, explain, imply. Show: MakerDAO's response to Black Thursday over the subsequent quarters—raising auction lot sizes gradually, widening collateral sets, introducing circuit breakers, and publishing detailed risk dashboards—replaced bravado with telemetry. Name: the *safety envelope*—the range within which a system can operate without harming users. Explain: a protocol is trustworthy when it can document its safe operating range (volatility, liquidity, gas prices) and the exact interventions it will take when variables breach thresholds. Implication: investors and contributors should rank protocols by mean time to recovery (MTTR), number of critical incidents per quarter, and the clarity of their "pause and patch" runbooks. What gets measured gets stewarded.

Stewardship continues with *legibility*. Hype loves opacity; stewardship loves daylight. In 2022 and 2023, as stablecoin issuers absorbed lessons from Terra's May 2022 collapse and USDC's March 2023 de-peg scare, several began publishing reserve breakdowns weekly, disclosing custodian concentration and redemption windows in plain language. Legibility is not a blog post. It is a file you can audit. A responsible project tells you who can halt what, for how long, with which signatures, and under what pre-agreed criteria. The behaviour is simple: document powers in one canonical place and keep that file versioned. The metric is simpler: *disclosure latency*—the time between a material governance change and a digestible public summary. Under a stewardship lens, a two-day latency beats a two-hour announcement if the slower note contains the procedures, not the hype.

Then comes *reversibility*. Finality is a feature, but systems that never allow controlled reversal are brittle and cruel. Stewardship reframes irreversibility as a spectrum, not a creed. Ethereum's Merge rehearsals built in timelocks and client-level escape hatches; MakerDAO's risk modules introduced "circuit breakers" to suspend auctions when oracles misbehaved. The salient metric here is a *reversibility envelope*: the percentage of total value subject to controlled pause or rollback under explicit, auditable conditions—paired with limits that prevent moral hazard. If 5 per cent of a treasury sits behind a 48-hour timelock with multi-sig guardians and mandatory post-mortems, that is stewardship; if 95 per cent sits behind a single admin key, that is extraction dressed as convenience. Measure the envelope, not the rhetoric.

Two named examples anchor the shift. First, the Merge (global, September 2022): client teams published pre-mortems, not just post-mortems, listing known unknowns, failure drills, and fallback steps. That is legibility before incident. Second, after Terra's failure (May 2022, Seoul and Singapore), major protocols hardened their oracle designs, diversified collateral, and formalised emergency powers. Some introduced public stress dashboards; others scheduled regular "chaos days" to simulate outages. These practices echo aviation rather than advertising. They nudge culture from launch theatre to reliability engineering. The implication is cultural as much as technical: the heroes of the next phase are stewards, not promoters.

The credible counter-example is the bull market platform that boasts "no admin keys, no pauses" while quietly centralising front-ends, relayers, and governance delegates. When a shock arrives—a chain reorg, an exploit, a sanctions order—users discover that "no admin keys" was a fig leaf. Extraction hides in path dependency: a single wallet, a single RPC endpoint, a single bridge. Limitation exposed, we reconcile: stewardship does not mean maximal control; it means *proportional* control, publicly bounded and routinely tested, with the narrowest necessary powers distributed across independent actors. Anything else is marketing.

To adopt a steward's scoreboard, investors and communities must change what they praise and pay for. Return on safety replaces return on spectacle. Three shifts matter. First, *fund lifecycle safety*, not only TVL. Ask for a quarterly *safety P&L*: spend on audits, client diversity, incident response, and user restitution. If the number is zero, the risk is not. Second, *pay for legibility*. Reward teams that keep a living "constitution"—powers, procedures, and precedents—in a repository with diffs. The visible behaviour is commits, not press releases. Third, *insure the envelope*. Set aside a capped, rules-based restitution pool funded by protocol revenues, released only after a transparent claims process with public evidence thresholds. Responsibility funds mercy. Mercy earns legitimacy.

Narratives must shift alongside numbers. An investor memo written in 2020 might have led with market size, token velocity, and moat. A stewardship memo in 2025 should lead with *failure stories owned*: the most instructive incidents a team has handled, the speed and candour of disclosure, and the subsequent design change. Teams that handle failure well will outcompete teams that fail to imagine it. The motif of this subchapter is the *flight recorder*. You want projects that keep one, read it, and publish extracts.

Legibility deserves sharper definition. It includes three layers: public documentation of governance powers (who can pause, upgrade, or seize); public interfaces that surface those powers to users at the point of risk (wallet warnings, timelock notices, signer diversity indicators); and public habits that ritualise transparency (scheduled disclosure days, rotating stewards, standing Q&A). These are not ornaments. They reduce asymmetric information and align expectations. The metric is *comprehension rate*: when you A/B test a user base with a one-page governance explainer, what percentage can answer five basic questions about who can do what? If fewer than 70 per cent pass, your legibility is fiction.

Reversibility calls for similar sobriety. Not every asset should be wrapped in reversibility; not every system should be pausable. Stewardship treats reversibility as *contextual ethics*. For high-risk, high-value actions—treasury transfers, protocol upgrades, cross-chain mints—delays and multi-party consent reduce catastrophic error without paralysing routine use. For censorship-sensitive payments by citizens, finality protects the vulnerable. The long-game scoreboard distinguishes *who* benefits from reversibility in each case and *how* moral hazard is contained—limits on claim size, cooling-off periods, compulsory incident reports. Put simply: mercy should be scarce, procedural, and visible.

The culture turn is already under way. After FTX collapsed (November 2022, Nassau), communities stopped applauding sponsored stadiums and started reading solvency proofs. The race to launch gave way—if only briefly—to the race to disclose. Stewardship seized a toehold. To cement it, communities need rituals that elevate caretaking. A monthly "maintenance day" where contributors fix documentation, rotate keys, and test backups; a yearly "stress week" that drills the full incident chain from alert to restitution; a public "governance day" where delegates report votes and conflicts. Rituals write values into calendars. Calendars write them into muscle.

There are limits. Safety can be gamed; dashboards can be theatre. A project can publish thick reports and thin practice. The antidote is *externality accounting*. Track *participation dispersion* (how many distinct wallets propose and execute), *remedy rate* (percentage of substantiated user harms reimbursed within a defined window), and *stress performance* (key metrics—latency, slippage, failover—during a known shock). Publish the raw data. Invite third-party replication. Stewardship thrives where comparison is possible. It dies in vibes.

Two additional examples sharpen the frame. In March 2023, when USDC briefly de-pegged after Silicon Valley Bank's receivership, protocols with pre-declared pause rules and oracles that smoothed anomalies avoided cascading liquidations; others that chased real-time "truth" magnified chaos. Safety, here, looked like *graceful degradation*. In contrast, the 2021 vintage of vampire-attack farming platforms that offered unsustainable yields left no restitution plans, no dashboards, and no guardians. Extraction wore a carnival mask until music stopped. The implication is hard-edged: if a system cannot describe its failure posture, it is not investable under a stewardship lens.

Stewardship is not risk aversion. It is risk choreography. It knows when to slow markets with circuit breakers and when to quicken them with automated market makers that absorb shocks. It knows when to diversify clients to avoid single points of failure and when to prune features to reduce attack surface. The scoreboard therefore values *deletion*—lines of code removed, permissions retired, powers sunsetted. Subtraction is a virtue. Count it.

Communities, too, must change their applause. Reward the team that writes an exemplary post-mortem within 72 hours. Celebrate the protocol that refuses a tempting integration because it blows the safety envelope. Back the delegate who declares a conflict and abstains. These are not small gestures. They are compound interest on legitimacy. Over time, systems with credible safety, deep legibility, and humane reversibility will attract cheaper capital and steadier contributors. The market will remember who kept their promises when the lights flickered.

The motif returns to the *flight recorder*. Stewardship records, reviews, and reforms. Hype discards. Which do you want flying your treasury, your livelihood, your movement? The forward test is simple and stringent. Before you fund, join, or deploy, ask: What is the documented safe operating range? Who can stop the machine, and how do we watch them? How, precisely, are harms remedied, and who pays? If those answers are vague, you are not investing—you are gambling with other people's lives.

The unresolved tension is productive. How much safety can you buy before you strangle velocity? How much legibility can you demand before you overwhelm attention? How wide should the reversibility envelope be before it invites abuse? A steward's answer will not be universal; it will be argued, iterated, and measured. That is the point. The scoreboard has changed. Winning now means staying upright when others fall, writing procedures that strangers can love, and building institutions that can apologise—and make it right—without losing their nerve.

Measuring Legitimacy

On 15 September 2022, the Ethereum network shifted consensus while the world kept working. The Merge—coordinated by the Ethereum Foundation and client teams distributed from Berlin to Singapore—completed without material downtime. In Bogotá three weeks later, Devcon VI treated it almost as old news. Yet something decisive had happened beyond the engineering feat. The public readouts—client diversity charts, shadow-fork pre-mortems, validator participation—made the operation legible to strangers. Measurement makes legitimacy finally audible. A system earned trust because it exposed how it worked, who led, and how it would cope if events went wrong.

Not all tests are so declarative. In March 2023, when Silicon Valley Bank entered receivership and USDC briefly deviated from its peg, the response across protocols became a living audit. Which teams published reserve breakdowns by the hour? Which DAOs paused or throttled integrations according to pre-declared rules? Which oracles smoothed outliers rather than amplifying panic? Within days, reputations hardened.

Some projects recovered with restored confidence; others looked fast, fragile, and incurious. The story was not price. It was measurement. When pressure rises, legitimacy is what remains after the dashboards are read.

Legitimacy is a social asset, but it compounds through data. It cannot be conjured by slogans, and it cannot be sustained by charisma. To measure it is not to reduce it. It is to give communities a common language for responsibility. Three families of indicators deserve disciplined attention: *participation dispersion*, *remedy rates*, and *stress performance*. Each links an abstraction to visible behaviour. Each invites iteration rather than theatre. And each can be gamed unless paired with a culture of scrutiny. Metrics do not confer virtue. They expose posture.

Begin with participation dispersion: who really governs. Many networks trumpet token-holder counts and "active users" while a handful of wallets propose, a handful execute, and a handful veto. Show, name, explain, imply. Show: in June 2020, Uniswap's inaugural governance votes revealed turnout dominated by large delegates, a rational outcome of stake-weighted rules. Name: *participation dispersion*—the distribution of agenda-setting, deliberation, and execution across unique actors over time. Explain: dispersion is not generalised voter turnout; it is the dilution of gatekeeping. It asks, across the last twenty proposals, how many distinct authors exist; across the last twenty on-chain executions, how many distinct signers acted; across a year, how concentrated is veto power? Implication: publish a quarterly dispersion digest with raw counts and a Gini-like index for proposal authorship and execution signatures. The goal is not perfect equality. It is visible pluralism.

Such numbers change behaviour. When the Optimism Collective, in 2023, began surfacing proposer diversity and delegate concentration in its public notes, new proposers entered and long-standing ones justified their stances with greater care. By contrast, in March 2020, the Steem community's governance was overridden after a new majority assembled hastily with the help of centralised exchanges. The move triggered a contentious fork to Hive. The counter-example is instructive: low dispersion and opaque delegation invited a legitimacy crisis that measurement, had it been public and salient, might have deterred. The reconciliation is not to prohibit concentration—stakes will concentrate—but to dilute agenda control and require those who hold it to be seen. Measured visibility disciplines power.

Remedy rates turn care into a contract. They ask not whether harm occurs—harm will occur—but whether the institution corrects it swiftly and fairly. Show: during MakerDAO's "Black Thursday" (12 March 2020), a subset of users suffered liquidation anomalies as auctions cleared at zero bids under network congestion. The DAO later introduced a governance process for compensating affected vault owners after community debate and forensic work. Name: *remedy rate*—the percentage of substantiated user harms remedied within a defined window, and the median time to resolution. Explain: it is not charity; it is stewardship quantified. It requires public criteria for what counts as harm, a claim submission pipeline, and a transparent corpus of decisions. Implication: protocols should publish remedy ledgers with case IDs, evidence, outcomes, and time stamps; investors and users should read them as closely as they read audits. Mercy, like safety, improves with practice.

Remedy metrics can be abused—teams may avoid acknowledging harm to protect their numbers. The antidote is to pair remedy rates with *disclosure latency*: time between incident detection and first public note. A project with high remedy rates and low disclosure latency is mastering responsibility. One with immaculate numbers and no narratives is massaging optics. Communities can correct for such gaming by sampling cases and conducting periodic meta-audits. The process is dull. It stabilises trust.

Stress performance is the third pillar. It moves legitimacy from promises to physiology. What happens when liquidity thins, when a bridge fails, when an oracle flickers? Show: during the USDC de-peg, some automated market makers widened bands and limited swaps to slow reflexive damage; others let pricing follow the spike-for-spike, producing forced unwinds. Name: *stress performance*—a bundle of telemetry captured during declared shocks: uptime, latency, slippage under load, failover rates for critical services, and mean time to recovery. Explain: stress data must be tied to triggers defined *before* the event (e.g., if collateral deviates by ±X per cent for Y minutes, capture metrics Z and publish within 24 hours). Implication: publish post-stress dossiers with the raw data and the design changes they inspire. Repetition is the point. Systems grow resilient because they revisit their scars.

Two named examples sharpen the point. First, the Ethereum Merge (global, September 2022): the public commitment to client diversity—no single client exceeding roughly two-thirds of validator share—gave a concrete, trackable threshold for stress resilience. Second, Gitcoin Grants (Denver, 2019 onward): by publishing matching outcomes and adversarial analyses of quadratic funding rounds, the organisers transformed distribution from black box to learning loop. Both cases demonstrate that legitimacy is performative only if unmeasured; when measured, it becomes cumulative memory.

A credible counter-example underlines the stakes. In 2021, several "algorithmic stablecoin" projects boasted unshakeable pegs while providing little stress telemetry and no remedy framework. When one collapsed in May 2022, wiping tens of billions, the response was narratives, not numbers. Users had no published path to restitution; investigators had no agreed data sets. Legitimacy evacuated the room because nothing had been prepared to hold it. The limitation is not unique to that design class. Any system that equates confidence with silence will discover, at the worst time, that it has none.

It is tempting to reduce legitimacy to a dashboard and be done. Resist the urge. Numbers can anaesthetise as much as they illuminate. A DAO with ten active proposers might still be captured if those ten are employed by the same sponsor; a near-perfect remedy rate can be manufactured by narrowing the definition of harm; stress performance can be flattered by choosing only comfortable shocks. Measurement must court falsification. The motif here is the *altimeter*. It keeps you oriented but cannot fly the plane. You still look out of the window.

How, then, should communities practise the craft? First, commit to *measurement cadence*. Quarterly is better than annual because it sustains narrative memory without exhausting attention. Second, tie metrics to decisions. If participation dispersion worsens over two cycles, alter delegation rules or incentivise new proposers. If remedy rates lag, grow the restitution pool or simplify claim proofs. If stress performance reveals a weak oracle or thin relayer set, diversify by mandate and schedule drills. Third, socialise the meaning of the numbers. Host briefings where stewards translate telemetry into plain speech and accept hostile questions. Legitimacy rises when institutions treat scrutiny as oxygen, not smoke.

A concrete scenario shows the mechanics. Imagine a public chain that tracks five shock classes: price collapse, gas spike, bridge outage, censorship event, and contract exploit. For each, it defines triggers. During the next event—say, a 30 per cent collateral drop in twenty-four hours—it records failover rates for nodes across three jurisdictions, measures block propagation latency at the 95th percentile, and time-stamps any emergency governance moves. Within seventy-two hours, it publishes the dossier with proposed rule amendments. A month later, it reports whether those amendments shipped. None of this makes headlines. All of it forms institutional memory.

Investors and contributors influence what is measured. If term sheets and grants require public remedy ledgers and dispersion digests, teams will build them. If exchanges and wallets surface legibility—displaying who can pause a contract at transaction time—users will demand better governance ex ante. If delegates publish voting diaries with rationale, minority opinions will survive long enough to win later. Measurement, again, is not accounting alone. It is pedagogy. It teaches those outside the room how the room behaves.

Measurement also dignifies maintenance. In most ecosystems, builders receive glory; caretakers receive fatigue. That is backwards. Keepers of the ledger, moderators of the forum, responders to alerts—they carry legitimacy between cycles. Recording remedy rates gives them grounds to argue for budget. Recording dispersion gives them grounds to insist on rotation. Recording stress performance gives them grounds to refuse reckless integrations. The altimeter keeps them honest and keeps them funded.

There is a deeper ethical reason to track as well as build. Legitimacy is a promise to strangers. It says: when you cannot judge us by character, judge us by habit. Show you your distribution of voice. Show you our work when we break. Show you how we repair. In cryptographic systems—where identities are fluid and borders porous—habits are the most portable form of virtue. They cannot be forged cheaply. They can be measured.

The unresolved tension is practical. How much measurement is enough before governance becomes self-surveillance? How do we prevent dashboards from ossifying innovation or becoming a cudgel for bad-faith critics? And when a shock arrives that falls outside the templates—because one always will—who decides what counts as success the morning after? The forward test is simple to state and hard to meet. Choose the three numbers you will defend in public after the next crisis; publish their formulas; rehearse their capture; accept their verdict. If you can do that, legitimacy will not be a speech. It will be a habit that compounds.

The Ethics of Default Settings

On 26 April 2021, Apple shipped iOS 14.5 and quietly inverted a business model. App Tracking Transparency required applications to ask before following users across other apps and websites. Overnight, most people declined. Advertisers fumed, publishers recalibrated, and privacy moved from policy to practice through one small change: a default. Defaults quietly decide daily conduct. A tick-box did not educate millions; it steered them. The lesson travels: if a single consent prompt in Cupertino can alter global behaviour, then the defaults in our wallets, exchanges, and governance tools will shape far more than UX. They will shape rights.

Show, name, explain, imply. Start with the core claim. Defaults are not neutral. They encode a thesis about who matters in edge cases and who bears the cost of mistakes. Name the ethic: *consent-preserving, safety-first defaults*. Explain: in decentralised systems, where finality can be unforgiving and exposure global, the absence of thought is still a choice. When a wallet auto-connects to a website; when a dApp requests unlimited spend approval; when a bridge selects the cheapest route without showing custody risks—each of these is a moral decision disguised as convenience. Implication: if you are building rails for strangers, you owe them defaults that keep them dignified under stress, not merely delighted at first use.

Consider two instructive precedents beyond crypto. The first is the Apple example: a system-level default that turned surveillance into a conscious choice changed market behaviour without banning anything (Flurry Analytics reported single-digit opt-in rates in early months, 2021). The second is WhatsApp's adoption of end-to-end encryption by default in April 2016, using the Signal Protocol. Billions of messages became unreadable to intermediaries with no training required. In both cases, the ethical stance was enacted in code, not merely declared in terms and conditions. Consent had to be given, not inferred. Safety was the starting point, not a premium tier. These are templates for our rails.

What, then, do defaults look like in decentralised finance and digital governance? Begin with approvals. The ERC-20 standard separates *approve* from *transferFrom*, enabling dApps to spend tokens on a user's behalf. Many interfaces request "infinite approval" as the default—one click now, friction removed forever. It is efficient, until it isn't. In December 2021, the BadgerDAO front end was compromised; users, conditioned by generous approvals, signed malicious transactions that drained tens of millions. The software did not force fraud. It normalised maximum exposure. A consent-preserving default would set per-transaction caps, present the requested allowance in human-friendly figures, and require re-authorisation above a threshold. It would trade smoothness for survivability.

The quiet motif of this subchapter is *the safety catch*. Firearms have them. Industrial machines have them. Our rails need them. A safety catch is valuable not because it is beautiful, but because it changes the speed at which injury can spread. In code, that involves timelocks on high-risk actions, mandatory simulation of transactions before signature, and social recovery paths that require human confirmation when a guardian is replaced or a vault is moved. These are defaults that prevent haste from becoming harm. The metric is not aesthetic pleasure; it is *mean time to clarity*.

A second class of defaults concerns visibility. Legibility is dignity. Hiding risk behind "advanced settings" tramples consent. Wallets should warn, in plain language, when a site can spend on a user's behalf, when a transaction routes through a custodial bridge, or when a contract is upgradeable by admins within short windows. Interfaces should default to *show* emergency powers and *name* the keyholders. The explanation is simple: informed consent demands that the risk of override is visible at the point of action, not buried in a PDF. The implication is sharper: teams that fear clarity fear scrutiny. And if scrutiny endangers a design, the design is the problem.

Reversibility is the third domain where defaults matter. Finality protects speech and commerce against arbitrary interference. It also punishes honest error. The ethical move is not to abolish finality but to bound reversibility. A protocol can default to a narrow "recovery envelope": a small percentage of funds, accessible via a slow, auditable path under strict criteria—say, court orders or supermajority social proofs—while the rest remains irreversible. Products can default to "slow funds" for large transfers: a 24- or 48-hour delay with out-of-band alerts that permit cancellation if the transaction was a mistake. This is not paternalism. It is mercy engineered. The behaviour to watch is *use of the envelope*: how often slow funds save users, how seldom they invite abuse.

A credible counter-example clears the fog. During the 2020–2021 bull market, many interfaces set slippage tolerances generously and auto-selected "cheapest route" across opaque bridges. Users saw speed and price; they did not see custody models or failure modes. When bridges were later exploited, losses cascaded through the very coincidences the defaults concealed—single relayers, admin keys, oracles with thin quorum. The lesson is not to paralyse design. It is to replace cleverness with candour. Default to showing the custody stack, the upgrade path, and the pause authority before any cross-chain move. If a route cannot tolerate that daylight, it does not deserve default status.

The ethics of defaults also govern governance. Voting portals often preselect delegates, hide abstain options, or collapse complex decisions into a binary. That scaffolding edits consent. A stewardship-oriented product defaults to *no delegate preselected, abstain visible, quorum rules explained,* and *conflicts declared*. It defaults to slow upgrades with published diffs and a human-readable changelog shipped with the binary. It defaults to public timetables for power—who can pause, how long, and what review follows. These defaults turn ritual into responsibility. They also set a measurable rhythm: *disclosure latency, diff comprehension, timelock coverage.*

To make defaults more than slogans, translate them into a checklist that can be read by builders and users without a lawyer in the room. In practice, that checklist reads as behaviour. New connection? Default to least privilege: do not auto-connect; present a narrowed permission set; display the unique risks of the dApp class (AMM, NFT marketplace, bridge). New approval? Default to cap by transaction and by day, with a path to raise limits. Large transfer? Default to slow funds plus out-of-band alerts—email, authenticator app, or a previously designated contact. New guardian? Default to a waiting period and multi-party acknowledgement, with a simple, printed backup for those who cannot manage hardware immediately. Upgrade? Default to timelock and diff with a plain-English explainer, and a simulation environment where high-stake users can test before the switch. Each line in that implicit checklist binds design to dignity.

Two named, positive examples can anchor the shift. WhatsApp's 2016 default to end-to-end encryption transformed a right into a routine, demonstrating that when protections cost users nothing, they endure at scale. Apple's ATT default in 2021 showed that consent can be restored without banning business models. Both moves were criticised as paternalistic by incumbents. Both strengthened public agency by asking first and assuming nothing. Defaults do not have to be anti-business to be pro-dignity; they have to be honest about who pays when things go wrong.

Measuring the ethics of defaults is not a philosophical exercise. It is a dashboard. Track *approval cap ratio* (share of approvals that are limited vs. unlimited); *slow-funds save rate* (percentage of large transactions cancelled during the delay window); *guardian diversity* (number of distinct guardians across jurisdictions); *disclosure comprehension* (share of users who answer five governance questions correctly after reading the explainer); and *recovery rehearsal rate* (percentage of users who have completed a timed recovery drill in the last year). These numbers are not theatre. They turn aspiration into iteration. If the save rate is zero, the window may be too short; if cap ratios skew unlimited, your defaults are lazy; if comprehension is low, your prose flatters itself. Adjust and measure again. Legitimacy compounds when measured.

There are limits. Defaults can condescend. They can over-protect to the point of attrition, smothering capability in prompts. The remedy is proportionality anchored to context. For negligible sums, speed may trump ceremony; for treasuries and life savings, ceremony is part of safety. Offer *graduated modes* that change defaults by risk tier—everyday spend, savings, organisational funds—while preserving the principle that moving "up" a tier requires clear consent and extra verification. Let users *opt out* of safety, but make the path deliberate and reversible. Freedom includes the freedom to choose risk. Dignity includes the dignity to refuse it.

The safety catch motif returns at the edge case that matters most: emergencies. When bridges halt, when markets lurch, when regulators issue notices, defaults should degrade gracefully. Products should transition to conservative modes automatically: widen slippage warnings, disable risky routes, surface status banners that link to signed statements. Governance defaults should slow: pause non-essential upgrades, extend deliberation windows, require larger quorums for irreversible steps. The tell is care for attention. In crisis, a dignified product asks less of its users, more of itself.

So the forward test is practical, not poetic. Before launch, ask three hard questions of your defaults. *Who is protected if a sober but tired person clicks twice too quickly?* If the answer is "no one", your default is extraction. *What must be shown, in words a teenager can parse, before money leaves the wallet or power shifts hands?* If the answer does not fit on a single screen, your default is obscurity. *How do we reverse a small subset of harms without creating a general veto?* If the answer is "we cannot say", your default is ideology, not engineering.

Defaults are not mere preferences. They are the first draft of our ethics—executed every time a stranger trusts the tool more than themselves. Build them so that a mistake does not become a life story. Build them so that consent is an act, not a checkbox. Build them so that when pressure arrives, the safety catch is already on, and dignity, not drama, governs what happens next.

Chapter 9
After Authority

In August 2021, a group of Afghan coders began quietly copying government databases onto decentralised storage. Kabul was falling; ministries were collapsing; the ledgers of civil servants, teachers, and students risked deletion or seizure. These volunteers—half terrified, half exhilarated—did not ask permission. They built parallel archives that no single general could erase. For a moment, authority scattered. What emerged was neither chaos nor utopia, but something subtler: a glimpse of *continuity without command*. When the formal state froze, informal code kept fragments of truth alive. That is the afterlife of authority—when the mantle of governance shifts from institutions to protocols, from ministries to networks, from trust in persons to trust in process.

The question is not whether authority disappears, but what inherits its obligations when it wanes. Every ledger, every DAO, every distributed system that outlives its founders becomes a miniature state. And yet, we have built these systems faster than we have learned to legitimise them. Central banks publish minutes; smart contracts publish hashes. Parliaments hold hearings; protocols hold votes. The vocabulary of responsibility lags behind the machinery of control. If decentralisation has been the technology of escape, its next act must be the architecture of belonging.

This chapter explores what it means to imagine institutions *after* institutions—how modular, interoperable commons might operate without reviving the very hierarchies they sought to replace. The post-institution imagination is neither anarchy nor automation. It is a sober kind of pluralism that accepts fallibility as a design parameter. A modular commons recognises that no community scales infinitely, that legitimacy degrades without feedback, and that any protocol that cannot describe its own failure modes is a faith, not a system. These are hard admissions. But they are prerequisites for freedom that lasts longer than a funding cycle.

The idea of "post-institution" is not a call to burn bureaucracy; it is a call to *miniaturise* it—to compress constitutions into code, to fragment stewardship into maintainable pieces. The pattern already exists in nature. Coral reefs, immune systems, and open-source projects all govern by distributed competence: many small checks, no single choke point. Each component is partial, fallible, but collectively adaptive. When one part dies, the whole survives. Digital commons must learn the same grace. They must cultivate replaceability as a virtue, not a weakness.

Yet, every modular system hides a paradox. The more we distribute power, the more we need to co-ordinate around shared standards—interfaces, not empires. Ethereum's EIP process, Wikipedia's editing norms, Mastodon's federation rules: each begins as a freedom experiment and ends as a form of law. The difference is not that they avoid authority, but that they earn it iteratively. Instead of demanding legitimacy upfront, they *accumulate* it through transparent revision. Authority becomes a verb, not a noun—a function of how disagreement is handled, not how commands are issued.

This is the temper of the post-institution imagination: a world where systems do not ask to be obeyed, but to be examined; where oversight is coded into operation; and where governance is treated not as theatre, but as maintenance. The risks are real. Modular systems can fragment faster than they federate. Commons can harden into clubs. Protocols can become oligarchies disguised as utilities. The antidote is not more ideology; it is better measurement—tracking participation dispersion, remedy rates, and the subtle health metrics of belonging. When legitimacy is observable, it can evolve. When it isn't, capture follows.

Still, technical composability alone will not make political maturity inevitable. We cannot outsource moral judgment to consensus mechanisms. The post-institution imagination therefore requires an ethical companion: *taking positions, not sides.* That phrase may sound modest, yet it redefines what citizenship means in programmable systems. To take a position is to commit to principles that can survive new evidence. To take a side is to treat loyalty as knowledge. The first makes you accountable; the second makes you tribal. As the rails we build mediate more value, speech, and labour, the discipline of principled revision becomes civic infrastructure.

Being "pro-freedom, pro-accountability, anti-fraud" sounds simple until we test it against the trade-offs of design. Freedom means users can exit; accountability means we can trace consequences; anti-fraud means we constrain harm even at the cost of friction. Each value tugs against the others. Absolute freedom breeds scams. Absolute accountability breeds surveillance. The task, then, is not to rank them but to balance them in context—to treat ethics as a set of tuning knobs, not commandments. A culture of revision—open, documented, and teachable—turns disagreement into a resource rather than a risk.

For builders, that ethic manifests as maintainable products: explicit powers, time-bound privileges, readable code, reversible errors. For policymakers, it means crafting rules that treat decentralised systems as laboratories for civic learning, not threats to be smothered. For citizens, it means resisting comfort—the comfort of centralised safety and the comfort of righteous outrage. The legitimate future of decentralisation will belong not to maximalists but to moderators: those who can argue in good faith, upgrade in public, and admit when the evidence has changed.

The motif of this chapter is a compass, not a flag. Authority, once lost, leaves behind direction but not destination. The institutions of the twentieth century were built to survive shocks through scale and secrecy. The institutions of the twenty-first must survive through transparency and iteration. They will not promise certainty; they will offer procedures. Their leaders will look less like presidents and more like maintainers—custodians of protocols that govern flows of value and trust.

What happens *after authority* is not absence but reconfiguration. Rules become composable. Accountability becomes continuous. Trust, long hoarded, becomes a renewable public good. The systems we inherit will be judged not by how loudly they proclaim decentralisation, but by how gracefully they distribute agency. The challenge—and the invitation—is to build worlds where the question "who decides?" is answered not by charisma or coercion, but by design.

This chapter, then, is not an obituary for authority. It is a rehearsal for its transformation. We will trace how modular commons can mature without metastasising; how ethical defaults can discipline freedom without suffocating it; and how post-institutional citizens can prototype polity itself—testing, measuring, and improving the fragile miracle of self-rule. The age after authority will not be leaderless. It will be leader-light: steered by principles that outlast their founders, and communities confident enough to rebuild themselves when the compass wobbles.

The Post-Institution Imagination

In March 2020, as the COVID-19 pandemic closed borders, a network of volunteers began building the Open Source Ventilator project. Originating in Dublin and soon spanning more than forty countries, it co-ordinated engineers, doctors, and makers through GitHub, Slack, and Telegram. No government mandate. No central procurement. Just thousands of strangers assembling blueprints, sourcing components, and testing prototypes. Within months, they had produced working ventilators certified for emergency use in Ireland and deployed in parts of India and Brazil. It was neither a start-up nor an NGO, but something hybrid—a modular, interoperable commons that learned in public. The project dissolved as the crisis eased, yet its structure lingered as a question: if we can prototype life-saving machines without a ministry, could we prototype governance the same way?

That question defines the post-institution imagination. It does not abolish authority; it atomises it into transparent, composable parts. The premise is pragmatic: institutions are brittle when they centralise trust, but they become renewable when they share it. A modular commons is not a utopia of code; it is a system where governance can fork, merge, and interoperate like open software. The scene in Dublin was not accidental—it emerged from a global culture of version control, shared protocols, and distributed verification. What began as an engineering emergency doubled as a rehearsal for a political future.

Show, name, explain, imply. Show: the Open Source Ventilator demonstrated a capacity to self-organise across borders without permanent hierarchy. Name: *the post-institution imagination*—a design stance that treats authority as a tool, not a throne. Explain: such imagination recognises that the machinery of coordination once monopolised by states or corporations can now be rebuilt as protocols, co-ops, and networks that share rules but not rulers. Implication: our challenge is not to dream statelessly, but to design *institutionally small*—to construct durable patterns of care without bureaucratic overgrowth.

Consider Ethereum's public goods experiments, such as Gitcoin Grants (founded Denver, 2017). Its quadratic funding mechanism distributes matching funds according to the breadth of community support rather than the depth of single donors' pockets. A thousand small contributions outweigh one whale. The behaviour is measurable: participation dispersion, match ratios, and contribution diversity become governance data, not press releases. The system iterates because it is modular—new rounds, new algorithms, new failure analyses. Another example: the Estonian e-Residency programme (launched 2014), a state-level attempt to modularise identity itself. It offers a digital citizenship layer usable for company formation, taxation, and signature across borders. Both projects show fragments of a post-institution future: one non-state and emergent, the other state-born but interoperable.

Yet modularity is not an unqualified virtue. The counter-example is instructive. During the 2022 collapse of Terra's algorithmic stablecoin, the promise of composability—of every DeFi protocol connecting seamlessly with every other—amplified disaster. Smart contracts trusted the wrong collateral; integrations propagated loss across dozens of projects. Modularity without governance became contagion. The reconciliation is not to abandon interoperability, but to encode *boundaries* as part of the commons. The ethic is proportionate interdependence: components should connect voluntarily, monitor each other, and fail gracefully, not catastrophically. The motif here is *the joint*, not the chain. Flexibility is strength.

The post-institution imagination must therefore hold two ideas in tension: radical openness and explicit constraint. It thrives not by erasing rules but by making them legible and editable. In this architecture, constitutions are thin documents that define the scope of consent, not the totality of control. Think of them as *credibility layers*: agreements about what can change, how it changes, and who gets to propose the change. When these layers are transparent, coordination becomes self-documenting. When they are hidden, corruption blooms. Every functioning commons requires this grammar of revision—without it, participation decays into ritual.

Risk becomes the tutor. A modular system that never encounters stress never earns legitimacy. The first wave of

DAOs (2020–2022) learned this painfully. Many copied governance templates wholesale—token voting, multi-signature treasuries, timed proposals—without adapting them to their size or mission. The result was paralysis masquerading as democracy. A few projects began to mature by publishing *stress post-mortems*—public logs of decision errors, exploit responses, and member attrition. These experiments mark the shift from enthusiasm to engineering. The post-institution imagination grows up when it values *iteration logs* over manifestos.

There is a moral reason for this. Institutions, for all their inertia, at least make responsibility visible. Post-institutional systems risk hiding it behind interfaces. To design responsibly, builders must expose not only the code but the human choices embedded within. Who maintains the oracle? Who can pause the contract? Who audits the auditors? These are not technicalities; they are the new separation of powers. Transparency without context is voyeurism; transparency with context is civics. A mature modular commons insists that every default, every admin key, every veto route be public knowledge. Authority does not vanish—it becomes inspectable.

A second tension arises between composability and cohesion. Too much interoperability, and norms dissolve; too little, and silos return. The answer lies in *semantic bridges*: shared standards for data, identity, and consent that allow independent communities to cooperate without surrendering autonomy. The Decentralized Identifiers (DID) standard approved by the W3C in 2022 exemplifies this approach. It enables portable reputations—verifiable, privacy-preserving attestations that travel between systems. Such standards are political artefacts disguised as technical protocols. They encode an ethics of minimal disclosure: reveal enough to participate, never enough to be profiled.

Still, every interoperable future must confront the problem of scale. Modularity lets us compose systems; it does not guarantee alignment. Without shared incentives, a federation of well-intentioned commons can degenerate into competition for liquidity, attention, or legitimacy. The post-institution imagination therefore extends beyond code to *culture*: the expectation that stewardship, not extraction, defines success. This is why projects like Nouns DAO—auctioning one NFT per day to fund public goods via open governance—matter less for their art and more for their cadence. They normalise patience. Governance as rhythm, not spectacle.

One can measure the maturity of a modular system by its *exit temperature*: how gracefully participants can leave. In a corporate institution, exit is an act of betrayal; in a modular commons, it is an act of renewal. Forking, migration, and replication are built-in safety valves. The ability to walk away disciplines those who remain. Yet this freedom carries a civic cost: attention fragments, and institutional memory resets. A future of endless forking risks replacing tyranny with amnesia. To avoid it, systems need archival mechanisms—versioned history, transferable context, and rituals of reunion. Remembering together is governance's quiet half.

The post-institution imagination is therefore not a fantasy of spontaneity but a discipline of design. It asks: can we build systems that are *strongly accountable and weakly centralised*? Can we compose governance as we compose software—testing, forking, and merging without losing moral coherence? It demands a shift from building things *for* people to building *with* them, from platforms to protocols, from ownership to stewardship. The challenge is to make these principles visible enough to teach, and flexible enough to survive disagreement.

Two centuries ago, Alexis de Tocqueville wrote that the health of democracy lay in "the habits of the heart" cultivated by associations, not decrees. The post-institution imagination revives that insight in code. It treats civic habit as modular software: reusable, auditable, and portable. When we talk of interoperability now, we are not merely speaking of APIs—we are speaking of moral interoperation, the ability of distinct communities to align around consent, fairness, and reversibility even when they diverge elsewhere. That is what makes this imagination plausible rather than utopian.

Yet sober possibility demands honesty about limits. Modular commons will not abolish power; they will redistribute it in new forms. Code can discipline incentives but cannot replace virtue. Communities can rotate stewards but cannot automate conscience. The danger is hubris: mistaking interoperability for justice, or composability for care. The most radical innovation may be restraint—the choice to keep systems small enough to comprehend and slow enough to correct.

The motif of *the joint* returns at the close. A joint connects without merging, flexes without breaking, bears load by design. Post-institutional systems must do the same: unite without uniformity, evolve without rupture, and translate without domination. The open ventilator project began as crisis response; it ended as a metaphor for what governance might become when connection replaces command. The forward test remains unresolved: can we construct a polity as adaptable as open software yet as humane as its best institutions once were? The answer will not arrive from theory, but from practice—from how well we learn to prototype the next generation of shared responsibility, one joint at a time.

Taking Positions, Not Sides

On 18 January 2012, Wikipedia went dark. For twenty-four hours the front page carried a single message opposing the Stop Online Piracy Act (SOPA) and the PROTECT IP Act (PIPA). The blackout, decided by community vote and executed from the Wikimedia Foundation's offices in San Francisco, helped stall the US bills in Congress within days. What mattered was not merely the outcome. It was the stance: an institution whose norms forbid advertising and advocacy took a public position when it judged that the infrastructure of knowledge was at risk. It chose freedom of expression over neutrality theatre, accountability over comfort, and it did so with a willingness to explain, document, and—if evidence warranted—revise. Positions are commitments under revision.

This subchapter argues for that discipline: pro-freedom, pro-accountability, anti-fraud. Not a factional slogan, but a working compass for citizens, builders, and policymakers designing decentralised systems. A compass is modest. It points; it does not march. It helps you reorient when the ground shifts. And the ground will shift—under legal regimes, under market stress, and under the cultural pressure of tribes who prefer sides to standards. Taking a position is harder than declaring allegiance because it binds you to trade-offs in public. The aim here is to show how to hold such a stance, test it against cases, and leave the page with a posture you can defend without becoming doctrinaire.

Begin with *freedom*. Show, name, explain, imply. Show: the Wikipedia blackout demonstrated that freedom of expression sometimes requires instruments of refusal—turning the lights off to illuminate the stakes. Name the principle: *freedom as exit and voice*. Explain: in decentralised systems, freedom exists when users can leave (export keys, switch clients, fork code) and speak (propose changes, audit decisions, publish dissent) without retaliation. Implication: design and policy should measure freedom not by rhetoric but by *switching costs* (time to migrate state), *fork friction* (governance and technical barriers), and *retaliation risk* (documented penalties for dissent). A project that boasts permissionless participation while locking assets behind proprietary bridges has chosen sides, not a position.

Now *accountability*. The Merge in September 2022 was executed after months of shadow forks, client diversity targets, and pre-mortems. That was accountability as practice: specify failure modes, simulate them, disclose who can pause what, and accept blame when necessary. Name the rule: *accountability as legibility under stress*. Explain: a system is accountable when outsiders can answer three questions from public materials alone—who decides, how they can be replaced, and how harms are remedied. Implication: insist on *disclosure latency* (time from incident to first public note), *remedy rates* (share of substantiated harms made whole within a defined window), and *steward rotation* (turnover or reconfirmation of keyholders and delegates). Without these behaviours, "accountability" is a press release.

Finally *anti-fraud*. Fraud is not just theft; it is the deliberate manufacture of opacity for gain. The Terra/UST collapse (May 2022, Singapore and Seoul) showed how reflexivity, marketing, and thin disclosure can detonate a market. Name the counter-value: *anti-fraud as predictable verification*. Explain: users should be able to verify reserves, admin powers, and upgrade paths without privileged access or insider gloss. Implication: favour designs with *verifiable disclosure* (on-chain proofs or audited statements with named custodians), *bounded promises* (yields and pegs with clearly stated dependence), and *recovery envelopes* (strictly limited, rules-based mechanisms for partial restitution). A culture that treats "DYOR" as absolution is taking sides against the public. Anti-fraud demands shared safeguards.

With the compass drawn, test it. In March 2023, USDC briefly de-pegged after Silicon Valley Bank entered receivership. Some protocols slowed integrations, widened bands, and published dashboards; others chased "real-time truth" into reflexive liquidations. The pro-freedom, pro-accountability, anti-fraud stance would have asked three questions in order: Can users exit safely right now? Who can pause exposure and on what triggers? What disclosures convert rumours into facts? The visible behaviours would have been *temporary safety-first defaults* (automatic conservative modes), *signed incident notes* within hours, and *post-event dossiers* tying design changes to observed failure. Sides would have offered slogans. Positions would have offered procedures.

Consider a second case with different stakes: the European Union's Markets in Crypto-Assets (MiCA) regulation adopted in April 2023 (Strasbourg/Brussels). Builders divided into camps—celebrate clarity or decry overreach. A position, by contrast, parses the text and sets measurable tests. Freedom: does MiCA preserve self-custody and open-source publication? Accountability: do stablecoin issuers face regular reserve attestations and redemption rules? Anti-fraud: are marketing claims enforceable as commitments? The implication is a civic project: civil society should track *MiCA conformance dashboards* the way developers track uptime—how many issuers publish attested reserves on schedule, how many exchanges surface governance powers at the point of trade, how many consumers win remedies. If the numbers trend well, revise the position in favour; if not, iterate the statute. Revision is core.

The credible counter-example is tribal capture: the 2015–2017 Bitcoin blocksize conflict, in which "big block" and "small block" camps hardened into identity. The debate produced technical exploration—Bitcoin XT, Classic, Unlimited—but it also produced social fracture. A position-led approach would have committed, publicly, to criteria independent of faction: throughput targets under stress, propagation times across geography, orphan rates, and node costs. It would have published *thresholds for change* ("if X and Y are met for Z months, we support adopting proposal A") and *thresholds for refusal*. Sides escalate rhetoric; positions specify barometers. The eventual SegWit activation and the endurance of Bitcoin's conservative approach tell a simple story: standards outlast slogans.

Positions also carry duties for citizens. The individual stance is not "believe in decentralisation" but *behave for it.* Behaviours can be trained: refusing unlimited approvals, reading one governance explainer per month, rehearsing recovery quarterly, and voting with delegation you can publicly defend. Track your own *consent diary*: when did you last review emergency powers in the contracts you use? Which delegate represents your view of reversibility and remedy? Civic muscle strengthens with repetition; untrained, it defaults to trust theatre.

For builders, the manifesto trims to four verbs: *publish, limit, rotate, repair*. Publish powers and procedures in a living constitution with diffs. Limit what default connections can do until users opt in with comprehension. Rotate stewards and keys on a clock, not a mood. Repair harms through a public claims process with evidence thresholds, and report remedy rates. The metrics keep you honest. If you cannot hit them, explain why and ship a plan. That is what positions demand: not perfection but *accountable intent*.

Policymakers require a different grammar. The stance is *permission to experiment, obligation to disclose*. Sandbox regimes—like the UK's FCA sandbox (launched 2016, London)—succeed when they trade regulatory indulgence for rigorous measurement and open results. A principled policymaker's position sets guardrails for citizen risk (caps, disclosures, timelocks) while allowing controlled variance in design. It funds *public reference implementations*—open, audited tooling for identity, consent, and reversible wrappers—so that safety is not a private luxury. It publishes *regulatory pre-mortems* for high-impact rules, spelling out intended outcomes, failure modes, and test metrics. Then it revises. Not once, but on schedule. Evidence governs.

The motif returns: the compass. Sides are flags; they rally and they bind. Compasses are quieter. They keep you from walking in circles. To normalise compasses, communities can ritualise revision. Quarterly "position audits" where delegates present what evidence changed their minds; biannual "policy drills" where regulators and builders simulate an exploit and test the path from alert to remedy; annual "freedom checks" measuring switching costs across the dominant wallets and bridges. These are not spectacles. They are the infrastructure of correction.

Sceptics will say this is naïve. Tribes deliver energy; procedures deliver boredom. But boredom—structured, measured, documented—is what keeps systems from betraying strangers. The alternative is theatrical conviction that outpaces reality and leaves citizens paying for someone else's learning curve. A defensible position does not promise harmony. It promises legible friction: the confidence that when values clash, we have a way to talk, measure, and choose again without burning everything down.

Two further examples offer proof and caution. First, Apple's App Tracking Transparency (Cupertino, April 2021) showed how consent defaults can move billion-dollar markets toward user agency. A position reads this not as corporate virtue but as *engineering of choice*: a repeatable pattern for wallets and dApps to adopt—ask, cap, time-limit, and explain. Second, Canada's freezing of certain convoy-related accounts (Ottawa, February 2022) revealed how state power can overreach in emergencies. A position resists sides—neither romanticising the movement nor minimising abuse risk. It recommends *graduated reversibility*: narrow, court-supervised remedies; explicit time bounds; transparent appeals; and strong protections for small donors. Freedom and accountability are tuned, not traded. Anti-fraud is honoured, not weaponised.

What, finally, makes a position defensible? Four traits. It is *principled*—anchored to freedom, accountability, and anti-fraud. It is *operational*—expressed as behaviours and metrics, not adjectives. It is *falsifiable*—stated in a way that evidence could overturn. And it is *teachable*—shareable with a colleague without your charisma. You should be able to say: "I support reversible wrappers for treasuries with 48-hour timelocks and supermajority guardians, but I oppose generalised reversals for retail payments; here are the incidents that would change my mind." That sentence contains a future.

The forward test is direct. Before your next vote, integration, or policy draft, write the compact version of your stance on one page. Name the rights you protect first when values collide. List the three metrics that would make you change your mind. Commit to a review date. Then act. If you cannot do this, you have a side, not a position. If you can, you have built yourself a compass—quiet, stubborn, and ready for the weather.

About the Author

Sameer Khalid writes about power, trust, and technology with the calm focus of a systems thinker. Raised between bureaucracies and bazaars, he learned early how institutions both enable and constrain ordinary lives—a sensibility that animates his work on decentralisation. His essays read code as political text and incentives as moral choices, drawing lightly on sources from Ibn Khaldun to Elinor Ostrom to make today's design debates intelligible. He champions privacy as civic infrastructure and autonomy as a discipline, not a slogan. When he is not mapping governance patterns, he mentors builders on writing constitutions that people can actually live with.

www.ingramcontent.com/pod-product-compliance
Lightning Source LLC
Chambersburg PA
CBHW031342230926
51848CB00002B/341